Not on the Map

Not on the Map

The Peculiar Histories of De Facto States

Michael J. Seth

LEXINGTON BOOKS
Lanham • Boulder • New York • London

Published by Lexington Books
An imprint of The Rowman & Littlefield Publishing Group, Inc.
4501 Forbes Boulevard, Suite 200, Lanham, Maryland 20706
www.rowman.com

6 Tinworth Street, London SE11 5AL, United Kingdom

Copyright © 2022 The Rowman & Littlefield Publishing Group, Inc.

All rights reserved. No part of this book may be reproduced in any form or by any electronic or mechanical means, including information storage and retrieval systems, without written permission from the publisher, except by a reviewer who may quote passages in a review.

British Library Cataloguing in Publication Information Available

Library of Congress Cataloging-in-Publication Available

ISBN: 978-1-7936-3252-4 (cloth)
ISBN: 978-1-7936-3254-8 (paper)
ISBN: 978-1-7936-3253-1 (electronic)

Library of Congress Control Number: 2020945006

Contents

1	A World of States	1
2	Mountain Republic: Nagorno Karabakh (Artsakh)	15
3	Breakaway States from a Breakaway State: Abkhazia and South Ossetia	37
4	Shoestring of Europe: Transnistria	65
5	Born of Ethnic Cleansing: Kosovo	85
6	Divided Island: Turkish Republic of Northern Cyprus	107
7	State in Waiting: Sahrawi Arab Democratic Republic	125
8	Not Being Somalia: Somaliland	147
9	One China, Two Countries: Taiwan	171
10	Not Quite De Facto States	195

Conclusion: What Can We Learn from De Facto States?	215
Bibliography	225
Index	233
About the Author	239

Chapter 1

A World of States

INTRODUCTION: "I CAN'T FIND IT ON MY MAP!"

"I can't find it on my map," a friend said after I told him I was going to Nagorno Karabakh. Not his fault, as it doesn't appear on most world maps. Nagorno Karabakh does not officially exist. No United Nations (UN) member recognizes it, and it belongs to no international organizations. When I arrived in the country, my iPad kept giving the time in Azerbaijan, not in the different time zone of Nagorno Karabakh. Yet it existed. I got a visa for it in an embassy-like building in the Armenian capital of Yerevan. There was a capital city, Stepanakert. I stayed next to the national parliament, across the street from the presidential office. It had a flag, and it had an army which I watched parading down the street. It all seemed real enough. Yet, if it is not recognized by other states or even on the map, is it a real country?

Nagorno Karabakh belongs to the world of de facto states, that is, states that are not universally accepted as one of their own by the community of sovereign countries yet function as independent entities. Each of these de facto states possesses a territory it controls, a population that identifies with it, and most of the things one expects to find in a country: customs posts; a national flag and a national anthem; armed forces; and a government that administers the schools, collects taxes, and maintains the roads. This book looks at some of these states. Not just because they are interesting anomalies, which they are, but also because they reveal much about what a country is, how nations and national identities come into being, and about the international community that we all live in.

A WORLD OF STATES

When we look at the map of the world, we see land masses neatly divided into different countries. What we notice is that there are so many of them. How many countries are there? In 2020, there were 193 members of the UN, that is, 193 states recognized by the global community as sovereign independent states. This is many more than existed several generations ago. When the UN was formed in 1945, there were fifty-one members plus a few states such as Switzerland that were not members for one reason or another. The number of sovereign states has grown for two related reasons. First, the age of empires ended after World War II. The majority of states today were part of larger empires then. Second, the growth of ethnic and national consciousness has meant that more and more groups of people have sought to be self-governing, which is why empires have mostly disappeared. But not just empires, even within states there have been many separatist movements as ethnic groups try to form their own nation-states. Some of these movements such as in Bangladesh or more recently South Sudan have been successful, most such as in Quebec, Tibet, Kurdistan, and Catalonia have not—at least not yet.

In addition to these 193 UN members, there are a few oddities: the de facto states with most of the trappings of being a separate country but not recognized by the international community, or by a significant portion of it, as one. There are not many of these, and most are quite small; yet their very existence makes us think about what it means to be a sovereign state, a country, and a nation. Our main focus will be on nine of them: Nagorno Karabakh, Abkhazia, South Ossetia, Transnistria, Kosovo, the Turkish Republic of Northern Cyprus (TRNC), the Sahrawi Arab Democratic Republic (SADR), Somaliland, and Taiwan. They are places that straddle the boundaries of what is generally accepted as an independent country. They all have defined territories and a government in control over the people in them. The people in the states recognize and identify with them. While most are modest in size, they are all bigger than many recognized states, and they have all the things we generally associate with being a country. Furthermore, they have been around for a while, in most cases long enough for an entire generation to have grown up in them.

De facto states are known by other labels as well. Sometimes they are referred to as "contested states."[1] One study of them refers to them as "so-called states."[2] Another writer labels them "invisible countries."[3] They can be distinguished from what Robert Jackson has called "quasi-states." These are states that have all the symbols of statehood—flags, anthems, ambassadors—and are also recognized by the international community but do not exercise effective governing authority over the territory they rule. Quasi-states are mostly poor countries that have failed to develop or lost the institutional capacity to control all of the people within their legally recognized borders.

Examples might be the Democratic Republic of the Congo or the more extreme case, Somalia.[4] As Scott Pegg has pointed out, de facto states are the opposite—they have a government that governs the territory and is in control of the people within it, but they just do not have international recognition as a sovereign political entity.[5] De facto states are also different from short-lived secessionist states, in that they have endurance and stable boundaries.

Our de facto states are geographically, culturally, and in many other ways very different places. Three are in Europe, two in Africa, one in Asia, and three are located where Europe and Asia meet. Somaliland is among the world's poorest countries, Taiwan among the richest. Transnistria is small, smaller than Delaware, and Somaliland is territorially larger than half the countries of Europe. Northern Cyprus is a popular tourist destination, but Nagorno Karabakh, a beautiful and safe place to travel, sees few visitors. Kosovo enjoys widespread diplomatic recognition, but several of our de facto states are not recognized by a single UN member or major international organization. Six are usually not on the map at all: Nagorno Karabakh, Abkhazia, South Ossetia, Transnistria, the Turkish Republic of Northern Cyprus, and Somaliland. One, the Saharawi Arab Democratic Republic, often appears on maps as "Western Sahara" or more strangely is left unlabeled. Two, Kosovo and Taiwan, can be found on most maps but are not full-fledged members of the international community.

Nonetheless, for all their differences all these states have some shared characteristics. All are the products of empires that came to an end—in some cases suddenly, violently, and chaotically, in other cases more gradually and orderly. Most, and one can argue all, are products of "frozen conflicts," unresolved wars in which active fighting has ended but there has been neither peace nor an agreed settlement. All were secessionist states that broke from a "parent" state which refused to recognize it. Each finds itself in awkward geopolitical circumstances in which recognition has major international complications. And all of them find themselves entangled in the ambiguities, the rigidities, and the failures of the international state system.

In broad historical perspective, these de facto states are the products of several developments that have profoundly shaped the world we live in: the creation and universalization of the modern state system, the emergence of nationalism and the nation-state, the end of empire, and the failures of the international community to resolve conflicts.

WHAT'S A COUNTRY?

If Nagorno Karabakh does not exist on the most maps and is excluded from most lists of countries, it raises the question—what qualifies as a country?

The answer is: there is no universal agreement on this. We can begin to work toward defining a country by calling it a state. While some scholars make a distinction between the two, "country" is normally used interchangeably with the term "state." Of course, a state can also be a subunit of a country such as the states of Brazil, India, or the United States. But in other contexts, state is synonymous with country. States first appeared in Mesopotamia and Egypt five thousand years ago and a little later in India, China, Peru, and Mexico. Gradually over the next several thousand years, they became the fundamental political unit for most of humanity.

While there is no universally agreed definition of a state or what constitutes "stateness," it is generally accepted to be a type of political organization that controls a defined territory. But rather than try to refine a definition of something that can never be precisely defined in a way to satisfy every situation and every author, it is easier to look at some of the basic characteristics of states. First, a state (or country) needs to possess a clearly defined territory. This might seem obvious, but not always. Rebel movements might declare themselves a state but if their boundaries are constantly shifting or they hold isolated pockets of territory rather than a clearly marked bloc they do not really constitute a country. In the past, states often had vaguely defined boundaries including areas where the central government held only marginal control or where more than one state claimed possession, but this is generally not the case of modern states. Borders are fixed, usually marked; they have customs and immigration controls. It is usually pretty clear where one state ends and another begins.

A country needs to have a population that it exercises some measure of control over. That is, it not only has a territory but a permanent population that lives in it. The size of both territories and populations can vary. Russia has 17 million square kilometers (6.5 million square miles)—a vast land mass that spans eleven time zones. Monaco has less than 2 square kilometers (1 square mile) but is generally regarded as a country. China has 1.4 billion people which is 140,000 times that of Tuvalu with only 10,000 inhabitants. Yet, both have one vote in the UN General Assembly; both are regarded by the international community as independent states. The population within the state should somehow acknowledge its existence. This poses the question of whether or not the people in a state have to know that they are part of the state. What about noncontacted tribal peoples in the Amazon that might not know they live in Brazil or Ecuador? The rule seems to be that a state can claim the population within it, as long as most of that population recognizes that they live in that state whether or not they are happy with this fact.

A state has to have a government that controls the territory and its population. That is, it effectively administers it, providing the basic services that a government can provide. Just how much control it needs to have varies. Most modern states exercise far more control over the people they govern than states in the past. Rather than just collect taxes and provide some defense, modern states support education, promote public health, administer justice, carry out policing, and build and maintain infrastructure such as roads and water works. But governments don't always control all the territory and population of their country. The government of Myanmar for the past half century has not been able to exercise control over much of its rugged mountainous and jungle periphery where the ethnic minorities who live there often contested its authority. Still it is considered the government of all the areas within its official boundaries. Somalia has not had a central government that can control the County since 1991. The authority of the government of Afghanistan has often been so limited that the president is often called "the mayor of Kabul."[6] These are exceptions. In general, we can say that to be a country the government needs to effectively control most of the population within a given and fixed territory and that most of the population needs to recognize it as their government.

A state to be considered an independent country must possess sovereignty—that is, its government is the ultimate authority in that territory. But sovereignty is harder to identify than the first three requirements. The term is a complicated one, associated with the rise of the modern state system (discussed below). It does not mean that a state has complete unlimited authority over everyone and everything within its boundaries. It is generally accepted that no state has the right to commit genocide. Nor can a state carry out activities that would endanger communities outside its boundaries even though they are taken place within it, for example, sending dangerous chemical toxins into the atmosphere. So, in practice, and in international law, no state is completely independent or autonomous. However, a state must have the ability to act in a way that is within what is generally acceptable by the international community without interference from another state to be sovereign.

This is not just a matter of definitions and theories. Governments and international organizations have come up with two ways of deciding whether a country is, in fact, a sovereign state. One is called the *declarative principle* of state sovereignty. It was drawn up in the 1930s and became adopted by the League of Nations in 1936 as the basis for deciding if a place constitutes a sovereign state. Under this principle, a state must have (1) a permanent population, (2) a defined territory, (3) a government, and (4) a "capacity to enter into relations with other states."[7] This means if a political entity has the hallmarks of a state, and if it *could have* ambassadors and diplomats and be a responsible member of the international community, it is a sovereign state even if other states don't recognize it. Our de facto states are, therefore, by this definition, real countries, that is, sovereign states even if they are not widely recognized as such and, in some cases, cartographers won't acknowledge their existence.

IT TAKES ONE TO KNOW ONE

By this declarative principle, most of the de facto states we are going to discuss are real countries. But there is another way of deciding if a state is a real one or not, which is called the *constitutive theory* of state sovereignty. It means, in practice, an independent country is a sovereign state if it recognized by other members of the international community of states as such.[8] It is only the internationally recognized community of sovereign states that decides if a political entity is one of them. Or in other words, it takes one to know one. Under this definition, there are, as of 2020, 193 internationally recognized sovereign states. All are members of the United Nations. So, the world is made up of 193 states that recognize each other as such. That of course leaves out our nine political entities.

In practice then, UN membership is the real standard for joining the club of recognized states. There are some complications in this club of 193. The People's Republic of China is not recognized by fourteen members, Israel is not recognized by thirty-one members, Cyprus is not recognized by Turkey, and North and South Korea do not recognize each other. But generally, if a country joins the UN, it is broadly accepted as a legitimate member of the international community. States can be excluded from the UN and still be recognized by other countries. For example, Kosovo, which declared independence in 2008, is recognized by 110 members, the Republic of Abkhazia, which declared independence from Georgia in 1999, is recognized by five members, the Republic of South Ossetia, which declared independence in 1991, is also recognized by five members, the Turkish Republic of Northern Cyprus is recognized by one, Turkey. In addition, the state of Palestine is recognized by 136 members and the Sahrawi Arab Republic (Western Sahara) is recognized by forty-seven members. Then there are two oddities: the Pridnestrovian Moldavian Republic, or as we will refer to it Transnistria, proclaimed in 1991 and recognized by only non-UN members: Abkhazia, South Ossetia, and Nagorno Karabakh, and the Republic of Nagorno Karabakh proclaimed in 1991 and recognized only by the three non-UN members: Transnistria, Abkhazia, and South Ossetia. Thus, Transnistria and Nagorno Karabakh are de facto states that are recognized only by three other de facto states. There are also some other oddities such as Andorra. France and Spain are co-princes and have to approve defense and internal security treaties and have some say over its diplomatic representation. And yet it's a UN member. France is responsible for Monaco's defense, but it too is a UN member.[9]

But if a state is not a UN member, it is still something short of being a full member of the international community. And this has real consequences. Nonmembership means not only being excluded from participating in this international forum but from most of its affiliated organizations: World Health Organization, World Bank, the International Monetary Fund, the United Nations Education, Science and Cultural Organization, the International Labor Organization, and many others. It means not having a voice in international affairs, and of having difficulty carrying out business transactions and all kinds of other activities. For example, there are no ATMs and credit cards don't work in Somaliland. Nonmembers are generally not members of the Universal Postal Union. Letters to the Turkish Republic of Northern Cyprus are sent via an address in Turkey. Non-UN members can join the Universal Postal Union but only if they are supported by two-thirds of the UN members and if that was the case, they would probably be in the UN itself. Being non-recognized means having no internet country domain. It generally means being excluded from the International Olympic Committee—Taiwan was permitted to participate in the Olympics but only under the banner China-Taipei. It means exclusion from the International Federation of Association Football (FIFA). In short, it means isolation. Often for its citizens it means being trapped as well since their passports are not recognized.

There is a sort of second-tier membership as a permanent observer to the UN. Observers can attend meetings and make speeches but cannot vote. Switzerland was one from 1946 to 2002 since it did not want to compromise its cherished policy of neutrality by voting in the General Assembly. But the Swiss found that the advantages of membership outweighed the risk to their country's reputation. South and North Korea were observers since both claimed to be the government of all of Korea. They managed to work this out among themselves and were admitted as full members in 1991. In 2020, there were only two permanent observers—the Vatican City, which has been one since 1964, and the state of Palestine, which became one in 2012. Palestine's bid for full membership was blocked by the United States.

MODERN STATES ARE MODERN

Our de facto states are the product of two modern developments: the rise of the modern nation-state and the emergence of the international state system. We take as natural and for granted that the world and all of humanity is divided into states with clearly defined borders that exist in a kind of global community of nations. Yet it is a modern development. Until two to three centuries ago, most states had porous, often ill-defined, and fluctuating boundaries. They were surprisingly weak and disengaged from the life of the inhabitants. Few rulers knew how many people lived under their authority and often did not care. They collected taxes, as much as they could without inciting rebellion. As the result of the emergence of modern science and the scientific-rational mode of thinking, ruling groups became more systematic and efficient in organizing themselves. States were more bureaucratic, more efficient at record keeping. By the end of the eighteenth century, they began to take censuses, numbering and keeping track of their citizens. European states in between the 1600s and the 1800s gradually become more concerned with expanding their economies and thus more involved in trade and finance. They started to become modern states—far more intrusive, more involved in the life of ordinary people, passing health and safety regulations, compulsory schooling for children, issuing licenses and regulations for lawyer, doctors, engineers, teachers, and other professionals. Taxes were collected more efficiently, and most modern states required military service for young men. They demanded ever more loyalty from the people they governed. States in the nineteenth century became far efficient at controlling their peripheries, patrolling their boundaries, establishing custom and immigration posts, and began issuing passports to control exits and entries. They became states as we know them today.

They also became nation-states. Nationalism has been a driving force that has broken up empires and led to the creation of most modern states. At its core, nationalism is the belief by a group of people that they belong to a nation; a nation is a community that shares a common heritage and believes it shares a common destiny. What binds a nation together? Membership in a state and the shared experience of belonging to that state often contributed to the development of a sense of nationhood. Language, in the majority of cases, is important in defining a nation—a community that uses the same written and/or spoken language may consider itself a nation. Other factors contributing to a sense of common nationhood include shared customs, religion, or a belief in a common ancestry. Nationalism became one of the most emotionally powerful forms of identity in the modern world. Probably no other identity has generated more conflicts and struggles or done more to shape international politics in the nineteenth, twentieth, and twenty-first centuries.

It is hard to say just when modern nationalism began. Historians can be roughly divided into two camps on this. Some historians, such as John Armstrong and Anthony Smith, regard nationalism as having deep roots. This is what is sometimes called the traditionalist or primordial view of nationalism.[10] While recognizing that many cultures Japanese, Korean, Chinese as well as French and English had elements of nationalism, most historians understand it as a modern development. For them it is the product of modern centralized intrusive states; modern concepts of popular sovereignty;

and the demands of modern capitalism for a literate workforce speaking a standard language and sharing common patterns of behavior. To satisfy the last of these demands, governments created national education systems that also served to reinforce a common identity and loyalty to the state.[11] These historians holding a "modernist" view of nationalism often trace it to the French Revolution, and certainly by the early-nineteenth-century nationalism was emerging as a powerful force in Europe and the Americas. By the early twentieth century, nationalism was becoming a powerful force in Asia, the Middle East, and Africa.

RECOGNIZING EACH OTHER AND GETTING ALONG: THE STATE SYSTEM

A second major development was that states became sovereign entities. As the first modern states emerged in Europe, along with them emerged the modern set of rules, practices, and concepts that historians call the European state system. The key element of the state system was the concept of state sovereignty. For more than a century, religious wars raged in much of Europe culminating in the Thirty Years War 1618–1648. Almost every state in Europe participated in this confusing conflict. The war ended with the Peace of Westphalia of 1648. This marked a milestone in the evolution of the state system. The treaty recognized the principle of state sovereignty in which each state was solely in charge of its internal affairs. The Europeans then developed elaborate rules of diplomacy to govern the way states conducted their relations with each other. After 1648, European states continued to go to war with each other but began to adhere to rules of diplomacy and conflict. These were not new; many of the concepts of diplomacy—the stationing of permanent ambassadors and the concept of diplomatic immunity—were pioneered by the Italian states during the Renaissance. They now become more regularized and universally accepted as the normal way states conducted business with each other. A body of international law to establish rules of conduct between states emerged, a process greatly indebted to the pioneering efforts of the Dutch jurist Hugo Grotius (1583–1645), who believed in international laws governing all states based on natural law. As it evolved and became generally accepted, international law embraced practical arrangements that facilitated trade and diplomacy. For example, the high seas were considered free from any state's rule while by the early eighteenth century it was agreed that a state's territory extended only 3 miles from its coast, then the range of a cannon. States were required to issue formal declarations of war and provide causes for doing so. Eventually, international law was expanded to include such things as the treatment of prisoners of war. When Europeans became the dominant powers in world in the nineteenth and early twentieth centuries, their state system and its principles of sovereignty and international law became global.

TRIUMPH OF THE NATION-STATE

States seem solid and permanent, but they are, from a historical perspective, rather transient structures, rising up, disappearing, or morphing into something else. Only about a dozen or so of today's countries existed in anything like their current geographical form in 1500. All the rest of the literally hundreds of states, from tiny city-states and principalities to great empires, that existed have long vanished or changed beyond recognition. But one doesn't have to go back that far. Most of today's states didn't exist even one hundred years ago; a majority in 2020 are not as old as the average lifespan of a person.

In the twentieth century, the nation-state became the reigning system of political organization. Living in a world of sovereign nation-states seems so normal to us that we do not realize how recent it is. For most of the past couple of millennia most people lived in empires. At the start of the century, in 1900, more than four out of five people in the world were imperial subjects. The twentieth century saw the end of the age of empires that began with the early Chinese, the Persian, and Roman Empires and continued through the Incan, Ottoman, the Russian, the Japanese, the Spanish, the British, and so on. In 1945, empires still held about half the world's people (if we consider the Soviet Union as an empire). But today they are mostly gone. What happened? Nationalism, especially ethnic nationalism, destroyed them. It was combined with the idea of the government by consent of the governed to mean that a people had the right to freely choose their political status and their international status without interference. If a group of people identified themselves as a nation and wished to be a sovereign state, they had the right to be one.

The year 1919 is a good one to peg the beginning of the end of empires and the emergence of the world of nation-states. At the end of World War I, President Woodrow Wilson made the principle of national self-determination one of his "Fourteen Points" that were the aims of the peace settlement. The map of Europe was redrawn to accord with national aspirations of the various groups. The Austro-Hungarian and the Ottoman Empires disappeared. New states were created: Czechoslovakia, Poland, Estonia, Latvia, Lithuania, and Finland. Political boundaries of existing states were redrawn to conform to ethnic-national boundaries. At the same time, the new Bolshevik regime of Lenin in Russia denounced imperialism and offered support for nationalist independence movements.

However, the Western powers applied the principle of national self-determination only to Europeans and hung on to their colonial empires. In Germany, Italy, and Japan regimes came to power that glorified empire and sought to create or enlarge their own. But their defeat in World War II helped to discredit empire. Britain, France, and the Netherlands were too exhausted to hold on to theirs and the two superpowers, the United States and the Soviet Union, at least nominally championed sovereign nationhood as the only legitimate form of state. Nationalist movements of great intensity arose in India, Indonesia, Vietnam, Algeria, and elsewhere, and many new nations were born.

The principle of national self-determination was enshrined in the charter of the new UN organization in 1945. The great European colonial empires came to an end by the 1960s, with the exception of Portugal's which disintegrated in the mid-1970s. The last major empire, the Soviet Union, broke apart in 1991. The age of empire dating back to Sargon of Akkad in 2300 BCE in ancient Mesopotamia was over. The map of the world was now a map of nation-states or states that claimed to be nations. Each of our nine de facto states came about as the result of this breakup of empires. Abkhazia, South Ossetia, Transnistria, and Nagorno Karabakh emerged with the collapse of the Soviet empire. Northern Cyprus grew out of the end of Ottoman and the British empires. Kosovo was a product of the disintegration of the Ottoman and the mini-Serbian empire. Somaliland and the SADR are part of the legacy of the European colonial empires in Africa, and Taiwan is part of the legacy of the Chinese and then the Japanese empires.

IT IS SO HARD TO BECOME A STATE

As the result of the decline in empire, the number of internationally recognized states nearly quadrupled in the half century after World War II. But there have been few new states since the early 1990s. Mostly this is because empires are gone; it is also because international community has been reluctant to accept new members. Instead, there has been a tendency to stabilize the existing borders, bringing about what one writer calls "cartographic stasis."[12] In recent times, succession movements have garnered rather little support. When, for example, Biafra, the southeast region of Nigeria, seceded in 1967 declaring itself an independent state and fought valiantly for three years, it was recognized by very few countries. Most of the world, including the two superpowers of the time, backed the bloody efforts of the Nigerian government to suppress the rebellion.[13] The principle of self-determination seemed no longer to apply. In fact, since 1945, the international community has embraced the idea of national self-determination but only in a narrow meaning. Formal colonies such as those of the British and French colonial empires have the right to declare themselves independent states but not regions of a recognized member of the international community of sovereign states. The general operating principle has been that when a region has tried to secede, it is up to the state itself to decide how to respond. Between 1992 and 2020, only two secessionist movements succeeded in winning international recognition: East Timor in 2002 and South Sudan in 2011, although Kosovo has come close.[14]

The other side of this stability is that states are not likely to disappear. Unlike the past in which stronger countries conquered weaker ones without much need to justify their actions, today this is unacceptable. When Iraq invaded and attempted to annex Kuwait in 1990 to which it had a shaky historical claim, a vast coalition led by the United States liberated Kuwait and defeated the Iraqi armed forces. Russia's annexation of the Crimea in 2014 while not taking over a country was a forcible attempt to alter an international boundary. There was some justification for Russia actions—Crimea was ethnically and historically part of Russia and its assignment to Ukraine was rather arbitrary, and there seemed to be considerable support for the annexation by the local inhabitants. Yet the international community disapproved and placed costly economic sanctions on Russia. This rather unwelcoming attitude by the international community is one factor in explaining why our nine de facto states have been locked into their strange ambiguous status.

DEFINING DE FACTO STATES

De facto states are the political entities that are left out of the international community of sovereign states even though they seem to belong there. But what exactly is a de facto state? Unfortunately, there is no universally accepted definition. As a result, efforts to list them vary and each attempt adds or excludes one or more candidates. Generally it refers to a state that has achieved the basic requirements of a sovereign state: a well-defined territory, a population, and a government that exerts authority over it; it has state institutions that carry out the normal functions; it is effectively independent from external control, and it has the capacity to enter into relations with other members of the international community, but is not recognized by that community. Some would add that it actively seeks recognition. Nina Caspersen has added a few qualifiers. These include that it must be able to control at least two-thirds of the territory it claims and is recognized only by a patron state "and a few others of no great significance."[15] She also adds that it must be around for at least two years. The last is important that it must have a certain endurance to resemble a real state.

But these features are not as easily determined as they might sound. Does it have to have full control over all its territory? Does it have be completely free of outside control and how is that measured? How can the effectiveness of state's control over its population be determined? How actively does it need to pursue recognition and if that pursuit is a matter of expedience and not the real goal of the state, does it still count? And how long does a state have to exist before it can be distinguished from an insurgency or a temporary entity not an enduring one?

OUR NINE DE FACTO STATES

Nagorno Karabakh, Abkhazia, South Ossetia, Transnistria, Kosovo, the Turkish Republic of Northern Cyprus, the Sahrawi Arab Democratic Republic, Somaliland, and Taiwan each meet most of the criteria of a recognized state—they have clearly defined territories and, for the time being at least, stable boundaries.[16] They have permanent populations and governments that are in effective control of them and carry out the normal governing functions. Most are small; while Taiwan isn't—it has 23 million people—Republic of Nagorno Karabakh is, with only 150,000. But even this makes it bigger than fifteen UN members. They have the capacity to enter in relations with other states. Some have done so and have diplomatic relations with other states. Even those who do not such as Somaliland have informal relations with some countries that function like diplomatic ones. And they seem to be countries. They share not only most of the symbols and trappings of statehood but in most respects are viable as independent states. They appear to be rather permanent; most have been around, not for just two years, but for at least a quarter of a century. And that is long enough for a whole generation to grow up in them. If their situation is somewhat precarious, it is because they are not recognized by members of the international community. They do not all fit Caspersen's definition. The SADR controls only 15 percent of the territory it claims, and Kosovo enjoys considerable international recognition even if it is excluded from the UN. They are included because the SADR does have a stable effective government and strong sense of nationhood, and even if it is recognized by many important states Kosovo is still not an accepted member of the international community. All are in many ways unique entities making it difficult to be precise about what is or is not a de facto state.

The following chapters look at how these de facto states came about and their struggles to survive in a hostile international environment. They seek answers to several questions. Why has it become so difficult for them to gain international recognition? How have their governments and citizens managed to navigate in a world that does not accept their legitimacy? What common traits do they share? Are these sufficient to constitute a category of political entities distinct from others? And what do they reveal about the nature of the international state system that we inhabit? But these aren't the only reasons for studying them. Each of the unrecognized countries we are examining has its own special story that has resulted in its status. The following chapters will tell those stories.

NOTES

1. James Ker-Lindsay and Eiki Berg, "Introduction: A Conceptual Framework for Engagement with de facto States," *Journal of Ethnopolitics* 17, no. 4 (July, 2018): 335–42; George Kyris, *The Europeanisation of Contested Statehood: The EU in northern Cyprus* (London: Routledge, 2015).

2. Rebecca Bryant and Mete Hatay, *Suspended Sovereignty: Building the So-Called State* (Philadelphia, PA: University of Pennsylvania Press, 2020). The authors in the same text come up with another term: "aporetic" states.

3. Joshua Keating, *Invisible Countries: Journeys to the Edge of Nationhood* (New Haven, CT: Yale University Press, 2018).

4. Robert Jackson, *Quasi-States, International Relations, and the Third World* (Cambridge, UK: Cambridge University Press, 1990).

5. Scott Pegg, *International Society and the De Facto State* (London: Routledge, 1998).

6. "President Karzai, President of Afghanistan or Mayor of Kabul?" *The Guardian*, November 21, 2013, https://guardianlv.com/2013/11/karzai-the-president-of-afghanistan-or-the-mayor-of-kabul/, Accessed November 12, 2018.

7. Malcolm Nathan Shaw, *International Law* (Cambridge, UK: Cambridge University Press, 2003), 178.

8. Thomas D. Grant, *The Recognition of States: Law and Practice in Debate and Evolution* (Westport, CT: Praeger, 1999), 44–45.

9. Nina Caspersen, *Unrecognized States: The Struggle for Sovereignty in the Modern International System* (Cambridge, UK: Polity, 2012), 5.

10. John Armstrong, *Nations before Nationalism* (Chapel Hill, NC: University of North Carolina Press, 1982); Anthony D. Smith, *The Ethnic Origins of Nations* (Oxford, UK: Blackwell, 1986).

11. Examples are Ernest Gellner, *Nations and Nationalism* (Ithaca, NY: Cornell University Press, 1983); Benedict Anderson, *Imagined Communities: Reflections on the Origin ad Spread of Nationalism* (London: Verso, 1991).

12. Keating, *Invisible Countries*, 8.

13. James Crawford, *The Creation of States in International Law*, Second Edition (Oxford, UK: Oxford University Press, 2006), 415.

14. We will examine this last case further in chapter 5.

15. Caspersen, *Unrecognized States*, 11.

16. This is less true of the Sahrawi Arab Democratic Republic than of the others.

Chapter 2

Mountain Republic
Nagorno Karabakh (Artsakh)

INTRODUCTION TO ARTSAKH

Nagorno Karabakh may not be found on most world maps, but its physical existence is a reality. Wedged between Armenia to the west, Azerbaijan to the east, and Iran to the south, this former Armenian-speaking province of Azerbaijan declared itself an independent state in 1991, during the chaotic period that accompanied the disintegration of the Soviet Union. It is a small country, "officially" listed as having 4,400 square kilometers (1,700 square miles) that is a little smaller than the state of Delaware, 70 percent bigger than Luxembourg.[1] However, the state controls an area around 10,000 square kilometers (4,000 square miles) or about the size of Connecticut. It is mountainous highland, with less than 150,000 inhabitants, more than a third living in the capital Stepanakert. Outside of Stepanakert and a few other towns, much of the country is quite sparsely populated with the number of wolves and bears rivaling that of people.

Most of the world regards Nagorno Karabakh (Karabakh for short) as part of Azerbaijan. But Azerbaijan has had no control or presence in the area since its armed forces were driven out by Armenian and Karabakh troops in 1993. The people of this small republic are ethnically Armenian, and their original aim was to join their fellow Armenians in Armenia. But that did not happen; instead, they became their own little state. No one officially recognizes it, but Armenia supports it. Armenian troops defend it, and its only connections with the outside world are through Armenia. There are no trains or express buses to it. It has a brand new airport, but no plane has ever landed or taken off from it. There are two road connections with Armenia, and both are adventurous, narrow paths through rugged mountain country. There are little mini-buses that take one there or a traveler can hire a car and driver in the Armenian capital of Yerevan. Or it is possible to pay for a ride in an Armenian military helicopter to the Armenian military base not far from Stepanakert. Being a nonrecognized country, it has no internet domain name, no postal or telephone code, communications to it are routed through Armenia.

Nagorno Karabakh is also known as Artsakh—that's the name that appeared on my visa—although it is not often used outside the country. Artsakh is derived from an ancient Armenian province, a name that long predates the arrival of the Turks and the Russians in the area. Historically part of Armenia, it was absorbed by the Russian empire in 1813, before then it changed hands many times. The more common name used for the region—Nagorno Karabakh—reflects the cultural influences in the area. Nagorno is derived from the Russian *nagorny* meaning highland, *Kara* is Turkish for black and *bagh* is Persian for garden. Hence, the name literally translated is "highland black garden." The name is appropriate since it is a highland. Furthermore, getting there one crosses semi-arid mountains and then comes upon what is, by comparison to its barren surroundings, a comparatively lush garden land with dark forests.

Karabakh was an accidental country, born of a conflict between the Armenians and the Azeri Turks of Azerbaijan. Understanding Karabakh requires understanding this conflict. In turn, understanding this conflict requires some knowledge of the Caucasus region and its complex physical and human geography, who the Armenians are, the impact of the Armenian genocide on the Armenians, Soviet policy in the region, and the chaos that accompanied the disintegration of the Soviet Union.

MOUNTAIN OF LANGUAGES: THE CAUCASUS REGION

Nagorno Karabakh is situated in the Caucasus region, a mountainous area between the Black and Caspian Seas. Politically, the Caucasus region is divided into the northern Caucasus which lies in Russia and the southern Caucasus that consists of Azerbaijan, Georgia, and Armenia and Nagorno Karabakh. The Arabs have referred to the region as *Jabal al-Alsine* or the "Mountain of Languages."[2] And for good reason. It is an area that could fit inside France or Texas yet contains an incredible variety of languages, ethnicities, and cultures. The linguistic diversity is amazing—greater than the entire continent of Europe minus the Caucasus. There are Indo-European languages such as Russian and Armenian (which are very different from each other), as well as several Iranian languages, such as Ossetian. There are Turkish languages such as Azeri, Karachay, and others. Most of the languages spoken in the Caucasus, however, are not linked to languages spoken anywhere else. They form three language families completely unrelated to each other: Northeast Caucasian, Northwest Caucasian, and the Kartvelian languages which include Georgian. The Caucasus is not just an area of linguistic diversity but a kaleidoscope of cultures as well. It is where the Middle East/ Islamic and European worlds meet. The population includes Sunni Muslims, Shi'ite Muslims, Orthodox Christians, and the Armenians who have their own branch of Christianity.

The ethnic-linguistic diversity of the region is a product of its geography. It lies between the Russian steppe to the north, the lands of the Middle East to the south, between the Caspian Sea to the east, and the Black Sea to the west. The Black Sea connects the Caucasus to Europe and the Mediterranean while the Caspian Sea links it with Central Asia. The landscapes are as varied and the people. Two major mountain chains cross this area: the Greater Caucasus and the Lesser Caucasus. These are rugged ranges and include the highest mountains in Europe. In between are lush valleys, semi-arid plains, grasslands, and canyon country. Only in a few other places in the world can landscapes change so dramatically in such short distances.

Many independent states arose here from ancient times but in the past few centuries the region was divided between the Ottoman Empire, the Russian Empire, and Persia, with the Russians eventually gaining control of almost the entire area in the nineteenth century. After 1918, it was incorporated into the Soviet Union. When the Soviet Union fell apart, three countries emerged: Azerbaijan, Georgia, and Armenia in the south. The northern Caucasus remained part of Russia but was divided into a number of semiautonomous Russian republics. The complicated geography and the diversity of the area along with a resurgence of local ethnic-national identity made for a troubled region with many ethnic conflicts. Among the best known was the war in Chechnya, a small semiautonomous region of Russia where the 1.5 million Chechens, a Muslim people speaking a Northeast Caucasian language, fought an unsuccessful independence war. Another conflict was the war between Armenia and Azerbaijan over Nagorno Karabakh.

JUST SAY HI! WHO ARE THE ARMENIANS?

The people of Nagorno Karabakh are Armenians. There are about 8 million Armenians living around the world, including more than 1 million in the United States. The best-known Armenian-Americans are probably the singer Cherylin Sarkisian (better known as Cher) and Kim Kardashian. Three million live in Armenia, and 150,000 live in Nagorno Karabakh. They are an ancient ethnic group tracing themselves back nearly three thousand years to the state of Urartu in what is now eastern Turkey. Outsiders call them as

"Armenians," a name that was first recorded in a Persian inscription twenty-five centuries ago. However, they call themselves the Hay (pronounced "high"). The Armenians are a distinctive people with their own language, which despite being an Indo-European language is very different from the other members of the language family. Unlike the Romance, Germanic, or Slavic languages, there is little shared vocabulary, and it is not obvious that the language is related to most European languages. Not only do they have their own very distinct language, but Armenians have their own alphabet created in 405 CE by Mesrop Mashtots. Armenians are Christians with their own very old institution—the Armenian Apostolic Church. That is, they are not Catholic, Orthodox, or Protestant, but members of a distinct branch of Christianity. Christianity has deep roots; in fact, the premodern kingdom of Armenia officially adopted Christianity in 301, the first state to do so.[3]

Their ancient home was in a highland area of eastern Turkey extending into the Caucasus. Sometimes the home to an independent state, Armenia at other times was ruled by various powers. In the sixteenth to nineteenth centuries, it was divided between the Turkish Ottoman Empire and Persia (Iran). As a result of being divided into two antagonistic empires, Armenians split into eastern and western groups with separate dialects. The Persian part became part of the Russian Empire in the early nineteenth century and later part of the Soviet Union and then in 1991, the independent state of Armenia. Western Armenia disappeared in 1915.

In the center of their historical homeland is Mount Ararat, the tallest mountain in the Middle East. And what an impressive mountain it is, rising far above anything around it. To most people in the West, it is best known as the place where Noah's ark landed. Today the mountain is easily visible from much of the country but is not accessible to most Armenians for it lies in Turkey and across a fortified, tense border that is closed to them. It is a border that sadly separates the people of Armenia from this symbol of their identity and antiquity. Mount Ararat also is a reminder of the tragedy that has haunted Armenians for over a century: the Armenian Genocide.

THE ARMENIAN GENOCIDE

Nagorno Karabakh in an indirect way is the product of the first large-scale genocide of the twentieth century. In 1914, Turkey, still called the Ottoman Empire, went to war on the side of Germany and Austria-Hungary against the Allies: Britain, France, and Russia. At that time, the once mighty Ottoman Empire was in decline having fallen behind the nations of the West in science, technology, economic wealth, and political and military power. It saw its empire shrink as various groups—Romanian, Serbs, Bulgarians, and

Greeks—inspired by modern nationalism rebelled and formed independent states. In 1908, a reform-minded group of military officers, the Young Turks, took control and tried to modernize and strengthen what was left of their empire. They were becoming increasingly nationalistic, moving it in the direction of a Turkish ethnic state.

The Armenians living in the middle of what they considered their heartland were also becoming more inspired by nationalism and some sought an independent nation-state. From the point of view of the Turkish government, Armenian nationalism posed a threat to the territorial integrity of their state. Tensions between Armenians and Turks increased and there were periodic massacres of Armenians. During the war, the Ottoman rulers were fighting for the survival of their state with the Russians moving in on their eastern border. Some Armenians looked to Russia for help in securing their independence. Seeing all Armenians as potential enemy supporters, the government in 1915 ordered the arrest and execution of prominent Armenian leaders, then rounded up nearly the entire population and marched them into the desert where they perished. Historians estimate that at least 800,000 Armenians died with some estimates going as high as 1.5 million.[4] Turkey has denied the Armenian Genocide ever happened but many scholars consider it the first major genocide of the twentieth century; it may have served as an inspiration for Hitler's genocide of the Jews in World War II. For Armenians, the genocide was their great collective tragedy.

During the chaos that accompanied the Russian Revolution in 1917, Turks invaded the Russian-ruled eastern Armenia. It is not certain whether this would have led to another round of genocide, but in any case, the Bolsheviks intervened, and the Armenians were saved. After a brief period as an independent state, eastern Armenia became the Armenian Soviet Socialist Republic. When the Soviet Union was dissolved in 1991, it became the independent state of Armenia.

HISTORICAL KARABAKH

Karabakh has, during most of recorded history, been the easternmost part of Armenia. But separated by mountains and on the outer fringe of the Armenian world, it has been a bit different; today it has its own dialect.[5] The area of what is now Nagorno Karabakh is mentioned in inscriptions dating back to the first millennium BCE. The Greeks referred to it as Okhinstene. Although our evidence of this is shaky, it appears to have been inhabited by Armenian-speaking people from as early as the seventh century BCE. From 180 CE to the fourth century, it was Artsakh, one of the ten provinces of the Kingdom of Armenia. In fact, one of Armenia's famed rulers Tigran the Great, who ruled from 95 to 55 BCE, placed one of his four capitals in the province.[6] The ruins of this city, Tigranakert, are located about 48 kilometers (30 miles) northwest of Stepanakert and can be visited today.[7] The kingdom of Armenia went into decline, but Armenian culture continued, much of it centered in monasteries. These medieval monasteries still dot the region. In Nagorno Karabakh, the most impressive example of the rich tradition of monasteries is Gandzasar on a highpoint outside the northern town of Vank. Vank, incidentally, is the Armenian word for monastery.

After 1500, the region was part Persia. When the Persian state weakened in the eighteenth century, it became an autonomous Khanate of Karabakh ruled by a Turkish-speaking Khan in Shusha (Shushi) although still part of Persia. After 1813, under the Treaty of Gulistan, the area, like most of eastern Armenia, passed from Persian to Russian rule. Western Armenian lands remained under Ottoman Turkey's control.[8] By the early nineteenth century, the majority of the population were non-Armenians, mostly Azeri Turks. Armenian speakers were only a small minority. Encouraged by Russia, many Armenians left Persia and settled in the Russian territory including Karabakh. As a result, over the next century the Armenians went from being a small minority to a majority once again.[9] In 1918, the area was ethnically mixed with an Armenia majority and a large Muslim, mostly Azeri Turkish minority.

BACKGROUND TO THE CONFLICT

The conflict that created the current state of Nagorno Karabakh is not rooted on an ancient hatred between the Azeri Turks and the Armenian people of the region, although this is what most contemporary Armenians and Karabakhis believe. Rather it is a "modern hatred" based on events in the past century or so.[10] If a date had to be chosen for the start of the present conflict over Nagorno Karabakh, 1905 would be a good one to select.[11] The Russians promoted the Christians in the region whom they saw as being more loyal than the Muslims. But they became concerned about the growing sense of Armenian national identity. Like all empires in the late nineteenth and twentieth century, they found the growing sense of national consciousness among their subjects a threat. Meanwhile, in the late nineteenth century Russian Azerbaijan underwent an oil boom. The city of Baku on the Caspian Sea became the world's largest center of oil production at a time when a global demand for kerosene and for gasoline was emerging. Many Armenians came to Baku, being better educated they often took more professional and skilled jobs. The Azerbaijani nobility and the emerging Azeri middle class resented the growing Armenian domination in the economy.[12] This resulted in riots and armed conflicts between the two ethnic groups in 1905, a turbulent year in the Russian Empire that saw widespread unrest and rebellion in wake of Russia's defeat in the Russo-Japanese war. The so-called Armenian-Tatar War (Tatar was a common Russian term for Turkish-speaking Muslims) resulted in several thousand casualties.[13]

The conflict did much to foster a growing sense of Azerbaijani national identity as well as hatred of Armenians. Azeris a decade later became alarmed when tens of thousands of Armenians fled into the region escaping the Armenian genocide during 1915–1916. Then the Russian Revolution in 1917 saw a collapse of Russian authority in the region. In the absence of imperial authority, various long-repressed ethnic sentiments emerged along the periphery of the empire, including the Caucasus region. Left on their own, the leaders of Georgia, Armenia, and Azerbaijan formed a short-lived Trans-Caucasian Federation in 1918. This soon broke up into the Azerbaijan Democratic Republic, the Democratic Republic of Armenia, and the Democratic Republic of Georgia. During this chaotic time, Russian efforts to secure the oil fields of Baku resulted in Armenian-Azeri clashes that left thousands dead during the so-called Bloody March of 1918.[14] Then in 1919–1920, Armenia and Azerbaijan went to war over the disputed territories of Karabakh, Zangezur (which the Armenians call Syunik), and Nakhchivan, all areas of mixed populations. In 1920, Turkey invaded the Armenian Republic. It forced Armenia to cede territory to Turkey, give it control over its railways, and allow free passage to Turkish troops. The Bolsheviks who were consolidating power throughout the former empire intervened and took control preventing Armenia from falling under effective Turkish rule but ending its brief existence as an independent state.[15] By 1921, the Bolsheviks were able to consolidate power and reestablished central authority over the region.

KARABAKH UNDER SOVIET RULE

Nagorno Karabakh became a contested land in the 1910s between increasingly nationalistic Armenian peoples, fearful of the Turks that nearly surrounded them and of an emerging Azerbaijani nation. When most of the old empire was put back together by the Bolsheviks, they had to address the "nationality question" as they called the issue of how to rule a multiethnic state with many separatist movements. They did so by creating autonomous republics. Each of these would be allowed to have its own language made official along with Russian and was given some latitude toward promoting its own culture. In 1921–1922, Russia was reconstituted as the Union of Soviet Socialist Republics, with a giant Russian Federated Soviet Socialist Republic and some smaller ones. Within these "republics" smaller ethnic groups were given their autonomous regions.

The Bolsheviks made the briefly independent states of Armenia, Georgia, and Azerbaijan into Soviet republics. Boundaries in this ethnically complicated region often reflected perceived national and local political interests and not the wishes of the local population. In 1922, to the outrage of Armenians, Moscow gave Nakhchivan, a wedge of territory between Armenia, Turkey, and Iran with a large Armenian population, and Karabakh to the new Azerbaijan Soviet Socialist Republic. This decision was made in part to placate Turkey, which did not want to see this area come under non-Turkish rule. Since Karabakh had an Armenian-speaking non-Muslim majority, it was made an autonomous province of Azerbaijan in 1923. The area was small only about one half the size of historic Karabakh and was surrounded by Azerbaijan.[16] It remained a predominantly Armenian area in the Azerbaijani Soviet Socialist Republic. In 1989, 76.9 percent of the region's population, numbering 145,000, was Armenian, Azerbaijanis numbering 40,600 made up only 21.5 percent.[17] This proved to be a problem. The Armenian population in Nagorno Karabakh never accepted the idea of being part of Azerbaijan—the last thing any Armenian wanted was being ruled by Turks.

Armenians never accepted the loss of Karabakh. Karabakh Armenians unsuccessfully appealed to Moscow in 1936 and in 1947 to have their region reassigned to Armenia.[18] Armenian leaders had pressed for the transfer of Nagorno Karabakh to the Armenian SSR in the 1960s and 1970s.[19] In 1963, 2,500 Karabakh Armenians signed a petition to have the region transferred to Armenia. Demonstrations in support of the petition broke out in Stepanakert resulting in eighteen deaths. More protests took place in 1965 and 1977, and this was in the Soviet Union where public demonstrations were rare. That they took place at all is indication of the depth of feeling over the issue. In the 1980s, Armenians accused the Azerbaijan Communist Party boss, Heydar Aliyev of trying to settle Azerbaijanis into Karabakh and making it less Armenian. What many feared was that Karabakh could go the way of Nakhchivan, the exclave of Azerbaijan that many Armenians after the Bolshevik Revolution thought should have been given to Armenia. When Nakhchivan was made part of the Azerbaijan Soviet Socialist Republic in the 1920s, 40 percent of the population was Armenian. By the 1980s, there were hardly any Armenians left.[20] Then there were the memories among Armenians of the genocide, a genocide carried out by Turks and to many Armenians, the Azerbaijanis were Turks. Although the Azerbaijanis had nothing to do with the events of 1915, the fact that Azerbaijani Communist Party leader Heydar Aliyev denied the Armenian genocide ever occurred obscured that point.[21]

When Mikhail Gorbachev became the leader of the Soviet Union in 1985 and introduced the policy of allowing for freer expression and reducing political and social oppression, these old grievances came out in the open. A rise in Armenian and Azerbaijani ethnic expression led to protests and occasionally violent clashes. In 1987, organizers gathered thousands of signatures by Armenians in the republic and in Karabakh requesting reunification of Armenia and Karabakh. Gorbachev, however, stated the boundaries of the republics could not be changed. In February, mass protests took place in Stepanakert, the Karabakh capital reaching 100,000 on February 22—a huge number for such a small population. Demonstrations calling for the transfer of Karabakh to Armenia in Yerevan reached 1 million, a quarter of the population of Armenia—truly amazing in size and some of the largest demonstrations ever in the Soviet Union.[22] A group of Armenian intellectuals formed the Karabakh Committee to press for the issue. They were arrested in late 1988 but released a few months later. This committee became the most influential group in the resurgent Armenian national movement and its leader Levon Ter-Petrosian later became the president of Armenia. The slow Soviet response to the earthquake in the Armenian city of Leninakan (Gyumri) that destroyed much of the second city of Armenia on December 7, 1988, killing 25,000, only added to anger and frustration with Moscow.[23]

Tensions between Armenians and Azerbaijanis grew as Azerbaijani nationalism grew, in part, stimulated by the conflict with Armenians. A kind of vicious feedback loop occurred with each act of violence or revenge on the part of one side only further inflaming the nationalist passions of the other. In early 1988, following rumors that Armenians had attacked and driven out Azeri villagers in Armenia, Azeri mobs carried out an anti-Armenian pogrom in the oil refining city of Sumgait. Armenian homes and businesses were attacked; at least twenty-nine killed, perhaps many more and almost all the 14,000 Armenians there fled.[24] On April 24, the day Armenian commemorate as Armenian Genocide Day, Armenians nationalists began equating Azerbaijani Turks with Ottoman Turks—rhetoric only designed to instill more hatred. Violence continued including Armenian attacks of their Azeri and Kurdish minorities, eventually some 200,000 of them fled Armenia. Then in January 1990, what Armenians call "Black January" occurred in which another anti-Armenian pogrom took place in Azerbaijan, this time in Baku. One hundred and twenty Armenians were killed before the Soviet forces intervened. Most of the sizeable Armenian community in the oil production city were evacuated to Armenia.[25] By 1991, both Armenia and Azerbaijan had been "ethnically cleansed" but not Karabakh—this was the last place where the two ethnicities were neighbors.

WHO ARE THE AZERIS?

Just who are Azeris? They are Turks. Citizens of Azerbaijan are known as Azerbaijanis; the largest ethnic group in Azerbaijan is Azeris who make up about 90 percent of the population. Confusingly, all ethnic Azeris are also called Azerbaijanis. About 15 million Azeris live in Iran and 9 million in Azerbaijan. Azerbaijan, the country is a chunk of Persia that was annexed by the Russian Empire in 1828. Azeris in both Iran and Azerbaijan speak the same Azeri, a language closely related to Turkish, in fact, the two languages are mutually intelligible. What separates Azeris from the cousins in Turkey is religion—Azeris are Shi'a, whereas Turks are Sunni Muslims. Also, unlike their cousins in Turkey, the Azeris were heavily influenced by Persian and Russian culture.

Azeris were not confined to Azerbaijan but could be found in much of the Caucasus region. In fact, the mixture of peoples made drawing up states by ethnic lines difficult. This is reflected on the map which shows the section of Azerbaijan called Nakhchivan that borders Armenia, Turkey, and Iran, separated from the rest of the country by Armenia and Karabakh. Nagorno Karabakh itself was both at times, an Armenian and Azeri region. Historically, the people of the region defined themselves first by religion. And for Azeris what most distinguished themselves from the Armenians was being Muslim. Until more recent times, Azeris often called themselves simply Muslims rather than Azeris or Azerbaijanis. But for Armenians after 1915, they were also Turks. Armenians therefore felt hemmed in on two sides by Turks, Turkey to the west and Azerbaijan to the east. It wasn't just paranoia—there was a pan-Turkish movement that sought to unify all Turks. Azeri, for example, is written in the Latin alphabet rather than in Arabic script or in Cyrillic; this was adopted so that the written language would be closer to that of Turkey, which in the 1920s had adopted the Latin alphabet.[26]

"WE WERE HERE FIRST": HISTORY WARS AND IDENTITIES

Armenians are an ancient people, and the Azerbaijani have a long history as well, but their modern national identity is more recent. Both these identities and their claims to the Nagorno Karabakh region have been based on how they see their history. Armenian historians portray the region as being Armenian since ancient times while Azerbaijani historians regard this as a myth.[27] Azerbaijani scholars have determined that the Azeris have long historian roots in the area while Armenian historians see them as relative newcomers.

Azerbaijanis appear to have the weaker case for an ancient claim to the region. They reject the findings of most outside scholars that the Turks entered the South Caucasus in the eleventh century, instead arguing that Khazar Turks arrived in the sixth or seventh century (known as the Seljuq theory versus Khazar theory). According to their "Albanian theory," the territory of Karabakh was part of Caucasian Albania (no relation to the other Albania in the Balkans), the people became Turkified and Islamicized with the arrival of the Turks. Thus, the Azerbaijani people were formed as the fusion of the two, and Karabakh was in the center of that process. It was not Armenian until the Russian took control over the region 1810–1828 and brought in hundreds of thousands of Armenians. Thus, not just Karabakh but much of Armenia itself was originally Azerbaijani. Some Azerbaijanis refer to both as Western Azerbaijan.[28] On the basis of these historical interpretations, the Azerbaijanis cultivated the idea that Armenians were "treacherous and ungrateful guests."[29] They were "guests" since they entered what was an ancient heartland of Azeri Turks and then took over.

The Armenian Karabakhis understand it differently. They see themselves as descendants of Caucasian people who were Christianized and Armenianized when they adopted Armenian Christianity in the early Middle Ages, long before the Turks arrived. In fact, the ethnic origins of the region are a bit murky, but the historical evidence supports that Armenian interpretation with some caveats. The Turks do appear to have entered the region long after the ancestors of modern Armenians lived there. Furthermore, Azeri historical claims to the area are complicated by the fact that there was no Azerbaijani state until 1918. Unlike the Armenians who had various states with a distinctive Armenian identity in ancient and medieval times, the last disappearing in 1375, there was never an Azerbaijani state. However, the dynasty that ruled Persia in the eighteenth and nineteenth century, the Qajar, were ethnically Azerbaijani so this is used to justify the idea that the area was under Azerbaijani rule. This, of course, is a bit of a stretch.

Yet one of part of the Azerbaijani historical argument does hold up. According to the Russian census of 1823, the first we have of the region, only 9 percent of the population of Karabakh was Armenian at that time, the rest were Azeri and Kurds. By 1880, 53 percent were Armenians.[30] Armenians explain this, by arguing that thousands of Armenians were displaced to Persia in the sixteenth and seventeenth centuries,[31] which is also supported by historical evidence. So rather than accepting the fluid ethnic nature of the region, both sides create a narrative of ethnic continuity. Rather than falsify history, they each select that part of it which supports their claim to the region.

THE KARABAKH WAR

The Union of Soviet Socialist Republics, successor to the Russian Empire, had consisted of fifteen so-called autonomous Soviet Socialist Republics: the Russian Soviet Republic which had half the population and four-fifths of the area and fourteen smaller ones. There, however, was never any doubt that the Soviet Union was a predominantly Russian state. While many republics and autonomous regions had their own language, which was taught in schools and used in the media, all citizens learned Russian, and Russian was the main language of government, business, and the professions. Most Soviet citizens, even if they had a different mother tongue, spoke Russian fluently. Most of the leadership was ethnically Russian, but not all—Stalin, for example, was Georgian.

In many respects, the Soviet Union was simply another modern empire, or a modernized version of the Russian empire of the tsars. The Soviet leadership did not see it that way and made efforts to create a new Soviet nationalism that would replace the ethnic-based loyalties of the Russians, Ukrainians, Armenians, Uzbeks, Lithuanians, and so on. It was not entirely unsuccessful. Many people did identify with the Soviet state as their nation. Yet the very fact that the Soviet Union preserved the fiction of being made up of autonomous states provided the institutional bases for new states to emerge. Many ethnic groups, such as Muslim Tadzhiks or Lithuanians who had a very different culture and a history of being an independent state, never fully assimilated. In fact, the ethnic identities remained strong. When Gorbachev loosened the censorship on expression, there was an outburst of ethnic-national pride as well as pent-up grievances. Old ethnic animosities reemerged almost overnight.

Gorbachev also inadvertently undermined the Soviet Union when he shifted more authority to the republics and allowed freely contest elections to take place in them in 1990. People turned out to feel more loyalty to their republics than to the Soviet Union and so the system unraveled in late 1991. As the Soviet Union began disintegrating, old ethnic conflicts, previously suppressed under Moscow's tight rule, flared up. A process thus occurred much like that which happened seven decades earlier when the Russian Empire collapsed in 1917. Few disputes emerged so quickly and intensely than the tensions between the Armenians and Azerbaijanis over Karabakh. In November 1991, the Azerbaijan government abolished the Nagorno Karabakh Autonomous Oblast placing the region under its direct control. It renamed the territory Xankandi, the old Turkish name for Stepanakert.[32] The Turkish name suggested to many Armenians that this was a prelude to an attempt by Azerbaijan to ethnically cleanse Karabakh. The following month the alarmed Armenian population held a referendum on independence. Almost all ethnic Armenians voted in favor, the Azeri minority boycotted it. On December 10, 1991, the Armenians proclaimed the Nagorno Karabakh Republic. Baku sent troops to crush the rebellion, Armenia intervened to support it, and war broke out between the two newly independent states. Full-scale fighting began in 1992.[33]

The war was serious business. Neither country had well-organized armed forces, but they quickly developed them. Both sides had considerable surplus Soviet military equipment, much of it bought extremely cheaply on the black market. Most Azeri and Armenian men had served in the Soviet Army; some had fought in Afghanistan. Both Armenia and Azerbaijan also employed Russians mercenaries. Overall, Azerbaijan had many advantages: it was much bigger, more than 8 million people opposed to Armenia's 3 million and it was a large oil producer, so it had money to purchase arms. And although it was a secular state, some Muslims volunteered to help Azerbaijan, including about one thousand Afghan mujahedeen. The Armenians, however, gained the upper hand in the fighting and launched an offensive in December 1993 that overran the Azerbaijani positions in Karabakh. The Azeri stronghold of Shushi fell, Azerbaijani forces fled the area along with almost the entire Azeri population.[34]

All the while this conflict was occurring, the Armenians were worried about Turkey intervening, forcing Armenia to keep troops along the Turkish border. But although there was strong popular sentiment to help their fellow Turks in Azerbaijan, the government in Ankara decided not to intervene. The war was an Armenian-Karabakh victory. When a ceasefire was arranged with Russian assistance on May 12, 1994, all of Nagorno Karabakh was in Karabakh and Armenian hands. Armenians not only helped drive the Azerbaijanis out of Karabakh, they also seized control of other borderlands. Hundreds of thousands of Azeris fled from these areas. About 14 percent of Azerbaijani territory was held by Armenia.[35] Much of it became a depopulated no-man's land as the Azeris fled. More than 1.5 million Azeris became refugees, most living in refugee camps in Azerbaijan.[36]

INDEPENDENT NAGORNO KARABAKH

Azerbaijan never recognized the independence of Karabakh or the Armenian annexations of territory; the two countries (three if we include Nagorno Karabakh) remain to this day in a state of war. This makes it, after the Korean War, the longest continuing conflict between sovereign nations in the world today. On and off negotiations have continued since the end of war, but tensions and occasional military clashes along the border continue. The world was reminded of this in April 2016 when a military engagement between the Nagorno Karabakh Defense Army and Azerbaijan refugees over a disputed territory erupted; it was joined by the Armenian military as well. Four days of fighting resulted in an estimated 350 casualties.[37]

Negotiations over ending the conflict between Armenia and Azerbaijan have been conducted since the 1990s under the auspices of the Organization of Security and Cooperation in Europe (OSCE), and by the Minsk Group which includes European Union (EU) and United States representatives. The status of Nagorno Karabakh is the key issue blocking peace. Azerbaijan maintains that Nagorno Karabakh is a rebel province. It has recognized Karabakh as a third party in armistice talks but never as an independent state. The Azerbaijani government has promised to give the people of Nagorno Karabakh "the highest degree of autonomy" but they must accept their incorporation into the Azerbaijan state.[38] The position of Armenia is that the fate of the territory should be decided in a referendum by the Karabakh people. Most Armenians regard Karabakh as a historic and rightful part of their homeland and support annexation, but the Armenian government fears annexing it will jeopardize the prospects for a lasting peace. Both Moscow, Armenia's most important patron and military ally, and Washington, which has good terms with both Armenia and Azerbaijan, also opposed annexation. Then there is the issue of Azeri refugees. Among the Karabakhis who regarded the Azeris (or "Turks" as they simply call them) as outsiders who settled in this Armenian region more recent centuries, there was no desire to see them return.

Karabakhis created their republic not as an end, but as a means of detaching themselves from Azerbaijan as a first step to joining their ethnic cousins in Armenia. Thus, the state they established was a conditional one, just a temporary situation until that time. Everything about the new country spoke of its provisional status. It chose to use Armenian currency. The postal system and other parts of the administration were designed so they could be integrated into Armenia once the two countries emerged. Even the flag was based on the Armenian flag, with a jagged line across the center indicating the split in the Armenian nation. One could say the Nagorno Karabakh was an accidental state. The people who fought and died for it did so not to create an independent state but to join Armenia. They saw themselves as Armenians living in the eastern most extension of the historical Armenian homeland but living under Turkish (Azeri) administration. Their aim was to join the other surviving Armenians in their own state. There has been strong public support in Armenia for annexing it; however, this has been resisted by the Armenian government as endangering the prospects for a peaceful settlement.

So where does that leave Nagorno Karabakh? In 2006, a referendum was held for a new constitution; 87 percent participated, and 98 percent approved. The election was observed by monitors from NGOs and by foreign journalists who reported it to be conducted fairly. More than 100 nongovernmental international observers and journalists who monitored the poll evaluated it positively, stating that it was held to a high international standard. The first article of the document describes the Nagorno Karabakh Republic as "a sovereign, democratic legal and social state."[39] The referendum was criticized by the EU and Turkey since the thousands of Azeri refugees that had fled were excluded. Yet, it is clear, that the overwhelming majority of Karabakhis accept their country's current status as an independent state, at least for now. Their independence may be one of expediency, yet it does satisfy one overriding concern for them—being free of Azeri rule.

AN UNRESOLVED CONFLICT

As of 2021, Armenia (and Karabakh) remained at a state of war with Azerbaijan. The government in Baku is determined to get Nagorno Karabakh and other lost territories back. And there is the issue of the half million refugees. Many still live in substandard temporary refugee housing, and others still hope to return to the hometowns. This sense of Azerbaijani victimization is fostered by the government in Baku, which is, incidentally, a family enterprise. When it became independent in 1991, its local Communist Party boss Heydar Aliyev became president and ran an authoritarian regime. Upon his death in 2003, he was succeeded by his son Ilham Aliyev. Although socially liberal and on good terms with the United States and the EU as well as with Russia, Azerbaijan is a dictatorship. The country is rich in oil and natural gas which has brought prosperity to the country. However, father and son Aliyev have found appealing to anti-Armenian sentiment, reminding people of the loss of their land and of the loss of Karabakh province, and constantly pointing to the hundreds of thousands who lost their homes is a useful diversion from questioning their family regime. Every now and then they create incidences to keep the tensions alive. For almost all Armenians, returning Nagorno Karabakh to Azerbaijan is out of the question. Karabakhis do not just oppose living under Baku's authority—they fear reprisals, repression, ethnic cleansing, and perhaps genocide.[40]

A peculiar feature of the Karabakh conflict is that both sides—the Armenians and the Azerbaijanis—have the same allies. Both remain on good terms with the Russians, although the Armenians depend on them more than do the Azerbaijanis who can afford to buy their weapons and are in less need of aid. They both are also on good terms with the United States. On the other hand, Azerbaijan has good relations with Armenia's nemesis Turkey while Armenia maintains good relations with Iran, a country whose regime is on bad terms with Baku. This might seem strange since the Azerbaijanis have religious links with Shi'a Iran as well as historical and cultural ones. But secular Azerbaijan remains an annoyance and even a threat to the Islamic state of Iran, while Iran's religion fundamentalism is a threat to the secular Azerbaijani regime.

NAGORNO KARABAKH AND ETHNIC CLEANSING

It is understandable that the Karabakhis desire to be free of Azerbaijani rule and control their own destiny, but there is the troubling issue of ethnic cleansing. In 1991, the ethnic composition of Nagorno Karabakh was 76 percent Armenian and 23 percent Azeri. It had a total population of 192,000.[41] Today, Karabakh is almost 99 percent ethnically Armenian. Karabakhis and Armenians argue that people voluntarily left, that there was no forced removal of the population. This might be technically true in most cases. There were fewer cases of civilians being deliberately targeted as happened to Kosovars in Kosovo (see chapter 5) or Bosnians in Bosnia or Rohingyas in Myanmar. Furthermore, just prior to the war almost all of Azerbaijan's Armenian minority had fled or was evacuated from Azerbaijan. Nonetheless, the result was the same, hundreds of thousands of Azeris lost their homes. Today visitors to the once Azeri majority city of Shushi see many abandoned houses and boarded up mosques giving the city a semi-ghost town feel. Even more troubling, the Karabakh countryside is dotted with totally abandoned villages, left behind by the tens of thousands of Azeris who once lived in them. Many still hope to return to their homes.

IS KARABAKH A COUNTRY?

Is Nagorno Karabakh a nation? Karabakh's entire identity is linked with Armenia. The local name for the country Artsakh is name for one of the ten historical provinces of ancient Armenia. Both Armenians in Armenia and Karabakhis regard the role of Nagorno Karabakh as central to Armenian history. The National Museum in Stepanakert presents much of its history as that of an Armenian province. Historical displays on the history of the region usually place it within the context of Armenian history.[42] Nagorno Karabakh is depicted as a special place, with a uniquely ancient and rich historical heritage but an Armenian place whose history is part of the story of the Armenian people. Its foremost historical site is the ruins of Tigranakert, the ancient Armenian capital. Karabakhis speak a distinctive dialect but it is easily understood by other Armenians, they use the same Armenian alphabet and almost all are at least nominally members of the Armenian Apostolic Church. Thus, Karabakhis share the same markers of identity with other Armenians: their seventeen-century-old form of Christianity, their unique written script, pride in their ancient history, and the sense of victimhood in modern times at the hands of the Turks (Ottoman or Azeri).

Interestingly, Nagorno Karabakh is one of the few functioning democracies in the region, albeit an imperfect one. It has a National Assembly which is unicameral. The Assembly is small, fittingly so for a small country, with thirty-three members who are elected for five-year terms. It has freely contested elections and a multiparty system. Five political parties were represented in the Assembly in 2019: the Free Motherland Party, the Democratic Party of Artsakh, Movement 88, the ARF, and the National Revival Party. Elections in Karabakh have been monitored and deemed fair by the EU and by observers from a number of countries. It has been recognized by Freedom House as more democratic than the semi-democratic Republic of Armenia, or than Azerbaijan which is not democratic at all.[43]

It has its own armed forces of 18,000–20,000 personnel. However, about 10,000 are actually from Armenia, only about 8,000 Karabakhis are on active duty at a time, but then this is a high percentage for a country of only 150,000. Almost all Karabakh men of proper age serve in the reserves. The army is well equipped with hundreds of tanks, armed vehicles, and artillery. It is clear to even the casual visitor that this is a heavily armed state. The sight of military vehicles moving through the streets of the capital and along the roads is very common.[44] Karabakh depends on Armenia to equip its forces. Disturbing reminders of the conflict are landmines. Thousands are left from the Karabakh war. One hundred and seventy-seven people have been killed and 381 injured by mines between 1994 and 2015. Again, a high number for a small country.[45] The UK-based demining NGO Halo works to help find and defuse mines. Their blue signs written in Armenian, Russian, and English warn visitors of areas where landmines are believed to be.

Relations with Armenia have been so close that the Karabakh leader Robert Kocharian, a hero to many Armenians became the president of Armenia in 1998 and served to 2008. The flag of Nagorno Karabakh is, as mentioned, the Armenian flag with a jagged white across it, indicating a piece of Armenia separated from the rest. In conversations with local people in 2015, the general sentiment among Karabakhis was that they were Armenian first. Joining Armenia was the desired goal. Of course, over time, they could become accustomed to governing themselves and increasingly identify with their own state. One Karabakh historian expressed concern that there were already a few, especially those that were enjoying the status and privileges of holding government offices, who might be quite comfortable with a permanent Karabakh state.[46]

A clue to the sense of national identity may be found in the capital, Stepanakert. It's a pleasant modern city of 55,000. Traffic is light, and it has a small-town feel.[47] In the center of the city is a parliament, a presidential office, and the basic ministries of an independent state and several museums. Nearby the Artsakh State Museum emphasizes the antiquity of the state and its history as part of Armenia rather than its history as a distinct region. A Museum of Fallen Soldiers has walls lined with photographs of men and women who died in the 1990–94 war. Behind it is the Museum of Missing Soldiers. Overall, the story that is being told is of Armenians fighting for freedom. So next to the institutions of a sovereign state are reminders of its Armenian identity.

Nagorno Karabakh's independence is also qualified by its dependency on Armenia. It is only possible to access the landlocked country through its patron. Stepanakert has a new modern airport that as of 2020 remained unused. This is because Azerbaijan has threatened to shoot down planes that attempt to fly in and out of it. Armenian troops defend the country; it uses Armenian money, and to put it simply it could not exist as a separate state without Armenian support. Armenian financial support comes not in the form of foreign aid packages but as a regular allocation built into the budget as if Karabakh was part of its administrative territory. Karabakhis travel abroad on Armenian passports. The elites of the two countries are connected; in fact, when Lev Ter-Petrosian became the first president of independent Armenia many of the officials he appointed were from Nagorno Karabakh.[48] Financial support from Armenians abroad, both Karabakh and non-Karabakh, along with the remittances of Karabakhis working outside the country form the basis of its economy. That is, it is not just the support of the government of Armenia but the Armenian diaspora that keeps the country viable.

Of course, no country is totally sovereign since all have to deal with economic, political, and cultural pressures for other states and supra-state entities such as international bodies, multinational corporations, and NGOs. So, the question of whether Nagorno Karabakh is a sovereign state is a matter of legal definition and judgment. Whether it is a nation is also difficult to state with any certainty since nationhood is subjective. If a people's regard themselves as a nation, they are one. By this measure, Nagorno Karabakh may not be one. Karabakhis identify too strongly with Armenia to have a sense of their own identity as a separate nation. But identities are malleable and changeable and overtime it is possible that they will develop a sense of themselves as a people apart, a nation within a larger Armenian identity, a community bonded by their long collective struggle to exist independently of Azerbaijan and by their long experience with self-rule.

WILL NAGORNO KARABAKH EVER BE RECOGNIZED?

Will Karabakh become an internationally recognized state? Will it be annexed by Armenia? Returned to Azerbaijan? Or will its current status continue almost indefinitely? As of 2020, this remains uncertain. Its return to Azerbaijan seems unlikely since the population would unanimously and violently oppose it, as would Armenia. And although thousands of Azeris might hope to return home someday, it is not clear that even they believe this will happen. Armenia would like to annex Karabakh, of course, but the geopolitical situation makes that virtually impossible. Russia opposed this since it would aggravate tensions in the region and Armenia depends on Russia. It would so outrage Turkey that supports the Azerbaijani claims that it could even lead to war with that neighboring country. Nor does the United States or the EU support this, since both recognize Azerbaijan's claim to the land. If Armenias could have annexed it, they probably would have. Only a dramatic change in the international and regional situation would make that possible. For all these reasons, at the start of the third decade of the twenty-first century it appears unlikely that the international community would recognize the independence of Nagorno Karabakh. Not one government has shown interest in doing this. Not only would this inflame passions in the region, but—and this is an important point for understanding all our de facto states—it is a bad precedent for an international community that promotes the territorial integrity of its members.

Azerbaijan still calls for the return of Nagorno Karabakh but this is a nonstarter. Armenia's leadership has insisted that Karabakh's independence is "an irreversible reality." A peaceful resolution to the conflict is not impossible. A framework for a settlement has been worked out by international negotiators in which seven districts of Azerbaijan held by Armenia or Nagorno Karabakh are returned in exchange for Baku's recognition of Nagorno Karabakh's right to determine its own status—whether as an independent state or as part of Armenia. However, Armenia and Nagorno Karabakh have insisted that no peace settlement can be worked out without Karabakh representatives involved, but Azerbaijan has been unwilling to negotiate directly with Karabakhis. Furthermore, the Karabakhis have stated that they would not give up any territory they hold.[49] So talks get nowhere. The conflict itself is an enormous strain on Armenia, a poor country which, like Nagorno Karabakh, relies on remittances from compatriots working abroad. This is a contrast with Azerbaijan, a country three times its population and a much bigger oil-fueled economy. In 2011, Azerbaijan spent more on its military than Armenia's entire national budget.[50]

Meanwhile in 2019, the government of Nagorno Karabakh began to seek recognition from Russia. It also began to open relations with the Russian-supported state of Abkhazia and was even was considering relations with the two breakaways states of Donetsk and Luhansk in Ukraine (see chapter 10).[51] The United States, seeking to line up Azerbaijan support against Iran, wanted to end Baku and Yerevan's conflict. It pressured Armenia to compromise on the Nagorno Karabakh.

A few communities have supported recognizing it. In 2014, the California State Senate voted unanimously on a Joint Resolution recognizing the Republic of Nagorno Karabakh and called on the president of the United States and Congress to do so.[52] Several other states have passed similar resolutions. But these are meaningless gestures to appease Armenian-American communities that support this. Karabakh prospects for recognition are hindered further by the ethnic cleansing that accompanied its independence, undermining the moral argument for recognizing it. It is hard to see governments recognizing the state unless it addresses the issue of Azeri refugees. And then there is the whole issue of the return of other territories that Armenia seized. And if Karabakh's independence were recognized, what would its boundaries be? Would they be the original boundaries of province that was surrounded by Azerbaijan? Or the much larger territory it controlled until 2020.

Nagorno Karabakh faced an unwelcoming international community that generally supports Azerbaijan's claim to it. Neither its annexation to Armenia nor its independence is in anyone's interest. Its "countryness" and its sovereignty are compromised by both its dependence on Armenia and by its own people's lack of a national identity although after decades of self-rule one could develop. It was an accidental state created when the efforts of the majority of the autonomous region to join Armenia resulted in being trapped in a limbo. It was not quite a full-fledged state but not part of any other. In the fall of 2020 fighting resumed as Azerbaijan launched an assault on Armenia and Nagorno Karabakh, Stepanakert was shelled, and there were heavy casualties on all sides. Turkey supported Azerbaijan with weapons. After pushing back the Armenians forces Azerbaijan seized Shushi and considerable Karabakhi held territory; only Russian intervention saved the de facto state. Nagorno Karabakh's future suddenly began to look more precarious.

NOTES

1. The present state holds the territory of the former Azerbaijan autonomous province plus additional territory that was not part of Armenia but that connects it to Armenia and provides military buffer zones.
2. "Caucasian Peoples," *Encyclopedia Britannica*, https://www.britannica.com/topic/Caucasian-peoples, Accessed September 5, 2019.
3. Simon Payaslian, *The History of Armenia: From the Origins to the Present* (New York, NY: Palgrave Macmillan, 2007), 35.
4. John G. Heidenrich, *How to Prevent Genocide: A Guide for Policymakers, Scholars and the Concerned Citizen* (Westport, CT: Greenwood, 2001), 5.
5. Bernard Coulie, "The Quintessential Conflict-A Cultural and Historical Analysis of Nagorno Karabakh," in Michael Kambeck and Sargis Ghazaryan, editors, *Europe's Next Avoidable War: Nagorno Karabakh* (New York, NY: Palgrave Macmillan, 2013), 35–42, 35.
6. James Forsyth, *The Caucasus* (New York, NY: Cambridge University Press, 2013), 117–18.
7. Some historians have challenged this interpretation believing it is the ruins of a later but still ancient city. See Robert H. Hewsen, *Armenia: A Historical Atlas* (Chicago, IL: University of Chicago Press, 2001), 58, 73, map 62.

8. Ohannes Geukjian, *Ethnicity, Nationalism and Conflict in the South Caucasus: Nagorno Karabakh and the Legacy of Soviet Nationalities Policy* (Burlington, VT: Ashgate, 2012), 38–39.

9. We will see this part of shifts in both ethnic composition and in ethnic identity with most of the de facto states.

10. Uwe Halback, "A Case Sui Generis: Nagorno Karabakh in Comparison with Other Ethnic Conflicts in Eastern Europe," in Michael Kambeck and Sargis Ghazaryan, editors, *Europe's Next Avoidable War: Nagorno Karabakh* (New York, NY: Palgrave Macmillan, 2013), 43–60, 45.

11. Emil Souleimanov, *Understanding Ethnicpolitical Conflict: Karabakh, South Ossetia and Abkhazia Wars Reconsidered* (London and New York, NY: Palgrave Macmillan, 2013), 94–97.

12. Souleimanov, *Understanding Ethnicpolitical Conflict*, 97.

13. Souleimanov, *Understanding Ethnicpolitical Conflict*, 97–98.

14. Souleimanov, *Understanding Ethnicpolitical Conflict*, 99–101.

15. Forsyth, *The Caucasus*, 421–22.

16. Souleimanov, *Understanding Ethnicpolitical Conflict*, 101.

17. Souleimanov, *Understanding Ethnicpolitical Conflict*, 105.

18. Souleimanov, *Understanding Ethnicpolitical Conflict*, 106.

19. Arsene Saparov, *From Conflict to Autonomy in the Caucasus: The Soviet Union and the Making of Abkhazia, South Ossetia and Nagorno Karabakh* (London: Routledge, 2015), 123.

20. Thomas De Waal, *Black Garden: Armenia and Azerbaijan through Peace and War* (New York, NY: New York University Press, 2003), 133.

21. De Waal, *Black Garden*, 79.

22. De Waal, *Black Garden*, 23.

23. De Waal, *Black Garden*, 64.

24. De Waal, *Black Garden*, 37–41.

25. Souleimanov, *Understanding Ethnicpolitical Conflict*, 109.

26. Forsyth, *The Caucasus*, 663.

27. Geukjian, *Ethnicity, Nationalism*, 33.

28. Souleimanov, *Understanding Ethnicpolitical Conflict*, 102–3.

29. Souleimanov, *Understanding Ethnicpolitical Conflict*, 103.

30. Svante E. Cornell, *The Nagorno Karabakh Conflict* (Uppsala: Uppsala University Press, 1999), 208.

31. Souleimanov, *Understanding Ethnicpolitical Conflict*, 103–4.

32. De Waal, *Black Garden*, 130.

33. Souleimanov, *Understanding Ethnicpolitical Conflict*, 110.

34. De Waal, *Black Garden*, 179–81.

35. De Waal, *Black Garden*, 239–40.

36. Estimates for the number of refugees vary considerably.

37. "Background Briefing on the Nagorno Karabakh Conflict," *U.S. State Department*, May 16, 2016, https://2009-2017.state.gov/r/pa/prs/ps/2016/05/257263.htm, Accessed December 29, 2016.

38. "Nagorno Karabakh," *Ministry of Foreign Affairs of the Republic of Armenia*, www.mfa.am/en/martsakh/, Accessed November 15, 2019.

39. Karine Ohanian, "Karabakh Defends New Constitution," *Global Focus: Caucasus*, January 11, 2007, https://iwpr.net/global-voices/karabakh-defends-new-constitution, Retrieved June 13, 2018.

40. This fear is compounded by the issue of Shahumyan Province, an area out the former Nagorno Karabakh Autonomous Region with an Armenian population that Nagorno Karabakh claims but failed to capture in the war. Most of its Armenian population has since fled.

41. Donald E. Miller and Lorna Touryan Miller, *Armenia: Portraits of Survival and Hope* (Berkeley, CA: University of California Press, 2003), 7.

42. Based on visits to the country's main historical museums: National Museum in Stepanakert, the National Martyrs Museum, the Shushi Museum and the Tigranakert Museum, and to the National University in Stepanakert.

43. *Freedom House*, "Freedom in the World: Armenia," 2009, https://freedomhouse.org/report/freedom-world/2009/armenia?page=22&year=2009&country=7557, Accessed June 13, 2018.

44. Based on my conversations and observations in Nagorno Karabakh May 2015.

45. *Land Mine and Munition Cluster Monitor*, August 2, 2017, http://www.the-monitor.org/en-gb/reports/2017/Nagorno Karabakh/view-all.aspx, Accessed August 5, 2019.

46. Interview Ashot Harutunyan, Shushi, June, 2015.

47. Nina Casperson reported that it "looks more like a dusty provincial town than a capital city," Caspersen, 1.

48. Fuad Chirigov, "The Nagorno Karabakh Conflict is Destroying Armenia," *National Interest*, June 9, 2019, https://nationalinterest.org/blog/buzz/Nagorno Karabakh-conflict-destroying-armenia-61407, Accessed August 17, 2019.

49. "The Conflict in Nagorno Karabakh," *Economist*, April 15, 2016; "A Mountainous Conflict," *Economist*, September 6, 2014.

50. Sargis Ghazarayan, "Background: Setting the Geopolitical Stage," in Michael Kambeck and Sargis Ghazaryan, editors, *Europe's Next Avoidable War: Nagorno Karabakh* (New York, NY: Palgrave Macmillan, 2013), 10–23.

51. Chirigov, "The Nagorno Karabakh Conflict."

52. "California Assembly Recognizes Artsakh's Independence," *Armenian Weekly*, September 1, 2014, https://web.archive.org/web/20140902231538/http://www.armenianweekly.com/2014/08/28/calif-senate-recognizes-artsakhs-independence/, Accessed June 13, 2018.

Chapter 3

Breakaway States from a Breakaway State

Abkhazia and South Ossetia

ABKHAZIA

If Nagorno Karabakh remains isolated in the Caucasus, unrecognized and ignored by most of the world, it is not alone—there is Abkhazia. The Republic of Abkhazia is one of two states that broke away from Georgia; the other is South Ossetia. No less real than Karabakh, Abkhazia is a small state wedged in between the Caucasus Mountains and the eastern coast of the Black Sea, south of Russia and northwest of Georgia. It has an area of 8,660 square kilometers (3,340 sq. mi.) and has a population of 240,000, similar in size to Nagorno Karabakh. Its capital is Sukhumi—a port on the Black Sea.

There are many similarities between Abkhazia and Karabakh. Not only are both small, mountainous Caucasian states excluded from the international community, both were created out of the chaos that accompanied the breakup of the Soviet Union. Both were formed out of an autonomous region of another newly minted post-Soviet state. The birth of both states was accompanied by bloody conflict and large-scale ethnic cleansing. In each case, the state they succeeded from has not accepted the outcome of the war and has continued to claim sovereignty over it—a claim that is backed by most of the international community. The United Nations and most of the rest of the international community regard Abkhazia as a part of Georgia, and this is reflected in most world and regional maps. Georgia, although lacking any control over the territory, still considers it as forming the Autonomous Republic of Abkhazia within the Republic of Georgia. In another similarity, both have a patron—Karabakh has Armenia, and Abkhazia has Russia. Both are considered "frozen conflicts" that stubbornly refused to yield to a resolution.

Yet there are some differences. While no UN members recognized Karabakh, Russia recognizes the independence of Abkhazia. For what it's worth, so do Nicaragua, Venezuela, Nauru, and Syria. Another major difference between the two is that Karabakh is Armenian and its people regarded the creation of their state as a transitional stage to union with Armenia. By contrast Abkhazians from the beginning sought to become a state of their own. In short, unlike Karabakh, Abkhazia was, as we shall see a country by design, not accident. Abkhazia is the home of the Abkhaz, a distinctive ethnic-linguistic group. So, Abkhazia makes some sense as a country. Other than its small size, a little smaller than Connecticut and with less than a quarter of a million people, Abkhazia seems like a country. It has its own national language Abkhaz and a strong sense of Abkhaz national identity. In this way, it is more of a real country than Nagorno Karabakh. Nor is it quite as isolated since it has access to the Black Sea and international shipping and has an airport which actually does have international flights, mainly to Russia. Getting to the country by road is much easier than getting to Nagorno Karabakh. It is economically viable. The subtropical coastal area produces tea, fruit, and other marketable crops, and it has considerable tourist potential including beaches, mountains, and an agreeable climate.

MOUNTAINS AND THE SEA

The Abkhaz have a legend: when God was dividing up the world between the nations, the Abkhaz missed their chance of selecting a homeland because they were sleeping off a festive drinking party. When they awoke, everything was taken except that part of the world that the Almighty had been reserving for himself, which was, of course, literally "heaven on earth." When the Abkhaz explained they were drinking to his honor, a flattered God gave them this last scenic corner of the world.[1] And indeed, it is a beautiful land. Abkhazia is characterized by mountainous terrain, breaking up the land into semi-isolated valleys and with astonishing climate and geographical diversity within small areas.

Abkhazia is separated from Russia by the Greater Caucasus Mountain Range. These formidable mountains rise to 4,000 meters (13,000 feet), with some being permanently covered in snow and glaciers. The three spurs divided much of the interior into narrow gorges, well-watered valley contributing to the country's natural beauty. The mountains, which can be bitterly cold, shield the coast from the cold air masses coming from the Russian steppe. The result is a subtropical climate where even in winter temperature averages are above freezing. This coast is an easterly extension of Russia's Black Sea coast—the resort town of Sochi, where Vladimir Putin vacations and the site of the 2014 Winter Olympics is not far from the border. Then there is the narrow coastal plain where vineyards produce wine, and fruit, tobacco and tea are grown on the mountain slopes. Interestingly, Abkhazia has the world's deepest known cave, Krubera (Voronja) Cave ("the Crow's Cave"), which is 2,158 meters (7,080 ft) from the highest to the lowest point.[2]

MORE CONSONANTS THAN PEOPLE: WHO ARE THE ABKHAZ?

A little over one half of the population of Abkhazia is ethnically Abkhaz, the rest is Georgian, Russian, and others; however, the Abkhaz dominate the state. Who are the Abkhaz? They are an ethnic group, speakers of the Abkhaz language, a Northwest Caucasian language. This is a curious language group that is unrelated, as far as scholars can tell, to other languages. There are three other living Northwest Caucasian languages—Karbadian and Adygean spoken in the Russian parts of the Caucasian (and both referred to in older literature as Circassian), and Abaza, also spoken in Russia. All total they make up only about 2 million speakers. A fifth language Ubykh was spoken in the Sochi area but all Ubykhs were expelled to Turkey in the nineteenth century when the Russians took over the area and their tongue died with the last native speaker Tevfik Esenc in 1992.[3] These languages fascinate linguists because they have so many consonants and so few vowels. Abkhaz has fifty-eight consonants compared with nineteen in Spanish or Japanese and twenty-four in relatively consonant-rich English. Ubykh had eighty-one consonants but only two vowels! These languages have more consonants than any language in the world except those spoken by the Bushmen of southern Africa, and fewer vowels than any known. It is tricky enough to learn a language that has two or three unfamiliar consonants, but having to learn sixty would intimidate even experienced linguists. Abkhaz doesn't have quite so many consonants, but still it would be a challenging language to master. The Abkhaz language was written in the Latin alphabet, but the Soviet authorities switched it to the Georgian alphabet in 1938.[4]

Most Abkhaz are Orthodox Christians, some are Muslims, and others adhere to a revived indigenous religion of probably ancient origins. They call their country Apsny, "land of the mortals." Their state is the Republic of Apsny, the name Abkhazia is derived from the Russian rendition of the Georgian name Apkhazeti. That the country is known to most of the world (to the extent that it is known at all) by its Georgian derived name reflects the interlinked history of Georgia and Abkhazia. A history that the Abkhaz to some extent can be said to be trying to escape from.

HISTORICAL BACKGROUND

It may seem to be the indulgence of a historian to trace the issue of Abkhazia's odd international status to events dating back thousands of years. Yet, as with all our de facto countries, their creation is based on issues of identity rooted in conflicting versions of history. Ancient history matters because it matters to the Abkhaz and to their neighbors.

What is now Abkhazia emerged in the historical records over two thousand years ago as part of the Georgian kingdom of Colchis or Kolkha. Colchis was conquered by another Georgian kingdom Lazica, and Lazica was conquered in turn by the Romans in the first century CE. We know about this area mainly from Greek and Roman sources. Roman-era Greek writers have provided accounts of people living in this region whom they called the Absagol, which of course sounds something like the Apsny, and most historians have regarded them as the ancestors of the Abkhaz.[5] In any case, this area was important to Rome because this distant frontier was along the border with Rome's great rival to the East—Persia. Lazica gained independence from the declining Roman Empire in the fourth century but remained within the sphere of influence of Byzantium, the eastern successor to Rome. It became a contested area between Byzantium and Persia.

Abkhazia appears on the maps in the 700s when a kingdom by that name emerged. The kingdom of Abkhazia had a brief golden age, expanded much beyond its present borders, then in the late tenth century declined and was absorbed by Georgia. It reemerged as a principality in the fifteenth century at a time when the region was fragmented into little states. In the sixteenth century, when most of the Caucasus was divided into Ottoman and Persian spheres, Abkhazia came under the rule of the Ottomans. Like most of the Caucasus, this area was a patchwork of different and somewhat shifting ethnic groups, so it is not clear who lived in medieval Abkhazia. The Abkhazian nobility appeared over time to have been strongly influenced by Georgian culture and wrote if not spoke in Georgian.[6] Later princes of Abkhazia were from a Georgian Shervashidze dynasty, and the ruling class appeared to be ethnically Georgian.[7] The area was Christian from the fourth century, but under Ottoman rule much of the elite, including the ruling Shervashidze family, became at least nominally Muslim. Most of the peasants remained Christian, although Islam gradually made inroads into the general population.[8]

Under the Ottomans, the people of the region were largely left alone, since the Ottomans gave the local rulers a great deal of autonomy. This changed when the Russians entered the Caucasus in the early nineteenth century. The Russians annexed eastern Georgia in 1801, the neighboring western Georgia in 1803, and in 1810 the Russians got rid of a pro-Ottoman ruler and installed one to their liking who converted to Christianity. The Russians in the early part of the nineteenth century had replaced the Ottomans as the overlords of the western Caucasus and the Persians as overlords of the eastern parts. But the fiercely independent local rulers of the region, protected by their rugged terrain and their warrior traditions initially remained largely autonomous. Not for long, however, Imperial Russia began a long hard effort to establish direct control over the area. From 1817, the Russian forces carried out a half-century-long series of military campaigns that brought the region into their administration. Abkhazia was the last bit to fall in 1864.

WILD SWINGS IN ETHNIC POPULATIONS

As with the case of Nagorno Karabakh, the history of Abkhazia is part of the radical shifts in ethnic composition as the result of migrations, expulsions, massacres, and assimilation. Enormous demographic changes came with Russia's nineteenth-century campaign to consolidate control over the Caucasus, a campaign accompanied and followed by mass ethnic cleansing and resettlement. In some cases, such as with the Ubykhs who lived in the Sochi area, the entire population was expelled to Turkey. Not many Abkhaz were expelled at first. Then in 1866, the Russians proposed a land reform in which land not formally owned could be purchased by farmers. But many peasants did not have formal ownership to the land they worked on; it was theirs by custom so that they were being asked to buy land that they already believed they owned. In response, they revolted in what is known as the Lykhny Uprising. Russian authorities quickly suppressed the rebellion and carried out mass expulsions. A second wave of expulsions took place during the 1877–78 Russo-Turkish War when the Abkhaz rebelled again in support of Ottoman Turkey. It was a mistake; the Russian crushed the Turks in the war which took place mainly in the Balkans. Tens of thousands of Abkhaz were expelled to Turkey joining the thousands that had been forced to leave a decade earlier. Many did not take part in the rebellion but were simply guilty of being Muslim.[9] Almost all Muslims in Abkhazia, perhaps 40 percent of the population, were deported. Most of these *muhajirs* (Arabic for "immigrant"), as they were often called, settled in Turkey. By the late nineteenth century, less than a quarter of what the Russians described as the "wild and unsubmissive" Abkhazians remained in their homeland.[10]

So many Abkhaz were expelled that much of the land became vacant. As in the case of Karabakh, the Tsarist regime also welcomed and encouraged the settlement of Christians into lands that were previously mostly Muslim. Responding to this, ethnic Russians, Armenians, and Greeks moved in. Although not officially encouraged or necessarily welcomed, many Mingrelians, the people of western Georgia, also moved in becoming one of the largest ethnic groups in Abkhazia. As these outsiders settled in, the Abkhaz found themselves a minority in the much of their own land. Just how many of the people were living in Abkhazia was not certain until the 1897 Russian census. It found that there were 58,000 speakers of Abkhaz and 25,000 of Kartvelian (Georgian) languages as well as significant numbers of Armenians, Greeks, and Russians.[11]

Meanwhile, the Tsarist government carried out a policy of "Russification" requiring school instruction and religious services to be carried out in Russian, which became the common language of the ethnically diverse region. However, rather than becoming totally Russified, the remaining Abkhaz became nationalistic in the modern sense seeing themselves as part of an Abkhaz nation. Some of this was the result of Abkhaz resistance to Russian rule. But it was also partly the result of the contradictions in Russian policy. While promoting assimilation, Tsarist regime also took pride in the cultural diversity of its empire, and like many European imperialists of the era the Russians undertook scholarly studies of the peoples they ruled. Through the work of Russian scholars and the Commission for the Translation of Religious Books into Abkhaz, established in the 1890s, a written script was created for the previously unwritten Abkhaz language. The educated Abkhaz elite began to study their history and culture. All this had the effect of fostering ethnic-national identity among them. By the early 1900s, an Abkhaz language literature appeared and in 1917 the first Abkhaz language newspaper. Pride and identification with their language became an essential feature of their sense of Abkhaz identity.[12]

ABKHAZIA IN THE SOVIET ERA

Abkhaz nationalism was just emerging when the Russian Revolution of 1917 impacted the region. In 1918, Georgia along with Armenia and Azerbaijan became independent republics and Abkhazia was within the territory of Georgia. When Georgia proclaimed its independence in 1918 in the aftermath of the Russian Revolution, it granted autonomy to Abkhazia in its constitution. But in the same year the Bolsheviks reestablished control over Georgia. For a short time, Abkhazia was its own Soviet Socialist Republic along with Georgia, Armenia, and Azerbaijan. Then in 1931, Stalin demoted it to the Abkhaz Autonomous Soviet Socialist Republic within the Georgian Soviet Socialist Republic. That is, it was in theory a politically and culturally autonomous part of Georgia. In practice, it had no autonomy, rather it was Georgianized. All students were forced to study in Georgian and Russian, and Abkhaz language materials ceased to be published. The ruling elite were largely wiped out in the 1937–1938 terror. It is interesting to note that both Stalin and one of his closest associates and later head of his security forces,

Lavrenti Beria, were ethnically Georgians and had no love for Abkhaz. Beria seems to have been personally involved in the purging of the Abkhaz.[13] In 1952, 80 percent of the 228 top party and government officials and enterprise managers within Abkhazia were Georgian, less than 15 percent were Abkhazian.

After Stalin's death and Beria's execution in 1953, repression lessened. Abkhaz sent appeals to Moscow in 1957, 1967, and 1978 to restore their status as a Soviet Socialist Republic that they had for a decade before being demoted to an autonomous region within Georgia. Moscow did not grant this, but it did make some concessions. It actively encouraged the revival of Abkhaz language and culture. Ethnically, Abkhaz were allowed their own schools, and there was a radio and a television station that broadcast in their language.[14] These measures were enough to promote Abkhaz national sentiment but not enough to satisfy it. And they were modest. In 1966, only 66 of the 365 schools in the autonomous republic held instruction in Abkhaz.[15]

Under the Soviet Union, the ethnic Abkhaz had become a shrinking minority in their own eponymous territory. A 1989 Soviet census listed a population of 525,061 divided into thirty ethno-national groups. Georgians were by far the largest, making up 45.7 percent of the population. Abkhazians accounted for only 17.8 percent, Armenian and Russians each 14–15 percent, Greeks about 3 percent, and the remaining 5 percent were other ethnic groups.[16] The dream of some Abkhaz nationalists that they could once again be politically and culturally dominant seemed highly unrealistic, but thirty years later they were. How such a small minority was able to reclaim political and cultural control over their ancient homeland is a remarkable and unlikely story. It came about as the result of the extraordinary upheavals that accompanied the collapse of the Soviet Union.

BREAKAWAY STATE 1990–2008

So how was this small minority group able to achieve majority status and political control over their ancestral land? The chain of events that led to it began when Gorbachev carried out his policy of opening the Soviet Union to free expression—his famous *glasnost* policy. In doing so, he unwittingly unleashed long-suppressed expressions of nationalist sentiment. This happened with the Armenians and the Azerbaijanis and the same happened with the Georgians and Abkhaz. Georgian nationalists sought independence from Moscow and Abkhaz nationalists sought independence from Georgia. In June 1988, prominent Abkhaz sent a letter to the Kremlin requesting the restoration of the Abkhazia Soviet Republic. Abkhaz nationalists argued that they were going back to the Leninist principles, that each people had the right to national self-determination within the Soviet Union. In June 1988, in a letter known as the "Abkhaz Letter" addressed to Gorbachev, they explained the distinctiveness of the Abkhaz people and their need for their own republic separate from Georgia. Their request was rejected by Gorbachev for the same reason he rejected the Armenian and Karabakh request—he did not want to begin a complex and contentious process of redrawing boundaries. Nonetheless, in March 1989 another letter was sent this time by a new nationalist movement Aydgylara that organized a mass meeting in at a place called Lykhny. Thirty thousand people signed this "Lykhny Letter" requesting the return of Abkhazia to its pre-1931 status.[17] Georgians became alarmed at this since it threatened the territorial integrity of Georgia at a time when Georgians were pushing for greater independence; moreover, it made the status of the Georgians in Abkhazia uncertain. On July 16, 1989, violence broke out in Sukhumi between Georgians and Abkhaz. Sixteen Georgians were killed and over 100 were injured when they tried to enroll in a Georgian university instead of an Abkhaz one. Soviet troops were sent in to restore order.[18]

Meanwhile, the increasing assertive Georgian nationalists held a referendum on independence in which most supported leaving the Soviet Union. But 52 percent of Abkhazia's population, almost all the non-Georgian population, voted to preserve the Soviet Union.[19] They were anxious about living as minority groups in an increasingly nationalistic Georgian state. A month later, Georgia declared its independence under the leadership of Zviad Gamsakhurdia a former Soviet dissident. Gamsakhurdia, however, worked out a power-sharing arrangement in Abkhazia in which the ethnic Abkhaz were given representation in the regional legislature that was larger than it would be based on their modest population. They were to hold twenty-eight seats in the Supreme Soviet, Georgians twenty-six, and other ethnic groups eleven seats.[20]

At first this seemed to be a widely acceptable compromise but the initial calm in Abkhazia under the newly independent Georgia did not last long. In early 1992, Gamsakhurdia was ousted by opposition groups that installed Eduard Shevardnadze as the new head of state. Shevardnadze was a moderate who had served as foreign minister and close associate under Gorbachev, but the real power in the Georgian capital of Tbilisi was in the hands of hardline nationalists. The new government announced that it was abolishing the Soviet era constitution. Since this had guaranteed Abkhazia's autonomy, Abkhaz leaders reacted by enacting a new constitution for their area based on the 1925 one that gave Abkhazia equal status with Georgia—an implicit declaration of independence.[21]

Abkhaz fears of the more nationalist Georgian government were reinforced with plans by the government in Tbilisi to replace the 1921 constitution of the Soviet Republic of Georgia with that of the 1918 independent Republic Georgia, which was seen as a move to eliminate Abkhazia's autonomous status. On July 23, representatives of the Abkhaz on Abkhazia's Supreme Council declared the region's independence. Adding to the confusion of the time were supporters of the ousted leader Gamsakhurdia in Abkhazia who were also posing a threat to the Georgian government. Tbilisi sent 3,000 troops to restore order in August in 1992. This proved the trigger that started a war in the region. The undisciplined Georgian forces marched into Sukhumi and carried out looting and violence against ethnic Abkhaz.[22]

Abkhaz militia resisting the Georgians were defeated. However, armed Abkhaz regrouped and were supported by a newly created Confederation of Mountain Peoples of the Caucasus. The latter group, a reflection of the chaos in the region at the time of the disintegration of the Soviet Union, contained volunteers from the Chechen, Ossetian, Circassian, and other ethnic minority groups as well as Russian mercenaries. It should be pointed out, as in the case of the contemporary Karabakh conflict, most men in the region had military training in Soviet Union's formerly huge armed forces, and there were plenty of unemployed discharged soldiers and weapons floating around. Coupled with the general restlessness in the region, it made for a volatile situation. By the end of 1992, the Abkhaz and their Russian and Caucasian allies gained control of large parts of Abkhazia while Georgian forces held Sukhumi. There was a ceasefire; then in the summer of 1993, the Abkhaz launched an offensive against Sukhumi trapping President Shevardnadze inside. In September 27, 1993, Sukhumi fell, and Shevardnadze who had vowed to stay in the city barely escaped.[23] The victorious Abkhaz and their northern Caucasian allies then carried out two weeks of looting and massacres against the remaining ethnic Georgians—thousands were killed or missing. Georgia, which had to deal with an uprising of pro-Gamsakurdia supporters in the west of their country, lost all control over Abkhazia except for one small area—the upper Kodori valley.

The war was a disaster for the Georgians. About 190,000 of the 250,000 ethnic Georgians fled the country. The remaining 60,000 were mostly confined to the corner still held by Georgia. About 20,000 homes of Georgians were destroyed along with hundreds of churches, schools, and historical monuments. More fled in 1998 when separatists attacked some areas still ethnically Georgian. The Abkhaz and their allies eliminated the ethnic Georgians and most traces of their previous existence in the country. Since some other ethnic groups fled or left, the population of Abkhazia fell from 525,000 in 1989 to 216,000.[24] About 200,000 Georgians became refugees in Georgia, a number equal to the people remaining in Abkhazia. The ethnic Abkhaz had ethnically cleansed the country of an astonishing half of its population. Abkhazians were excited about their victory and independence, but it was achieved at a heavy cost—about 4 percent of their entire population perished in the conflict.[25]

WE WERE HERE FIRST: MORE HISTORY WARS

As in Nagorno Karabakh history or "memory," wars have been extremely important in the dispute over Abkhazia. Georgians see Abkhazia as part of their homeland. They interpret the ancient people of the area as being proto-Georgians, Kartvelian-speaking peoples ancestral to the modern people of Georgia. Ethnically Abkhaz peoples, according to their version of history, settled in the area only in the seventeenth century. At least this is the version of history popularized by Georgian nationalist historian Pavle Ingorokva and held by some ultra-nationalists. By contrast Abkhaz scholars assert that the Apsua people, first mentioned by classical writers, were proto-Abkhazians and that the Abhkaz are directly descended from the original indigenous people of the area. While the medieval kingdom of Abkhazia is considered a Georgian state by Georgians, to the Abkhaz it was a kingdom separate from the Georgian ones, formed by people directly ancestral to the modern Abkhaz.[26] As in the case of the Karabakh origin debate, both sides have some basis for their historical claims but ultimately neither matters. Both project modern identities and ethnic-national sentiments into the past and ignore the fluid and shifting nature of identities among the local people.

THE 2008 WAR AND ITS AFTERMATH

From 1994 to 2006, the ceasefire agreement was monitored by the UN and Organization for Security and Cooperation in Europe (OSCE). Georgia found the agreement worrisome since most of the peacekeepers were Russian, which meant that Russian troops were stationed in what they regarded as their sovereign territory. Georgian officials accused the Russian peacekeepers of supplying rebels with arms and financial support. Furthermore, Georgians suspected that what Moscow really intended was to eventually annex Abkhazia. There were good grounds to support these suspicions. Moscow began providing Russian passports to Abhkaz. By 2002, about half the population held them. Abkhazia adopted the Russian ruble as its currency.

Relations between Russia and Georgia worsened when in 2003 Georgia had its "Rose Revolution" which brought to power the pro-Western government of Mikhail Saakashvili. Upon becoming president, in 2004, Saakashvili was committed to eventually bringing the breakaway regions back under Tbilisi's control. Tensions between Russia and the Western-leaning government increased. Sporadic violence occurred from time to time. Tension further increased when in 2006, Georgian troops succeeded in gaining control over the Kodori Gorge region where a Georgian ethnic population remained. The two countries were now on the edge of direct conflict. Georgia accused Russia of violating its airspace with helicopters and attacking rebels in the Kodori Gorge. In April 2008, a Russian MiG shot down a Georgian aircraft, even though Russians were prohibited from Georgian or Abkhazia airspace.[27]

The conflict in Abkhazia was connected to that of South Ossetia—another region of Georgia with a separatist movement. As in Abkhazia, this smaller less populated mountainous region in the north fell into rebel hands, ethnic Georgians were expelled, and Russian peacekeeping forces sympathetic to the rebels kept protecting it. By the beginning of August 2008, pro-Russian separatists in South Ossetia began firing artillery on Georgian forces. On August 7, Georgia sent its army into South Ossetia in response and took control of most of the main city of Tskhinvali. Russia then launched a full-scale land and sea operation against Georgia on August 8. Russian and Ossetian forces fought the Georgian army in Ossetia while simultaneously Russian and Abkhaz forces attacked the Georgian forces in the Kodori valley and Russian naval forces blocked the coast. The Russian invasion was far from a model of efficiency. Communications broke down and military commanders had to communicate with their units on the private phones using the Georgian mobile phone networks. They also lost some planes.[28]

Russia carried out air attacks on targets within Georgia proper. On August 9, 2008, during the South Ossetia war, Abkhazian forces fired at Georgian forces in the Kodori Gorge. The following day 9,000 Russian forces entered Abkhazia, two days later Georgia evacuated forces and civilians from the Kodori Gorge which was under attack. Georgian forces were quickly overwhelmed, and the Russians rolled into Georgia capturing several cities in Georgia and moving toward the capital. Russians launched cyber-attacks against Georgia; it was the first war in which this was part of military operations.[29] On August 12, President Nicholas Sarkozy of France, who was holding the presidency of the European Union at that time, brokered a ceasefire.[30]

As the result of the 2008 war, all of Abkhazia except one small corner was in Abkhazian hands. Thousands of remaining Georgians fled, adding to Georgia's refugee population. Abkhazia was now a majority Abkhazian land. The UN and OSCE monitoring missions ended, and about 4,000 Russian troops were permanently stationed in Abkhazia. South Ossetia and Abkhazia were recognized by President Medvedev on August 26, 2008, following a unanimous resolution by the Russian parliament urging him to do so. This was condemned by North Atlantic Treaty Organization (NATO) nations and the OSCE and the European Council.[31] Only Venezuela, Nicaragua, Nauru, and Syria followed. Most of the international community continued to recognize Georgia's sovereignty over the territory. And this is where the situation remained. Abkhazia was a de facto independent state recognized and protected by Russia but unrecognized by almost all the rest of the world.

Georgia did not give up on its efforts to regain control over Abkhazia. On March 28, President Mikheil Saakashvili unveiled his governments' new proposals for giving Abkhazia the broadest possible autonomy; it included giving the post of vice president to an Abkhaz with veto powers. It was rejected by the Abkhaz leader Sergei Bagapsh, leading to charges by the government of Georgia that this rejection of autonomy and power-sharing reflected Russian influence, not the will of the Abkhaz people. In July 2008, the OSCE Parliamentary Assembly passed a resolution at its annual session supporting the territorial integrity of Georgia. In October 2008, the Georgian parliament passed a law that limited its responsibility for actions in the breakaway territories. In 2011, Georgia issued neutral passports that contain neither the name Abkhazia or Georgia and are recognized by the United States and some other countries.[32]

DE FACTO STATE

Russia's war with Georgia resulted in Abkhazia becoming a majority Abkhaz state with at least (very) limited international recognition. However, it began as a self-governing state in 1992. On July 23, 1992, the Abkhaz faction of the Supreme Soviet of Abkhazia proclaimed the country's independence; the Georgian representatives had boycotted the meeting, but nobody recognized it.[33] The Abkhaz later celebrated September 30, 1993, at the end of the 1992–1993 war with Georgia, as their independence day. The international community stood behind Georgia, and Russia, Abkhazia's only ally, still hoped to win Georgia over to its side while militarily protecting Abkhazia. Moscow did not encourage or openly support its independence. So, Abkhazia was a pariah state. Its leader was Vladislav Ardzinba. Ardzinba was a historian, graduate of the University of Tbilisi who specialized in the ancient societies of the Middle East. Working at the Institute of Oriental Studies in Moscow he became a Hittite expert. A Georgian-trained scholar of the ancient Hittites living in Moscow hardly seems a likely leader of the Abkhaz independence movement. But in 1987, he became director of the Abkhazian Institute of Language, Literature and History where he was an ardent supporter of Abkhaz history and culture. Ardzinba was elected to the Supreme Soviet of the Soviet Union in the body's first openly contested election. He used his position to make friends with Soviet hardliners and military people, a connection that proved useful. A charismatic figure, he became Chair of the Supreme Soviet of Abkhazia. There he quickly became the leader of the movement to succeed from Georgia.³⁴ At first, as Abkhaz leader, he was able to work out a compromise with Gamaskurdia for Georgian-Abkhaz power-sharing but then undermined it by creating an Abkhazian National Guard made up of only ethnic Abkhaz that gradually replaced ethnic Georgians in positions of authority. When the Georgian military invaded in 1992, he fled to a Russian military base and worked his connections to secure Russian military support. As much as anyone, the Hittite scholar was responsible for the ethnic cleansing of Abkhazia.

Under Ardzinba, Abkhazia had an appalling human rights record that with its ethnic cleansing provided his de facto state with a very bad reputation among Western governments. Actions such as the banning of Jehovah Witnesses in 1995 did not help matters.³⁵ In 1999, Ardzinba was re-elected, an easy victory since he ran unopposed. But then his health began declining. While personally popular, there were calls that he step down, but he waited to 2004 and endorsed Raul Khadjimba, his prime minister. The forty-six-year-old Khadjimba was from the coal mining town of Tkvarchelli. He trained at the KGB school in Minsk and served in the last days of the Soviet Union as a KGB agent in his Abkhazian hometown. He was pro-Russian and he ran a campaign with posters showing him alongside the picture of Vladimir Putin, the Russian leader with whom he shared a background in the KGB. He was opposed by former mid-level Communist Party official turned businessman Sergei Bagapsh. When the election results came in, Prime Minister Khadjimba won in a landslide. But the Supreme Court of Abkhazia reexamined the results, and it found Bagapsh the winner. Khadjimba supporters, who were not at all pleased by the decision, stormed the court building and the judges reconsidered it. A compromised was worked out and in a new election in 2005, Bagapsh ran again with Khadjimba as his vice-presidential candidate. They won with 90 percent of the vote.³⁶

Bagapsh was re-elected in 2009 with a new running mate, Aleksandr Ankvab who became president in 2011 when Bagapsh, who had cancer, died at age sixty-two. A major issue was how to deal with Abkhazia's remaining Georgian minority living in the Gali district. Hardline nationalists wanted them excluded from all public life and encouraged them to leave, but Ankvab took a more liberal attitude. In 2014, enraged extreme nationalists rallied around Khadjimba and forced Ankvab to flee. He took refuge in the Russian military base at Gudauta. Khadjimba was elected president.³⁷

Abkhazia is in reality an ethnocracy. Although the Abkhaz make a bare majority of the population, they completely dominate the government. In 2018, thirty-one of the thirty-five members of parliament were Abkhaz, three were Armenians. No Georgians or Russians were members. The government administration is almost entirely staffed by ethnic Abkhaz. The small Georgian minority in Gali not only had no representation but also were isolated since they had difficulty crossing the border—a situation made worse in 2017 when Abkhaz and Russians established checkpoints.[38] The military too is almost all ethnic Abkhaz. The Abkhazian armed forces number 5,000 permanent and 50,000 reserves—almost the entire adult male population. It uses mostly weapons supplied by Russia which has 1,600 troops stationed in the country.

IS ABKHAZIA A REAL COUNTRY?

Abkhazia is often viewed by the West and by Georgia as a small Russian outpost, rather than an independent state. It is dependent on Russia for sure. Moscow stations troops there and covers about two-thirds of the state budget. It has a huge new embassy building in Sukhumi.[39] Russian is still the main language of administration. Abkhaz watch Russian television (although they have their own as well). Many in Abkhazia kept their old Soviet passports and applied for Russian citizenship, a process Moscow made easier in 2002. Russian textbooks are used. Pressure has been placed on ethnic Georgians to abandon the use of Georgian language.[40] Russian along with Abkhaz has replaced Georgian in all schools. Yet it seems clear that the Abkhazians do not want to be absorbed by Russia. Many are grateful for and understand the necessity of Russia's support but also resent it. While they might prefer being part of Russia to being part of Georgia, they want neither. Their dependency on Russia is seen as a necessity.[41] Instead, the government has attempted to avoid "Ossetianization," that is, being effectively absorbed into Russia while remaining nominally independent as has been happening to their fellow Georgian successionist state South Ossetia (see below).[42]

Abkhazia has become highly dependent on Russia, so much so that Georgia and many Western countries fear that Russia plans to annex it. Russia issued thousands of passports to Abkhazians since they cannot travel on Abkhazian passports. Abkhazians can hold these but still are free of the obligations of Russian citizenship. They do not have to pay Russian taxes or serve in the military. Russia has been building a naval base at Ochamchire in response to a Georgian sea blockade in which Georgian coast guard has been detaining ships heading to and from Abkhazia. Russia began patrolling the sea to protect ships. While this has led some Abkhaz to worry that Russian influence is too great they prefer Russia's presence to that of Georgia.[43]

Yet, according to a 2010 study published by the University of Colorado, the great majority of the population supported independence rather than union with Russia. There was little support for union with Georgia even among ethnic Georgians. In 2014, Moscow offered new "integration treaties" that would give control of its borders to Russia. South Ossetia accepted this, but the government of Abkhazia did not. Russia provides security services to help police the border but Abkhazia carefully keeps its military and security services separate. A proposal by Moscow to make it easier for Russians to become Abkhazian citizens and buy property was also rejected.[44] A study by two foreign scholars in 2014 found that Abkhazians very much wanted to remain independent.[45] Several years later another visitor, journalist and author Joshua Keating, found the people "fiercely independent opposing integration back to Georgia or Russia."[46]

Abkhaz leaders have sought to have relations with the wider world for economic reasons, to gain international recognition as an independent state and to counter their need to rely on Russia. Sergei Bagapsh in a March 2006 interview stated, "We have one aspiration—to be in Europe."[47] While Abkhaz would love to see European Union (EU) countries trade, vacation, and provide economic support and recognize their claims to independence, the European community has been less than welcoming. The central issue is Georgia. Almost all the world regards the government of Georgia as the rightful authority in Abkhazia. Sympathy for Georgia in the West was only solidified by the 2008 Russia-Georgian War in which Abkhazia and South Ossetia were seen as part of the Russia's gathering control over its "near abroad." Neither did the events of 2014 help when Russia annexed Crimea and supported succession movements in eastern Ukraine. It became generally assumed that Abkhazia's so-called independence was part of a larger pattern of Russian aggression and control over the former republics of the Soviet Union.

VIABILITY AS A STATE

As small as it is, Abkhazia is viable as a state. The mountains and coast create natural boundaries. It has considerable tourist potential and could easily be not just a Russian but an international vacation spot as well as an agricultural exporter. Thus Abkhazia could have a viable economy. The 2008 war ravaged the country but with the help of Russian aid and the tourist boom, new roads were built and within a few years much of the country recovered.[48] However, there were still many signs of conflict in 2016 such as abandoned blocks of apartments once occupied by ethnic Georgians.[49] It has a significant agricultural sector. Along the hills that begin to ascend quickly from the narrow coastal plains, grapes and tea are grown. The grapes are made into wine, one of its chief exports. It also produces and exports fruit, tung oil, tangerines, hazelnuts, tea, and tobacco. Its power comes from the Inguri hydroelectric power station operated jointly with Georgia and from Russia. There are some industries and coal mining. But the country's main economic asset is its natural beauty, and its economy depends on tourism, mainly from Russia. It competes with Turkey, Bulgaria, and Egypt in attracting Russians lured to coastal resorts by their low cost and by the lack of a visa requirement. In 2014, 1.1 million Russian tourists visited Abkhazia. Russians came to these resorts as well as to its sanatoria. It was especially popular as a vacation and convalescent destination for the military. Economically it is deeply tied to Russia. Russian companies have invested in tourist infrastructure and about two-thirds of its trade is with Russia (Turkey is second with about a sixth of its trade). Still even with its agriculture and tourism, it is heavily dependent on Russia for aid. Moscow provides for half of its state budget.

PROSPECTS FOR RECOGNITION

The Abkhaz with their own language and cultural traditions form a distinctive culture—they certainly can be regarded as a nation. And this is what most of the population apparently wants. However, Abkhazia is dependent on Russia which pays the pensions of its pensioners and contributes to much of its budget and economy; yet this dependency on Russia undermines its legitimacy as a state, at least from the point of view of most of the West. There is always the danger of being absorbed by Russia. Moscow would have several reasons for doing so. It has long ties to the land which has been a favorite vacation place for much of the Russian elite and of middle class.[50] Russia has a strategic interest in the country. Moscow is also concerned about the lawlessness and criminality in the country, as it is so close to the resort city of Sochi. As a result Abkhazia finds itself in a situation in which it both needs and fears Russia.

The Abkhaz have shown no desire to be absorbed by Russia. In a 2014 bilateral treaty with Moscow, the Abkhazian government resisted attempts to allow Russian citizens to buy property in their country. They would not allow their army to integrate into the Russian army. And they changed the title of the treaty from "On Alliance and Integration," to "On Alliance and Strategic Partnership."[51] Russia has been an obstacle to international recognition since outsiders see it as a puppet of Moscow. Russia's bullying of Georgia, its pro-Western government, and its efforts at democracy have earned it the sympathy of Europe and America, who support its claims on Abkhazia.

Then there is the ethical issue. Like Nagorno Karabakh, Abkhazia's independence is associated with ethnic cleansing. In 1992–1993 and again in 2008, tens of thousands of ethnic Georgians fled. The quarter-million refugees in Georgia outnumber the Abkhaz and Abkhazia.

Yet the Abkhaz cannot let the Georgians return without being a minority in their own country. Even now they are barely a majority. They have sought to encourage settlement in the somewhat depopulated country by the *muhajirs*. The great majority of these live in Turkey but smaller numbers are scattered elsewhere in the Middle East, in Russia and Europe. No one knows how many there are, but probably more than 500,000. Most are Sunni Muslims in a country where 60 percent are Christian and only 16 percent Muslim; few speak Abkhaz and so many generations have passed on that assimilation might be difficult. In any case, only a very small number have answered the call to return to their ancestral homeland. In the wake of the Syrian War, a few hundred Syrians of Abkhaz, Abazin, or Circassian ancestry were admitted. But efforts to bring Abhkaz diaspora home have had only limited success. In 2016, there were only 3,500 immigrants living in Abkhazia, a total of 8,000 expatriates had been issued Abkhaz passports.[52] Along with a low birthrate, the population of ethnic Abkhaz will remain small, and the state's survival without international recognition will remain a precarious one.

Georgia, of course, is determined to get both South Ossetia and Abkhazia back, and the fact that the ethnic Georgians of Abkhazia outnumbered the Abkhaz gives credibility to their claim beyond just a legalistic one. In 2010, the government of Tbilisi, in a plan supported by the EU and the United States offered to give neutral passports to any individuals from Abkhazia and South Ossetia who applied in Georgia. Although they were not officially Georgian passports, the fine print on them indicated that they were issued in Georgia. Progress in lessening tensions with Georgia was made more difficult when the hardline Saakashvili took on dealing with the Abkhaz and South Ossetians, but he lost an election in 2012 to a new Georgian Dream party led by Bidzina Ivanishvili. The Ivanishvili administration created a new Ministry of Reconciliation and Civil Equality to improve relations. Georgia made it easy for Abkhazians to enter Georgia proper and receive healthcare that they could not get in the small country. These attempts at reconciliation were ignored by Abkhaz who saw it as a trap to absorb them back into Georgia. Russia also proposed Western recognition of Abkhazia in exchange for its recognition of Kosovo; this proposal has not been taken seriously.

As long as it is an ethnicity-based state, and as long as the West is committed to supporting Georgia and sees Abkhazia as an extension of Russia, the prospects of international recognition for Abkhazia look dim. Abkhazia is caught between absorption in some form by Georgia and absorption by Russia.

SOUTH OSSETIA

South Ossetia, another little state in the Caucasus, is naturally paired with Abkhazia. Both were autonomous regions of Georgia that completed their succession from Tbilisi in 2008 during the Russia-Georgia War. Both are recognized by Russia, but the rest of the world regards them as still part of Georgia's sovereign territory. South Ossetia is much smaller than Abkhazia; the 3,900 square kilometer (1,500 square mile.) state has a population of only 53,000, of which 30,000 live in its capital Tskhinvali. Mountainous, landlocked, linked to the outside world by a single tunnel through the mountains that connects it to Russia and with a tiny population, it is less viable as an independent state. It is also different from the other breakaway region of Georgia because unlike Abkhazia where there is a general desire to create a nation-state that is accepted into the international community, South Ossetia's aim is to join Russia, specifically the autonomous Russian republic of North Ossetia-Alania.

South Ossetia boundaries are based on the former South Ossetian Autonomous Oblast with the Georgian SSR. It declared independence from Georgia in 1991. Georgia then stripped it of its autonomy and took over the region by force which led to the South Ossetian War 1991-1992 in which Georgia temporarily crushed the secessionist movement. Fighting resumed in 2004 and again in 2008, when Russia came to its support in the Russo-Georgian War freeing it from Georgian control. Shortly after the conflict, Russia recognized its independence quickly followed by Venezuela, Nauru, and Syria as well as its fellow internationally isolated states of Nagorno Karabakh, Transnistria, and Abkhazia. But no other nation did.

GEOGRAPHY

South Ossetia lies in the midst of the Greater Caucasus Range. Mountains cover most of South Ossetia, and there is very little flat land. In fact, of all the world's countries, only Bhutan is more mountainous. Less than 10 percent of the land is cultivable. Despite this, the economy is based on agriculture: cereals, fruits, and vines; forestry and cattle are also important. The vast majority of the population live above 1,000 meters (3,281 ft). The mountains are quite formidable with the highest point Mount Khalatsa at 3,938 meters (12,920 ft), and just beyond the border in Georgia is the mighty Mount Kazbek at 5,047 meters (16,558 ft)—Europe's second tallest mountain. The crest of the Greater Caucasus Mountain Range forms the northern border with Russia. On the Russian side is the Russian Republic of North Ossetia-Allania, the two Ossetias are connected by a road through the Roki Tunnel. Despite the high altitude, much of the county has a mild climate since the Greater Caucasus blocks cold air from the north while air from the Black Sea and the Middle East warm things up. The foothills and mountainous areas experience cool, wet summers and snowy winters with snow cover often exceeding 2 meters in many areas. Yet neither season is the wettest—that would be spring and autumn.

HISTORY

Although part of Georgia, the Ossetians are ethnically quite different. Ossetian is an Iranian language distantly related to Persian and Kurdish, and therefore completely unrelated to Georgian. The Ossetians trace their origins to the Alans, a Sarmatian Iranian tribe. The Alans or Alani were contemporaries of the notorious Huns and maintained a formidable kingdom in the North Caucasus until it was destroyed by the Mongols in the thirteenth century. Modern Ossetians are proud of their long and, at least to their mind, glorious history. Originally, the Ossetians settled on the north side of the Greater Caucasus Range and a half million still live there in the North Ossetia-Alania Federated Republic of Russia.

As with most people in the Caucasus, the South Ossetians themselves claim to be an indigenous people living in the area since ancient times, but this is generally not supported by professional historians. Another claim by Ossetian historians is that they came to the area during the Mongol invasions of the thirteenth century, but this too is not accepted by most historians.[53] The people of South Ossetia are, in fact, descended from Ossetians who migrated over the mountains into Georgia in the seventeenth century. Most were peasants who settled in the lands of Georgian feudal lords. In 1772, the Baltic German explorer Johann Anton Guldenstadt found the area still Georgian but with many Ossetians especially in mountainous areas. Ossetian migration into what is now South Ossetia continued after the Georgian Kingdom of Kartli-Kakheti was annexed by the Russian Empire in 1801.[54]

The present conflict has its roots in the collapse of the first Russian empire that of Tsars in the early twentieth century.[55] During the short-lived Democratic Republic of Georgia, 1918–1921, Ossetian peasants rose up against their Georgian landlords in 1919 and 1920. Ossetians attacked Tskinvali and other towns with their largely Georgian populations. They received covert support from the Bolsheviks. Georgians responded by carrying out massacres in which between 3,000 and 7,000 were killed and perhaps as many as 20,000 Ossetians fled. This would have amounted to a large percentage of the Ossetian population. Thousands more died of famine and disease following the victory of Georgian forces.[56] Although some scholars regard these numbers as an Ossetian exaggeration, the events of this period were fuel for later Ossetian grievances against the Georgians.[57]

Many southern Ossetians joined the Bolshevik forces when they regained control over Georgia; however, their support did not win their freedom from the Georgians.[58] As the area was absorbed into the Soviet Union, the Bolsheviks incorporated it into the Georgian Soviet Socialist Republic as the South Ossetian Autonomous Oblast. Ossetia north of the mountains became a North Ossetian autonomous region of the Russian Federated Soviet Socialist

Republic. Thus, the southern Ossetians became not only geographically cut off from their ethnic kin but also politically separated. In 1925, Ossetians in Tskhinvali and in Vladikazkaz, the administrative center of North Ossetia, sent a joint petition to Moscow asking for the unification of both North and South Ossetia. But this was ignored.[59] With the collectivization of agriculture, Ossetian peasants were no longer working for Georgian landlords but Georgians still holding most of the official posts in their region. It is not surprising then that Ossetians still felt dominated by Georgians. Nonetheless, during most of the Soviet era, there was a great deal of interaction and intermarriage among the two ethnicities.[60]

CONFLICT

In the late 1980s, along with so many other ethnic groups Ossetians were animated by the reforms of Gorbachev and the freedom it gave them to express their identity, to organize and unfortunately to revisit old grievances. In 1988, some created the South Ossetian Popular Front (Ademom Nykhas). Ossetians were the majority in the region; a census in 1989 gave the population of the South Ossetian Autonomous Oblast at about 100,000—66 percent Ossetian and 29 percent Georgian.[61] With Georgia moving toward greater independence from Moscow, there was a resurgence of Georgian nationalism and a move to make Georgian the sole language of the state. This was alarming to Ossetians, who suddenly found themselves at a disadvantage since most did not speak Georgian. Under Soviet rule, they didn't need to, since everyone could communicate in Russian. Furthermore, the language policy seemed like a move that was meant to assimilate South Ossetia into Georgia. And in fact, most Georgian nationalists resented the idea of autonomous regions within their borders seeing both South Ossetia and Abkhazia as imposed on them by the Soviet Union. Georgians were even less receptive to the desire of South Ossetia for autonomy than they were for that of Abkhazians. For example, the early Georgian independence leader Zviad Gamsakhurdia accepted that the Abkhaz had rights. However, he thought the Ossetians should go return to their "homeland," meaning North Ossetia.[62] Georgians regarded the region is part of their historical heartland and the Ossetians as recent immigrants into it.

On November 10, 1989, the South Ossetian Regional Council asked the Georgian Supreme Council to upgrade the region to the status of an "autonomous republic." When this was rejected, the South Ossetians went ahead with a plan to transform themselves into a Soviet Socialist Republic, making them on equal terms and separate from Georgia. This was rejected by the Georgian parliament and received no support from Moscow. Furthermore, when political parties were legalized in 1990, the Georgian government banned regional parties. When elections were held in Georgia for a new parliament that year, the South Ossetians did not participate but held their own elections which the Georgian government under Gamsakhurdia declared invalid.[63] In September 1990, South Ossetian deputies met and appealed to Moscow to make their region a Soviet Republic, a request that was rejected.[64] In early 1991, fighting broke out when the newly created Georgia National Guard sent troops there. Moscow sent troops into the area to disarm both sides.

When Georgia gained independence in late 1991, full-scale violence took place between Georgian and Ossetian forces. Thousands of Ossetians fled to North Ossetia not only from South Ossetia but also from other parts of Georgia. In 1992, a ceasefire was arranged by Russia. Under its terms, peacekeeping forces from Georgia, Russia, the Russian Autonomous Republic of North Ossetia-Alania and from South Ossetia prevented further fighting. But the status of South Ossetia remained unresolved. South Ossetians held a reference on independence which was totally ignored by Georgia and the international community. In 1993, they created a constitution that established itself as an independent republic which no one recognized. Nonetheless, the South Ossetians held elections for presidency in 1996.[65] The situation in South Ossetia was the same as in Abkhazia. Most of it was in the hands of the local breakaway regime although Georgia remained in control of some areas. Its pretensions to independence were not recognized by any power—the international community regarded it as under Georgian sovereignty. Its autonomy was precarious as Georgia was determined to regain control over the territory and there was no solid commitment to its defense by outside powers.

It was an uneasy peace with clashes occasionally taking place. A serious one occurred in 2004. South Ossetia had been selling imported food and fuel from Russia on the black market as one of its main sources of revenue. When the Georgia authorities began to crack down on this activity, tensions flared into violence. South Ossetian militia, joined by freelance fighters from Russia, fought Georgian troops and peacekeepers. Dozens were killed in armed clashes and in bombings, shootouts, and hostage-takings. On August 13, 2004, a ceasefire was worked out, although violent incidents continued to occur.[66]

Meanwhile, South Ossetian leaders supported the idea of real independence. In 2006, they held a second referendum. Unlike the previous referendum in 1992, efforts were made for the international community to take it seriously. Observers from Germany, Austria, Poland, Sweden, and other countries were brought in to witness and verify the results. Authorities in Tskhinvali carrying out the election claimed a turnout of 95 percent with 99 percent voting for independence. However, the ethnic Georgian community, which made up about a quarter of the population, boycotted the elections undermining its credibility. Despite Ossetian efforts, the results were not recognized by the UN, the EU, NATO, or Russia. All questioned the legality of the vote since it was not recognized by the government of Georgia. Meanwhile, the ethnic Georgian villages held their own elections and voted for an alternative pro-Georgia president.[67]

Georgia, in 2007, tried to form a basis for negotiations with the South Ossetians by establishing a Provisional Administrative Entity of South Ossetia. It also created a state commission to work out an agreement on the status of the region. The peacekeeping forces at this time consisted of equal numbers of Georgians, Russian, and South Ossetians. But the Georgians remained apprehensive about the presence of Russian peacekeepers just as they did in Abkhazia. As relations between Russia and the pro-Western government of Georgia that came to power after 2003 worsened, so did Georgian suspicion that the Russians were supporting South Ossetian separatists. This view was also held by the United States and the EU, which did not believe the Russians were a neutral party in the dispute in either South Ossetia or Abkhazia.

The 2008 war between Georgia and Russia which broke out in South Ossetia was disastrous to the Georgians living there. During the war and afterward, South Ossetian authorities and irregular militia carried out a campaign of ethnic cleansing against Georgians in South Ossetia where Georgian villages around Tskhinvali were destroyed after the war ended. South Ossetian leader Eduard Kokoity said he would not allow the Georgians to return.[68] Note that ethnic cleansing is only too common in the stories of our de facto states.

SINCE INDEPENDENCE

The South Ossetian leaders seem to have been unclear whether their goal was independence or union with Russia. The idea of unification with the larger North Ossetia, governed as a semiautonomous Republic of North Ossetia-Alania within the Russian Federation was appealing to some. And it seemed that this was the plan. On August 30, the deputy speaker of the new state's parliament, Tarzan Kokoity, announced that the state would soon join Russia and unite with North Ossetia. The inhabitants of Akkalgori, the largest remaining ethnically Georgian town, were given the choice of accepting Russian citizenship or leaving. But this was quickly contradicted by Eduard Kokoity who stated that South Ossetians had shed too much blood for independence to give it up.⁶⁹ Moscow did not seem to be too enthusiastic about the idea of annexation, but instead gave recognition to South Ossetia as an independent sovereign state. Nicaragua recognized its independence in late August and Venezuela in September 2009 later Nauru and Syria followed. But no one else did other than the three other international pariahs: Transnistria, Nagorno Karabakh, and of course Abkhazia and South Ossetia recognized each other. All other nations continued to support Tbilisi's insistence that it was part of Georgia. Russia's recognition of the South Ossetia was condemned by NATO, the Organization for Security and Co-operation in Europe, and the European Council. Meanwhile, the Georgian parliament passed, and President Saakashvili signed a law requiring foreign citizens to enter the two breakaway regions only through Georgia proper. The law held Russia fully responsible for human rights violations and for the compensation to those who lost property or suffered losses as a result of the conflict.

Meanwhile, the republic went about its business like a normal country. It held its fourth presidential election in November 2011. Since Eduard Kokoity was not eligible to run for a third time, several others vied for his position. The two main candidates were Anatoliy Bibilov supported by Russia and the candidate supported by the opposition figures, Alla Dzhioyeva. Each received a quarter of the vote. When a run-off was held, Dzhioyeva won, but the Supreme Court of South Ossetia invalidated the election. A new election was held in 2012 in which Leonid Tibilov defeated David Sanakoyev in a run-off.⁷⁰ No one outside the country paid much heed or took these developments seriously.

This ambivalence about independence versus integration with Russia has remained. In 2014, Abkhazia signed an agreement with Russia that closely aligned the country with its large protector while still maintaining its independence, and the following year, 2015, it appeared that South Ossetia was following suit. On March 18, 2015, the presidents of Russia and South Ossetia signed an agreement that incorporated the South Ossetian armed forces into the Russian armed forces and integrated its customs services into that of Russia. Russia also agreed to pay salaries of South Ossetian state officials. Georgian called this agreement the "annexation," and the United States and the EU refused to recognize it. On December 29, 2015, South Ossetian president, Leonid Tibilov, proposed renaming the county South Ossetia-Alania to correspond with the North Ossetia-Alania the name of the Russian republic north of the mountains. He further proposed to hold a referendum on joining the Russian Federation. In April 2016, he announced plans to hold the referendum before August of that year but later postponed it until after the April 2017 presidential elections.⁷¹ The referendum was held and the country was rather awkwardly renamed the Republic of South Ossetia, State of Alania.

SOUTH OSSETIA AS A DE FACTO STATE

Before the conflict, about 25–30 percent of the population was Georgian and two-thirds Ossetian. The eastern quarter around the town of Akhalgori was predominantly Georgian while the central and western quarters were predominantly Ossetian. As a result of the conflict, it is estimated by the Georgian government that 15,000 Georgians fled to the republic; 30,000 Ossetians fled to North Ossetia; and 500 citizens were killed. However, Russian investment into the de facto state may have encouraged some Ossetians to move back. In 2020, there were also about 3,700 Russian soldiers stationed there. Some estimates give the population as 80,000 but that was probably too high; as previously noted is believed to be closer to 53,000. Like Nagorno Karabakh, it has become ethnically homogeneous. The 1926 census gave the area as 69 percent ethnically Ossetian a figure that held until recent events. It is now estimated at 90 percent Ossetian with small Georgian and Russian minorities.[72]

The economy has struggled. It is one of the poorest parts of Europe, if not the poorest. There are few jobs; electricity from Georgia has been cut off, a cable to North Ossetia supplies power. The majority of the population lives at subsistence farming or is unemployed. A third of the government revenue comes from levying customs duties on goods most of which passes through the Roki Tunnel. The country relies on Russian assistance. There are a few small factories but most of those ceased functioning after the 2008 war. There is a South Ossetia State University in Tskhinvali but education officials planned after 2008 to place most post-secondary students in Russian institutions.

The status of South Ossetia remains unclear. It is small and isolated, linked to the outside world by a single tunnel through the mountains to North Ossetia in Russia. The economy is not viable, there are few resources, and it is largely dependent on Russia. The modest population is shrinking as people leave for work elsewhere. Most of the world sees it as a territory of Georgia occupied by Russia. Even Russia, the only major power to recognize South Ossetia, appears to do so only because it finds it of some strategic value; its troops there are a useful as a pressure point on Georgia. One way of looking at South Ossetia is that it is a pawn in Moscow's attempt to bring the former Soviet republics—what it refers as its "near abroad"—within its sphere. Pro-Western Georgia has been an irritant in this project of President Vladimir Putin to regain some measure of control over the former republics of the Soviet Union, a policy with considerable support among the Russian public.

Furthermore, it is not clear that South Ossetia even wants to be an independent state. South Ossetians for a century have wanted to be reunited with the Ossetians in the north. This still seems to be what many if not most want—which would mean being part of Russia. In fact, foreign journalists visiting the country in 2014 found that the "overwhelming majority" south hoped for annexation by Russia.[73] Unlike Abkhazia which is the homeland of an Abkhaz nation, and more like Nagorno Karabakh, South Ossetia's independence was only tactical, a means to an end.

NOTES

1. Thomas Goltz, "The Paradox of Living in Paradise: Georgia's Descent into Chaos," in Svante E. Cornell and Frederick Starr, editors, *The Guns of August 2008: Russia's War in Georgia* (Armonk, NY: M.E. Sharpe, 2009), 10–27, 20–21. The Georgians have the same myth about their beautiful land.

2. Roman Dbar, "Geography & Environment," in George Hewitt, editor, *The Abkhazians: A Handbook* (Richmond, UK: Curzon Press, 1999), 23–36.

3. George Hewitt, "Introduction," in George Hewitt, editor, *The Abkhazians: A Handbook* (Richmond, UK: Curzon Press, 1999), 13–32, p. 17.

4. Saparov, *From Conflict to Autonomy*, 151.

5. Tom Trier, Hedvig Lohm, and David Szakonyi, *Under Siege: Inter-Ethnic Relations in Abkhazia* (New York, NY: Columbia University Press, 2010), 23.

6. Souleimanov, *Understanding Ethnicpolitical Conflict*, 116–17.

7. The term "Georgian" refers to the speakers of the Kartvelian languages, which include Kartveli spoken by most of the people of Georgia, Mingrelian spoken in western Georgia near Abkhazia, and two other tongues.

8. Franziska Smolnik, Andrea Weiss, and Yana Zabanova, "Political Race and Borderland practices in Abkhazia and Adjara: Exploring the Role of Ottoman Legacies and Contemporary Turkish Influences," in Franziska Smolnik and Andrea Weiss, editors, *Reconfiguration of Political Space in the Caucasus: Power Practices, Governance and Transboundary Flows* (London: Routledge, 2019), 94.

9. George Hewitt, *Discordant Neighbors: A Reassessment of the Georgian-Abkhazian and Georgian-South Ossetian Conflicts* (Leiden: Brill, 2013), 25.

10. Forsyth, *The Caucasus*, 195–96.

11. Trier et al., *Under Siege*, 26.

12. Trier et al., *Under Siege*, 56.

13. Souleimanov, *Understanding Ethnicpolitical Conflict*, 120; Goltz, "The Paradox of Living in Paradise," 10–27, 21.

14. Souleimanov, *Understanding Ethnicpolitical Conflict*, 130.

15. Trier et al., *Under Siege*, 57.

16. Trier et al., *Under Siege*, 17.

17. Souleimanov, *Understanding Ethnicpolitical Conflict*, 132.

18. Hewitt, *Discordant Neighbors*, 75.

19. Hewitt, *Discordant Neighbors*, 101.

20. Souleimanov, *Understanding Ethnicpolitical Conflict*, 134.

21. Goltz, "The Paradox of Living in Paradise," 22.

22. Hewitt, *Discordant Neighbors*, 123, 125–31.

23. Hewitt, *Discordant Neighbors*, 142.

24. "Demographics of Abkhazia," https://en.wikipedia.org/wiki/Demographics_of_Abkhazia#cite_note-6CHECK.
25. Hewitt, *Discordant Neighbors*, 152.
26. Trier et al., *Under Siege*, 19–21.
27. Hewitt, *Discordant Neighbors*, 224.
28. Pavel Felgenhauer, "After August 7: The Escalation of the Russia-Georgia War," in Svante E. Cornell and Frederick Starr, editors, *The Guns of August 2008: Russia's War in Georgia* (Armonk, NY: M.E. Sharpe, 2009): 162–80.
29. Johanna Popjanevski, "From Sukumi to Tskinvali: The Path to War in Georgia," in Svante E. Cornell and Frederick Starr, editors, *The Guns of August 2008: Russia's War in Georgia* (Armonk, NY: M.E. Sharpe, 2009), 143–61.
30. Felgenhauer, "After August," 7175–76.
31. "Russia Recognizes Abkhazia and South Ossetia," *Radio Free Europe/Radio Liberty*, August 26, 2008, https://www.rferl.org/a/Russia_Recognizes_Abkhazia_South_Ossetia/1193932.html, Accessed January 17, 2020.
32. *Radio Free Europe*, June 6, 2012, https://www.rferl.org/a/georgian-separatist-region-officials-slam-neutral-status-travel-documents/24605470.html, Accessed January 18, 2020.
33. *Radio Free Europe*, June 6, 2012.
34. Hewitt, *Discordant Neighbors*, 88.
35. "South Ossetia Joins Russia, Bans Jehovah Witnesses," *Euronet*, October 21, 2017, https://eurasianet.org/south-ossetia-joins-russia-in-ban-on-jehovahs-witnesses, Accessed December 10, 2019.
36. "Bagapsh Wins Presidential Election in Abkhazia," *Radio Free Europe/Radio Liberty*, January 13, 2005, https://www.rferl.org/a/1056827.html, Accessed April 23, 2019.
37. Hewitt, *Discordant Neighbors*, 213.
38. Thomas De Wall, "Uncertain Ground: Engaging With Europe's De Facto States and Breakaway Territories," *Carnegie Europe*, December 3, 2018, https://carnegieeurope.eu/2018/12/03/introduction-strange-endurance-of-de-facto-states-pub-77841.
39. De Wall, *Uncertain Ground*.
40. Giorgi Menabde, "Georgians in Abkhazia: A Choice Between Assimilation and Emigration," *Eurasian Daily Monitor*, August 6, 2019, https://jamestown.org/program/georgians-in-abkhazia-a-choice-between-assimilation-and-emigration/, Accessed December 11, 2018.
41. Trier et al., *Under Siege*, 14.
42. De Wall, "Uncertain Ground." Note the parallel with Transnistria and the Turkish Republic of Northern Cyprus which will be discussed further on.
43. Thomas de Wall, "Abkhazia and the Danger of Ossetianization," *Moscow Times*, July 16, 2019, https://www.themoscowtimes.com/2019/07/16/abkhazia-and-the-danger-of-ossetianization-a66437, Accessed April 16, 2019.
44. De Wall, "Uncertain Ground."
45. Gerard Toal and John O'Loughin, "How People in South Ossetia, Abkhazia and Transnistria Feel about Annexation by Russia," *Washington Post*, March 20, 2014.

46. Keating, *Invisible Countries*, 23.
47. De Wall, "Uncertain Ground."
48. De Wall, "Uncertain Ground."
49. Keating, *Invisible Countries*, 55.
50. Ben Fowkes, *Ethnicity and Ethnic Conflict in the Post-Communist World* (New York, NY: Palgrave, 2002), 139 cited in Souleimanov, *Understanding Ethnicpolitical Conflict*, 131.
51. Pal Kosto, "Biting the Hands that Feed Them," *Journal of Post-Soviet Affairs* 36, no. 2 (December 2019): 140–58, https://www.tandfonline.com/doi/full/10.1080/1060586X.2020.1712987.
52. UN Refugee Agency, "Abkhazia's Attempts to Bring Expatriates Home Meets Major Obstacles," *UNRFA*, March 16, 2016, https://www.refworld.org/docid/56ec0bae4.html, Accessed December 18, 2018.
53. Saparov, *From Conflict to Autonomy*, 29–30.
54. Frederik Coene, *The Caucasus: An Introduction* (London: Routledge, 2010), 125.
55. Souleimanov, *Understanding Ethnopolitical Conflict*, 112.
56. Souleimanov, *Understanding Ethnicpolitical Conflict*, 113.
57. Coene, *The Caucasus*, 151.
58. Souleimanov, *Understanding Ethnicpolitical Conflict*, 113; Hewitt, *Discordant Neighbors*, 38–39.
59. Souleimanov, *Understanding Ethnicpolitical Conflict*, 122.
60. Souleimanov, *Understanding Ethnicpolitical Conflict*, 122.
61. Hewitt, *Discordant Neighbors*, 13.
62. Coene, *The Caucasus*, 151.
63. Souleimanov, *Understanding Ethnicpolitical Conflict*, 123–24.
64. Hewitt, *Discordant Neighbors*, 92–93.
65. "South Ossetia," *Freedom House 2011*, https://freedomhouse.org/report/freedom-world/2011/south-ossetia, Accessed February 19, 2019.
66. Coene, *The Caucasus*, 154.
67. Coene, *The Caucasus*, 40.
68. "Ethnic Cleansing in South Ossetia," *New York Times*, August 15, 2008.
69. "Interview with Edward Kokoity," *RT News*, August 27, 2008, https://www.rt.com/russia/interview-with-eduard-kokoity-2008-08-2, Accessed April 11, 2029.
70. Hewitt, *Discordant Neighbors*, 269.
71. Liz Fuller, "South Ossetia Referendum on Name Change Stirs Clear of Thornia Issue of Unification," *Readio Free Europe/Radio Liberty*, February 8, 2017, https://www.rferl.org/a/caucasus-report-south-ossetia-referendum-name-change/28298590.html, Accessed April 14, 2019.
72. Hewitt, *Discordant Neighbors*, 44.
73. Toal and O'Loughin, "How People in South Ossetia."

Chapter 4

Shoestring of Europe
Transnistria

Even on a map, if it is on a map, Transnistria stands out as a peculiar place. It forms a long narrow strip of land on the east bank of the Dniester River (hence its name) wedged between Moldova and Ukraine. It is a state with many names—officially the Pridnestrovian Moldavian Republic (PMR), but it is also known as Transdniester, Trans-Dniestr, Transnistria, and Pridnestrovie. All meaning beyond (on the east side) the Dniester. Despite the name, a piece of it lies on the west side of the river, around the city of Bender. Transnistria is officially considered part of the Republic of Moldova by all members of the United Nations (UN). No country recognizes it, and it is usually shown on maps as part of Moldova. Moldova is one of the least visited and perhaps least recognized countries in Europe, but most people have heard of it. Few have heard of its secessionist state Transnistria and even fewer have ever been there. Even my spellcheck tries to correct this as it is written—there is no such word as Transnistria. None of the variations in the name are recognized either.

Transnistria belongs to the four "frozen conflict zone" states that were created amid the turmoil that accompanied the last days and fall of the Soviet Union—the others being Nagorno Karabakh, Abkhazia, and South Ossetia. These three are the only countries that recognize it; every other state regards it as part of Moldova. Yet, Transnistria is for all practical purposes an independent state with its own government in full control over a clearly defined territory with borders, immigration control, and customs. It has a parliament, its own military forces, police, postal system, and currency, and it issues its own license plates. Its flag is the only one in the world today with the hammer and sickle.

Transnistria is small. Only 4,163 square kilometers (1,607 square miles), it is a little smaller than Delaware, and it possesses a population, according to the 2015 census, of just 475,000. Yet it is not unusually small for an independent state. Besides having more people than Karabakh and Abkhazia combined, it is bigger than twenty-eight UN members by area and twenty-seven by population. Transnistria is a landlocked country wedged into a narrow north-south valley with Moldova forming its western border for 411 kilometers (225 miles) and Ukraine at its eastern border for a similar length. As the name implies, it is the land across the Dniester border. The Dniester forms a natural boundary for the country with the rest of Moldova, the exceptions being the city of Bender and six nearby villages which are on the west bank but are controlled by Transnistria and several small localities in the north that are on the east bank but are controlled by Moldova. It is an oddly shaped, a narrow strip of land that forms the eastern fringe of Moldova, a sort of miniature Chile, the famed "shoestring of South America."

A third of the population are native speakers of Moldovan (a dialect of Romanian), a little more than a third are native speakers of Russian, for many of the rest Ukrainian is their first language. Almost everyone can speak Russian which functions as the official language. It is not entirely isolated but connected by road and train with Moldova and Ukraine. Barring an incident, Transnistrians can travel without difficulty out of the country through Moldova or Ukraine, or Russia. Since no one recognizes their passports, most Transnistrians hold citizenship in another country, some in two other countries. Roughly two-thirds are Moldovan citizens, one-third are Russian, and about one-fifth are Ukrainian citizens. They are not connected by air and must use the airports at Chisinau in Moldova or Odessa in Ukraine.

HISTORICAL BACKGROUND

Who are Transnistrians and why do they claim to be a different country when most of the world regards the land as part of Moldova? This requires a bit of history.

Transnistria does not have any natural borders other than the Dniester River which forms a shallow valley. Valleys often unite the people on both banks, and most of the time the Dniester has done the same. The valley lies within a vast plain, part of the western extension of the steppe, the grasslands that start in Manchuria and Mongolia, continue through Kazakhstan, southern Russia, and Ukraine and stretch across Moldova, northern Romania, and Hungary. It was an open land through which many people passed through, some settled down, and others stayed a while and left. So, it was a land of fluid ethnic compositions: Scythians (Iranian-speaking pastoral peoples), Goths, Romans, Huns, Slavs, Germans, Turks, and Mongols. The grasslands were excellent for grazing, and so many nomadic peoples with their cattle, horses, sheep, and goats lived there. But it was also fertile and supported agriculture. It had a good location. The river afforded good transport and connected the area to the Black Sea. Lacking in natural barriers, the valley was open to invasion and peaceful migration on almost all sides. As a result, it went through a kind of seesaw pattern—farmers would settle, grow wheat, barley, and rye, and trade with the people along the Black Sea. The pastoral people mounted on their horses would overrun the area, the population would decline, and it would revert to mainly pastoral land.

The Greeks were here and left behind the name of the capital Tiraspol which means town on the Dniester in Greek. The Romans were there too, incorporating the area into the province of Lower Moesia. German-speaking Goths in the fourth century AD took over the area, reverting it to pastorage and using it as a base for attacks on the declining Roman Empire. In the eleventh century it became part of the first Russian Empire based in Kiev—at least we think so—since our information on the Dniester region in the Middle Ages is sketchy. As that empire crumbled, it became primarily the home of nomads again. The Mongols came in 1241 and briefly made it part of their empire. Then it came under Turkish rule becoming part of the Crimean Khanate. Later it was ruled by the principality of Moldavia, a state that reached its peak in the fifteenth century, and then by Polish-Lithuanian Commonwealth, a state that in the fifteenth and sixteenth century was the largest in Europe, stretching from the Baltic to the Black Seas.[1] In the mid-sixteenth century, Transnistria was a border area for the Ottoman Empire.

The Dniester remained a frontier area. West of it the lands were predominately Romanian speaking but east of it was a more confused, shifting mixture of people. This is an important point since while today Romanian-speaking Moldova claims the area as part of its historical/ethnic Romanian homeland, the truth is that it was a bit beyond the lands of Romanian-speaking peoples.[2] On this frontier was the town of Bender; Bender is a Turkish name meaning "port." It has sometimes been referred to by another name—Tighina. The earliest record we have about Bender dates to 1408 when a check post is mentioned there. In 1558, the Ottoman sultan Suleiman the Magnificent built the great fortress that still stands. It was later used by the Russians who decommissioned it in 1897 but it has been used by the Transnistrian forces in recent years. Currently, the impressive fortress serves as a museum and tourist attraction.[3]

The great fortress of Bender has an interesting history. In the early eighteenth century, Peter the Great began moving into the region although he didn't get as far as the Dniester. Between 1700 and 1721, Peter fought a war with Sweden, at that time a major power, in fact, the dominant power in the Baltic. Its ruler was Charles XII of Sweden, a famed warrior king. The war, which Peter won, was a turning point in history since it gave Russia access to the Baltic, a new capital at St. Petersburg, and marked the country's arrival as a great European power. During that war, Charles was defeated at Poltava not far from modern Transnistria and fled under Turkish protection to the fort of Bender. There for a few years he remained, ruling Sweden from the shores of the Dniester. One could say the Transnistrian city of Bender was at one time the effective capital of Sweden.

In 1812, the Russians pushed the Turks out of the Dniester and in a sense never left. From this time on, the history of the region comes into clearer focus. The Dniester basin after 1792 was part of an immense, multiethnic Russian Empire. When the Russians acquired it, the region was sparsely populated by mostly Moldovan, Ukrainian, and some Turkish peasants. The Russian encouraged the development of the region by bringing in Russian peasants as well as Germans and Jews. Thus, Transnistria with its mix of Slavs, Turks, Germans, and Moldovans came to reflect the ethnic diversity of the Russian Empire. It is still an ethnically diverse land.

BECOMING MOLDOVAN

To the international community, Transnistrians are Moldovans. Who are the Moldovans? And why do Transnistrians insist they are different? Moldovans are Romanian-speaking peoples, whose language is derived from Latin. Modern Romanian speakers, including Moldovans, entertain a romantic idea (no pun intended) that they are descendants of the ancient Romans who settled in the region. Historians have challenged this assertion, but for our purposes it might be enough to say that the Dniester valley—both sides of it, the Moldovan and Transnistrian—was the home to Slavic, Romanian, and some German and Turkish speakers.

But the story of the region in modern times is intertwined with the rise of Romania and Romanian nationalism. To simplify a complex story, the Romanian speakers lived in two main states, Moldavia and Wallachia, which merged in 1859 to form an autonomous part of the Ottoman Empire. It adopted the name Romania in 1862. In 1878, this new state was internationally recognized as the independent Kingdom of Romania. Wallachia made up the southern and western part of the country and Moldavia the northeastern part. When Romania became an independent state in 1878 by uniting two autonomous regions of the Ottoman Empire, the Russians, who helped the Romanians gain their independence, controlled the eastern part of Moldavia east of the Prut River that runs through the country. This eastern region was known as Bessarabia. It had an ethnically Romanian majority although many other ethnic groups settled there. Then in World War I Romania was an Allied power along with Russia, Britain and France. Romanian nationalists regarded Bessarabia—present Moldova—as part of their greater homeland. When Russia in 1917 plunged into revolution and dropped out of the war, Romania, with Allied blessings, took advantage of the situation to annex it. However, a small piece of it—east of the Dniester—remained in Russian hands.

When the Bolsheviks took over and reinvented the Russian Empire as the Union of Soviet Socialist Republics, they took this remaining piece of Bessarabia and created the Moldavian Autonomous Soviet Socialist Republic. It had over 9,000 square kilometers of area, over twice the size of modern Transnistria, and included parts of what is now Ukraine. The purpose of this small autonomous region was to be used as a base for eventually acquiring the rest of Bessarabia.[4] It seems that it was Moscow's hope that they might induce the peoples of Bessarabia (current Moldova) to join the socialist paradise in the Soviet Union.[5] If that was the case, they were disappointed. Still they got back Bessarabia in 1940 with the approval of Germany with which Moscow had signed the Molotov-Ribbentrop Pact the previous year. The Romanians were hardly pleased at being pressured by Hitler to give up part of their territory but had a chance to regain it the following year when Hitler turned on his new ally and invaded the Soviet Union. The Romanians seized all of Bessarabia including Transnistria.

It was a brutal occupation. Between 150,000 and 250,000 Ukrainian and Romanian Jews were deported to Transnistria where the majority were executed or died in concentration camps.[6] Tiraspol had a large Jewish population—in fact, it was as much an ethnically Jewish city as it was an ethnically Romanian one. In 1944, the Red Army reconquered the area and all of Bessarabia now became part of the much larger Moldavian Soviet Socialist Republic. This Soviet region became the basis for the modern country of Moldova. The little Moldavian Autonomous Soviet Socialist Republic became part of the Moldavian SSR, one of the fifteen republics that made up the Soviet Union.

As part of the Soviet Union, life was harsh for the people of the Moldavia SSR. Partly because they had fought with the Romanians and their Nazi allies Moldovans were treated with great hostility by Moscow. Hundreds were executed as fascist collaborators, many thousands were sent to the Gulag. Those left behind had to endure the loss of the land and businesses as the region became communized. Farmers were forced into state-run collective farms, and 115,000 peasants died of hunger in 1946–47 during collectivization period.[7] What happened was a severe drought reduced crop yields at the time. Soviet officials ignored this and confiscated huge amounts of produce leaving behind far too little for the Moldovans.[8] Things did not get better. From 1949 to 1952 under the supervision of Leonid Brezhnev who served as secretary of the Moldavian Bolshevik Party (renamed the Communist Party in

1952), the Soviets carried out mass deportations. Named "Operation South" rich peasant families were deported to Kazakhstan and Siberia. In just two days alone, July 6 and 7, 1949, 11,000 families were abruptly sent to these distant parts of the Soviet empire.[9] Brezhnev, after carrying out this brutal task, went on to become the leader of the Soviet from 1964 to 1982.

Under the Soviet Union there was an effort to create a Moldovan identity, separate from Romanian. This was part of the Soviet Union's project to replace the Russian empire with a multinational Soviet state where theoretically all ethnic groups were equal, although in practice the Russians dominated and Russian was the official shared language that everyone had to learn and use but non-Russian areas were also taught their own language. Newspapers, magazines, and books were printed in both Russian and the local language, which was Moldovan. We have seen how complicated this was in the Caucasus region where there were so many ethnic groups and political boundaries often lumped different groups together. The Moldovan situation was somewhat different. It was not so much a matter of satisfying different ethnic and nationalist groups as it was creating an entirely new identity where one did exist before. Moldova was simply the eastern slice of the Moldavian region of Romania that the Russian had taken. The Moldovans spoke Romanian. But the Soviets promoted the idea that Moldovan was a distinct language from Romanian. Behind this was an effort by Moscow to avoid any attempts to unite Moldova with Romania by making a new Moldovan identity. This was done by writing the language in Cyrillic not the Latin alphabet as Romanian was and introducing some changes in vocabulary.

Yet despite the difference in script and some new vocabulary, Moldovan is virtually identical in grammar and pronunciation and shares the vast majority of its vocabulary with Romanian.[10] At the same time Moldovans were encouraged to identify themselves as Soviets first and Moldovans second, and not as Romanians at all. However, despite Moscow's efforts, it never fully succeeded in either creating a strong sense of Soviet national identity or a distinct Moldovan one.

TRANSNISTRIA BECOMES MORE RUSSIAN

When the Soviets intentionally tried to create a nation called Moldova by taking off a slice of Romania, they unintentionally created Transnistria. Under the Soviet Union, many ethnically Russian and Ukrainian people settled in Moldavian SSR but the great majority of the people were ethnically Romanian. Moldavia (as Moldova was called under the Soviet Union) was one of the poorer regions of the country, mostly rural and agricultural. Its economy was based on exporting agricultural products to the rest of the Soviet Union, especially wines for which the region was famous. After World War II, the Transnistrian region underwent industrialization forming the industrial heartland of Moldova. The Soviet established a large industrial base focused on armaments, making weapons for the vast Soviet military forces. This included a large steel mill. Although it possessed only 12 percent of Moldova's territory and had only 17 percent of the population, the region produced 40 percent of its gross domestic product (GDP) and 90 percent of its electricity and most of its industry.[11] The area was also the headquarters of an important Soviet military force, the 14th Soviet Army. Thus, the eastern part became very different than the rest of Moldova, military-focused, industrial, and having a large ethnically Russian population. In the 1989 census, Moldovans made up only 39.9 percent of the population, while Russians and Ukrainians were 53.8 percent.[12] The result was that under the Soviet Union, especially after 1945, the Transnistrian area became different from the rest of Moldova, both economically and ethnically.

THE END OF THE SOVIET UNION AND THE BIRTH OF MOLDOVA AND TRANSNISTRIA

Then in the late 1980s came Gorbachev and his reforms which included giving more authority to the local and regional governments and allowing some free local elections. As was the case in the Caucasus and elsewhere, this had the unintended consequence of stirring up long-suppressed feelings of national identity among the ethnically non-Russian peoples. With the new freedom to organize and express themselves, political and cultural groups of all sorts emerged throughout the Soviet Union in the late 1980s. In the Moldavian SSR, the most prominent movement was the Popular Front of Moldova formed in the spring of 1988. It advocated for the exclusive use of Moldovan as the official language rather than Russian and Moldovan, a switch back to the Latin alphabet, and recognition that Moldovans and Romanians had a shared ethnic identity. Returning to the use of the Latin alphabet was a move with great symbolic importance for it represented the reorientation of the country from looking to the East to looking to the West. It meant using the same writing system as Romania and this meant in effect, a linguistic reunification with their cousins across the Prut River. In other words, Moscow's efforts to create a separate Moldovan identity oriented toward Russia failed. A forty-year effort to erase their Romanian identity was unraveling.

On August 31, 1989, the Supreme Council of the Moldavian SSR, a previously powerless body that rubber-stamped decisions from Moscow, made Moldovan the only official language, ordered the return to the Latin alphabet, and declared a shared Moldovan-Romanian linguistic identity. In April 1990, it adopted a new flag for the republic that resembled the Romanian flag. And it adopted Romania's new national anthem as its new anthem. Later in 1990, the Supreme Soviet of the Moldavian SSR renamed it the Republic of Moldova.

This was alarming to the Soviet authorities since it suggested that the region might break off from Moscow altogether and rejoin Romania. At first, most people had little enthusiasm for joining Romania since that country was ruled by the grotesquely oppressive Nicolae Ceausescu. Under his regime Ceausescu built enormous monuments to himself while his population sank into poverty. But with the overthrow of the egotistic dictator in December 1989 that prospect became more appealing. In May 1990, Moldovans and Romanians began crossing the border between the two countries which had previously been closed, all suggesting an inevitable move toward unification.[13]

All these developments alarmed the Russian-speaking minority as well as the Ukrainians and the small Turkish-speaking Gagauz people who live in southern Moldova. The move to exclusively use Romanian (that is Moldovan) put the Russian speakers at a disadvantage since few had ever bothered to learn the Romanian language. As was the case with the Ossetians in Georgia, they didn't need to since most business and work were conducted in Russian which nearly everyone spoke. Possible unity with Romania also would reduce them to a tiny group in a much larger Romanian-speaking state. Even more ominously, radical factions within the Popular Front of Moldova talked of expelling the non-Moldovans. The Slavic population formed the Yedinstvo (Unity) Movement calling for equal status to be given to both Russian and Romanian. Feelings were especially high in Transnistria where unlike the rest of the country, ethnic Moldovans made up less than 40 percent of the population and even some of these Moldovans only spoke Russian. The exclusive use of Moldovan would leave the population of the region, most of whom could not speak or write Romanian, marginalized.[14]

In the spring of 1990, Moldavia had its first free elections, ever. The Popular Front won these and gained control of the Supreme Soviet, the legislative body of the republic. Mobs attacked ethnic Russian members of parliament. Ethnic minorities found they could not rely on the police for protection. So, they took measures to protect themselves. Leaders in Transnistria organized an ad hoc assembly called the Second Congress of the People's Representatives of Transnistria which proclaimed the Pridnestrovian ("Across the Dniester River" in Russian) Moldavian Soviet Socialist Republic on September 2, 1990. The small Gagauz Turkish minority did the same proclaiming their own separate Gagauzia state in southern Moldova. In October, the Popular Front began recruiting volunteers to form an armed militia to put down these breakaway states. No one was declaring independence yet. The region was still a part of the Soviet Union, and the leaders of Transnistria and Gagauzia were careful to apply for recognition as autonomous republics within the USSR. With the situation escalating toward violence, President Mikhail Gorbachev decided to intervene. He issued a decree annulling the new Transnistrian Soviet Republic. But with so many things going on at this time in the Soviet Union, and wishing to avoid bloodshed, Gorbachev did not send any troops to enforce his order. For all practical purposes Moldova was functioning as an independent state, and Transnistria a mini-state within it.[15]

Gorbachev outlawed the Transnistrian state in December 1990 hoping to prevent the outbreak of fighting, however, violent conflict had already begun. The first armed clash began in the town of Dubasari in November. The Transnistrians armed themselves and were joined by volunteers from Russia who saw it as a struggle of their fellow ethnic Russians. The situation became worse the following year. In August 1991, a failed coup against Gorbachev by hardline members of the Communist Party set in motion a chain of events that led to the breakup of the Soviet Union. The Soviet Union's fifteen republics became the new states of Russia, led by Boris Yeltsin and the smaller ones like Moldova which was one of the first to declare its independence on August 27, just days after the failure of the coup.

THE TRANSNISTRIAN CONFLICT

As one of its first acts as an independent state, the Moldovan government arranged to have the leader of Transnistria, Igor Smirnov, and another high-ranking official arrested while they were visiting Ukraine. They were brought back to Moldova for imprisonment but were released when Transnistrian women led a protest march. One interesting feature of this conflict was the role women played. Transnistrian women were often at the forefront of events. A Women's Strike Committee headed by Nina Andreeva was instrumental in bringing about a separate state when it blocked railway lines.[16]

Moldova, which was just trying to organize a police and military force, was not ready for open conflict. But it soon had weapons. At the end of 1991, Moscow recognized all the new republics and formally dissolved the Soviet Union. When it did this, it divided the military arsenal among the new republics. Moldova now acquired international recognition as an independent, sovereign state possessing a military. In the spring of 1992, it created a Defense Ministry and received military equipment from the Fourteenth Soviet Army that had been stationed there.[17] But the Transnistrians were hardly defenseless. There was still a Russian army, part of the former Soviet Fourteenth Army, stationed in their breakaway state. The Russian forces were ordered to stay out of any conflict, but sympathetic officers aided the Transnistrians with weaponry.

Serious fighting took place from March to July 1992. The two sides were now heavily armed with Moldovans possessing 25,000–30,000 troops, the Transnistrians about 9,000-plus unofficial support from of the Russian troops stationed in their country. Armed clashes took place in three areas. One of these was in the Bender area which became a center of the conflict. Bender was the part of the region west of the river and therefore more difficult to defend. After several months of fighting, a ceasefire was signed on July 21, 1992, leaving Transnistria effectively independent. By that time hundreds of soldiers and civilians on both sides had been killed.[18]

Russian support for the Transnistrian cause was rather confused. Officially Russia was neutral but elements within the government were sympathetic to the ethnic Russian Transnistrians. Russian vice president Rutskov in a speech on the region's Russian language TV channel called for Russian forces in the area to defend the Transnistrians although this was contrary to official policy.[19] The Russian military commander of the Fourteenth Army, Alexander Lebed, openly supported the Transnistrians. In exaggerated statements he accused the Moldovans of committing ethnic cleansing. Although he was also critical of the Transnistrian leadership, he took the role of the defender of the Russian minority. At one point he told a Russian newspaper that "the Transnistrian people are being systematically, hypocritically, and brutally annihilated."[20] After he left his command, he used the notoriety he gained during the crisis to launch an unsuccessful bid for the Russian presidency. Lebed is still regarded as a hero in Transnistria, where an exhibit about him is prominently displayed in the national museum.

Transnistria might have been effectively independent, but it was an international orphan. Moldova joined the United Nations and all its members recognized Transnistria as part of its national territory. Not a single nation gave official diplomatic recognition to Transnistria. Yet it was a heavily armed, de facto independent state. In Western Europe and the United States there was hope that a settlement could be worked out and Transnistria could be peacefully reunited with Moldova. The Organization for Security and Co-operation in Europe (OSCE) began negotiating a settlement. As a step toward peace and reconciliation on May 8, 1997, Moldovan president Petru Lucinschi and Transnistrian president Igor Smirnov signed the so-called "Primakov Memorandum" or more formally the "Memorandum on the principles of normalization of the relations between the Republic of Moldova and Transnistria." This established legal and state relations between the two countries, but its provisions were interpreted differently by the two sides. To the Transnistrians this amounted to an admission by Moldova that their state was independent, but it did not mean this at all to the Moldovans. Moldova regarded the agreement as just a practical arrangement allowing the Transnistrians to trade and travel to the rest of Moldova and even to use the international airport at the Moldovan capital of Chisinau. Meanwhile, in 1999, Ukraine signed a treaty with Moldova which respected Moldova's territorial claims.[21] Thus Transnistria was surrounded on one side by Moldova which regarded it as a renegade region and on the other side by Ukraine which supported Moldova's position.

The United States and the European Union were generally unsympathetic to the Transnistrians' concerns for autonomy. Russia, their main supporter, was more ambivalent. In 2003, the government of Vladimir Putin suggested a federation of the two with Transnistria having a veto power over laws that were not in its interest. This went nowhere and was abandoned. Meanwhile, Russia decided to maintain its military base in the country which meant in practice that Moscow was providing some military protection to the breakaway state. Talks between Moldova and Transnistria began in Geneva in 2011, along with representatives from Ukraine, Russia, and the OSCE to work out problems. The United States and the EU participated as observers hence they were called the 5 + 2 talks. But negotiations become complicated with the Russian invasion of Crimea in 2014. However, negotiations continued and as of 2019 the OSCE was reporting they were making progress toward reaching a settlement.[22]

Attitudes in Moldova and Transnistria only hardened over time. Moldova passed a law in 2005 that declared most of Transnistria an autonomous territory within Moldova. No Transnistrians were consulted on this and they have generally ignored attempts to reenter the state as an autonomous region. The following year, in 2006, the government of Transnistria held a referendum in which 97.2 percent of the voters supported independence from Moldova and free association with Russia. But the EU and other countries refused to recognize the referendum results.[23]

It is easy to see the conflict in purely ethnic terms—a Russian speaking majority section of Moldova sought to separate for the emerging independent Moldova state. The reality is more complex. For example, John Mackinlay and Peter Cross, who conducted a study based on casualty reports, found that many ethnically Russians and Moldovans fought together on both sides of the conflict.[24] So that while it had an ethnic component, the sense of loyalty to Transnistria was also a sense of local loyalty to the industrial region, not just an ethnic identity. In this it differed from separatist movements in Nagorno Karabakh, Abkhazia, and South Ossetia.

TRANSNISTRIA TODAY

By all measures, Transnistria is a strange place. To travel there requires getting a visa at the border. It is usually necessary to have a confirmed hotel reservation. The visa is limited to the period of this reservation. Other than a few business people, the country does not receive many visitors. If one is looking for a place in Europe to avoid the tourist crowds this is it. A visitor may not encounter any other tourists at all. Yet, it is a pleasant, safe place to travel with a friendly population.

Transnistria has been described as a mini-Soviet Union. The capital Tiraspol, a city of about 160,000, is filled with Soviet monuments. One guidebook describes it as a "veritable Lenin-loving theme park."[25] The main street 25 October Revolution is named after the date of Bolshevik Revolution and is flanked at both ends by statues of Lenin. One is at a park and the other Lenin stands in front of the main government building, the House of Soviets. Another Bolshevik leader Kirov also has a statue in a park named after him. The main street in Bender is named after Lenin; the country's only luxury hotel is the Russia Hotel. Restaurants serve Russian and Ukrainian food. The uniforms of officials and the military parades are all reminiscent of the former Soviet Union. And it is not just the monuments and the uniforms that make it Soviet-like, former Soviet officials have found jobs there. In the 2000s the minister of state security was General Antufeyev who had once had the job of cracking down on dissent in Soviet controlled Latvia.[26]

The capital Tiraspol served as the capital of the Moldavian ASSR from 1929 and 1940, it is the second-largest city in Moldova after Chisinau. The name, as mentioned, is Greek but the modern city was founded by Russians in 1793 as a military outpost.[27] It still acts as an outpost of the Russian military who maintain troops there. The other major town Bender, the part of Transnistria that isn't beyond the Dniester is especially contested. While Moldova has been willing to consider Transnistria an autonomous region, the 2005 law Chisinau passed recognizing its autonomy excluded Bender.

Transnistria has a democratic constitution, although it has not been a model of democracy. It has a multiparty system and a unicameral parliament called the Supreme Council with forty-three members elected from single-member districts. There is an executive president elected by popular vote for a five-year term. For four of those terms, the president was Igor Smirnov who lost in the first round in 2011. Smirnov was born in the remote eastern Siberian peninsula of Kamchatka. His family moved about the Soviet Union, but he did not move to Transnistria until as a plant manager he was transferred there in 1987. Smirnov administration was marked by corruption both his own and those of other members of his administration. At one time he had a monthly income of US$ 50,000 when most Transnistrians were earning three to four dollars a day.[28] His party the Republic Party controlled the parliament until 2005 when the opposition Renewal Party won more seats. The Renewal Party did even better in 2010 and its candidate Yevgeni Shevchuk won the presidency in 2011. All this looks very democratic and civilized but there have been questions about the degree of fairness in the elections. In the 2016 presidential elections, candidate Andrey Safonov was unable to register as one until a few days before the election.[29]

The human rights record has a lot to be desired. It has been criticized by several governments, and international organizations have been critical. Authorities have been charged with limiting freedom of expression, using torture and arbitrary arrest and detention, of imposing press restrictions, and opposition groups are reportedly seldom given permission for peaceful assembly. Minority religious groups have been harassed and found it difficult to register, homosexuality is illegal, gays and lesbians subject to governmental and societal discrimination. In 2018, the US-based Freedom House called Transnistria a "non-free" territory, with serious limitations on political rights and civil liberties. According to the Organization for Security and Co-operation in Europe the media climate is restrictive, and authorities continue to silence independent opposition voices and groups. Both major newspapers are controlled by authorities, as are most radio and television stations.[30] Russian is the main language, which helps set it apart from the rest of Moldova. There are is public education in Moldovan for the third or so of the population that speaks that language. But it is done in the Cyrillic script rather than in the Latin script in use in Moldova. Four of six schools that used the Latin script were forcibly closed by Transnistrian authorities in 2004. Students were required to use Cyrillic script. This action drew sharp criticism in Europe where one official called it "linguistic cleansing." Under EU pressure they were reopened.[31]

Transnistria is in a difficult physical situation. An inland country it has no seaport, no major international airport and is surrounded by two countries, Moldova and Ukraine, that do not recognize it. Yet it has an export economy producing steel, pipes, and other metal equipment to European countries. Goods initially could be shipped through Ukraine. However, on March 2, 2006, Ukraine introduced new custom regulations which would allow the importation of goods from Transnistria only if they had documents processed by Moldovan customs offices. The measure supported by the United States, the EU, and the OSCE was interpreted by both Transnistria and Russia as "economic blockade." Transnistria responded by blocking all Moldovan goods being shipped to Ukraine, since these had to pass through its borders. It lifted this after two weeks, but the Ukrainian measure remained in place causing economic hardship. Transnistria declared a "humanitarian catastrophe" which Moldova called "deliberate misinformation." Russia responded by sending cargoes of humanitarian aid.[32]

RUSSIA AS PATRON

Russia is Transnistria's big friend and protector. Moscow maintains a military presence in the country. This began as a peacekeeping mission at the time of the 1992 ceasefire. Moldova wanted the Russian troops to leave. Accordingly, in October 1994 Russia and Moldova signed an agreement that committed Russia to withdraw troops in three years but the Russian Duma (parliament) never ratified it and it never went into effect. The troops stayed although their numbers over time shrank to just 1,200. Still their presence remained a sore point with Moldova. Since the United States and EU recognized Transnistria as part of Moldova, the unwanted Russian troop presence is considered by these countries a violation of Moldova's sovereignty. Moldova has criticized Moscow for maintaining troops on what even Russia recognizes as legally part of Moldova's sovereign territory. Russia has argued these troops there as part of its peacekeeping mission. Moldova insists that no more than 500 can be considered peacekeepers and has even arrested Russian soldiers who have entered the country to use Moldova's airports.

North Atlantic Treaty Organization passed a resolution on November 18, 2008, urging Russia to withdraw its military presence from the "Transdniestrian region of Moldova." In 2011, US Senator John McCain in a visit to Moldova claimed Moscow was violating the territorial integrity of Moldova and Georgia and one of the "fundamental norms" of "international behavior." In 2015, Ukraine cut off transit to Russian troops terminating agreements it had with Russia.[33] Russia uses the Chisinau International Airport for the short overland journey from there to Tiraspol. Chisinau allows this but has occasionally blocked and deported soldiers who were not clearly identified as international peacekeepers or who have failed to give sufficient advance notice. Transnistria, of course, relies on the small Russian military presence as a sort of reinsurance. On June 27, 2016, the Transnistrian government created a new law that made disrespect or distortion about the positive role of the Russian Army's peacekeeping mission a crime punishable by up to three years imprisonment. In 2016 the government decreed that all laws must closely follow those of Russia.[34]

A SHADY REPUTATION

Transnistria acquired a reputation as having an economy that was based on contraband and gunrunning and is sometimes labeled a "mafia state." Reports and public comments in the West have been most unkind. It has been called as "a Stalinist backwater and a criminal Ruritania."[35] And has been labeled a "clearing house for illicit trafficking in arms, people, drugs, organized crime, money laundering and smuggling."[36] The country has been accused of being a "place where the Russian mafia launder money."[37] These allegations are denied by local officials and downplayed by officials in Russia and Ukraine. They may not be entirely fair, since Transnistria is located between two countries known for corruption and illicit trading of all kinds, it would be surprising if the country was not involved in illegal trade. There has been evidence of illicit production and trafficking of weapons into and from Transnistria. The country has an industry based on supplying the Soviet military but after 1991 it had no markets. Considering its ambiguous international status, support by nationalist elements in Russia, it is hardly surprising if it did make and sell weapons. Efforts by journalists and observers to find out just what is being manufactured at its big industrial complex have been blocked. International organizations have complained about this lack of transparency. However, a report by foreign experts working on behalf of the UN said these charges were exaggerated, although trafficking in light weapons was likely to have occurred before 2001. OSCE officials believe there is no arms trafficking today; in 2010 Ukraine's special envoy to Transnistria, Viktor Kryzhanovski, said there was no ongoing arms trafficking or drug trafficking through the Transnistrian section of the Ukrainian-Moldovan border. Another accusation has made that Transnistria is a significant transit point for human trafficking; this has not been confirmed.[38]

Transnistria does have a legitimate economic sector—steel, electricity, textiles, and so on. These companies were state-owned under the Soviet Union but were privatized in the late 1990s. The largest industry is steel, the Moldova Steel Works is the country's largest enterprise and accounts for much of the state's revenues. It is controlled by a Russian businessman Alisher Usmanov. The second is Tirotex, a textile company that claims to be the second-largest textile company in Europe. The energy sector is dominated by Russian owned companies. KVINT located in Tiraspol produces and exports brandy, wines, and vodka. Originally most of its trade was with Russia and its allies, this changed in 2014 when Moldova signed an Association Agreement with the EU allowing tariff-free exports to its member states. Ironically, although Transnistrians vehemently deny being part of Moldova, they were able to take advantage of the trade agreement since the EU considers it part of Moldova. As a result, the EU has replaced Russia as its largest trading partner.

A peculiar feature of Transnistria is the role of the Sheriff company. When the Soviet Union fell, former Soviet officials with connections gained control of much of the economy. This happened to Transnistria where two security officials linked to the KGB, Victor Gushan and Ilya Kazmal, formed the Sheriff company using their connections to acquire ownership of all kinds of enterprises: a construction company, a chain of gas stations, a chain of supermarkets, and food and beverage industries, as well as a mobile phone network, a TV channel, and other businesses.[39] The Sheriff company has had an enormous influence over the politics of the small country. They had strong ties with President Smirnov. Shevchuk tried to curtail its influence but it was he who lost power. In 2016, the Sherriff company successfully backed Vadim Kresnoselsky for president.[40] By the late 2010s the Sherriff conglomerate had obtained a large measure of control over both the presidency and the national legislature.[41] Meanwhile, the economy is far from flourishing. Unemployment reached 60 percent in the early 2000s; it has since declined but remains high, with wages low. Lacking jobs many young left, especially in the countryside where they left behind, aging, dying villages.[42] The economy has steadily deteriorated despite support from Russia.

TRANSNISTRIA—HOW VIABLE?

The people of Transnistria rebelled and created their own state in part as a response to the fear of being a tiny, discriminated minority of mostly Russian speakers in a unified Romania-Moldova. But after 1991, the movement by Moldovans to unite with Romania waned. Moldovans came to embrace the idea of a Moldovan nation. Transnistrian elites responded to these pro-Romanian, anti-Russian sentiments of the nationalist movement in Moldova creating and consolidating a separate state.[43] Yet there has become less reason for Transnistrians to worry about either of these since anti-Russian feeling has diminished as has the desire to unite with Romania. Moldovans became more tolerant of the Turkish-speaking Gagauz and Russian minorities. Russia supports the idea that Transnistria should be autonomous within Moldova. In fact, there is a sort of de facto federation between Moldova and Transnistria.[44]

To some extent, like Abkhazia and South Ossetia, Russia was crucial in sustaining Transnistria. Russia supplies military aid and its troops act as a guarantor of its independence. Russia supplies gas but that has created a financial debt the country owes to Moscow. At the same time relations between Russia and Moldova improved. This threatened to isolate Transnistria since Russia has been its only ally. Many Transnistrians three decades after declaring their independence would probably like to be affiliated with Russia in some way. However, it did seem unlikely that Russia would annex a territory that it does not border and whose annexation would antagonize potentially friendly countries in Eastern Europe as well as cause an international outrage. This became even less probable after 2014 when Moscow's annexation of Crimea brought about painful sanctions. This made it unlikely that Russia would want to risk more trouble for a less strategically valuable territory. The annexation of Crimea was popular with the Russian public, but they have less of an emotional attachment to Transnistria than they do to Crimea.

Transnistria has been a separate state long enough for its own sense of identity to emerge. In 2006, Natalia Cojocaru interviewed thirty-five college students and at Tiraspol University and found a sense of national identity emerging.[45] And at times Transnistrians have shown they were not marching to Moscow's tune. An example was the elections of 2011 when electorate rejected the Russian backed presidential candidate. Meanwhile, Transnistria over the years made progress from being something closer to a crime-infested "black hole," to becoming more "something akin to full-fledged statehood."[46] A state that carried out the normal functions of government, a somewhat normal, legitimate economy, and a state that has shown it can act independently of not only Moldova but of Moscow.[47]

Talks that began between Transnistria and Moldova have made some progress. However, it does not seem reunification is likely. As of 2020, it looks as if Transnistria would remain in its strange geopolitical situation, a de facto independent country that no one would recognize for the conceivable future.

NOTES

1. Nicholas Dima, *Moldova and the Transdnestr Republic* (Boulder, CO: East European Monographs, Distributed by Columbia University, 2001), 10–11.

2. Charles King, *The Moldovans: Romania, Russia, and the Politics of Culture* (Stanford, CA: Hoover Institution Press, 2000), 179.

3. Andrei Brezianu, *Historical Dictionary of Moldova* (Lantham, MD: Scarecrow Press, 2007), 349.

4. William H. Hill, *Russia, the Near Abroad, and the West: Lessons from the Moldova-Transdniestra Conflict* (Washington, DC: Woodrow Wilson Center Press, 2012), 48.

5. Dima, *Moldova and the Transdnestr Republic*, 23.
6. Brezianu, *Historical Dictionary of Moldova*, 355.
7. King, *The Moldovans*, 96.
8. Dima, *Moldova and the Transdnestr Republic*, 45.
9. King, *The Moldovans*, 9.
10. Dima, *Moldova and the Transdnestr Republic*, 96–98.
11. King, *The Moldovans*, 183–84.
12. King, *The Moldovans*, 183.
13. King, *The Moldovans*, 148–49.
14. King, *The Moldovans*, 187.
15. King, *The Moldovans*, 189.
16. King, *The Moldovans*, 187–88.
17. King, *The Moldovans*, 192.
18. Daria Isachenko, *The Making of Informal States: Statebuilding in Northern Cyprus and Transdniestria* (New York, NY: Palgrave Macmillan, 2012), 59.

19. King, *The Moldovans*, 194. Rutskoi later declared the intervention was a response to the Moldovans committing "a bloody slaughter" against the Russians.

20. King, *The Moldovans*, 200.

21. King, *The Moldovans*, 205.

22. Organization for Security and Cooperation in Europe, "Press Releases and Statements related to the 5 + 2 Negotiations Concerning the Transdniestrian Settlement," *OSCE Mission to Moldova*, October 2019, https://www.osce.org/mission-to-moldova/119488, Accessed January 21, 2020.

23. "Transnistria Votes on Independence," *New York Times*, September 18, 2006, https://www.nytimes.com/2006/09/18/world/europe/18RUSSIASUMM.html, Accessed March 18, 2019.

24. John Mackinlay and Peter Cross, *Regional Peacekeepers: The Paradox of Russian Peacekeeping* (New York, NY and Paris: United Nations University Press, 2003), 140–41.

25. Lonely Planet, *Eastern Europe*, 12th Edition (Franklin, TN: Lonely Planet Publication, 2013), 559.

26. "The Black Hole that is Transnistria," *Economist*, May 3, 2007.

27. Brezianu, *Historical Dictionary of Moldova*, 349–50.

28. Aimilia Papoutsi, *Frozen Conflict Zones: The Case of Transnitria* (Saarbrucken, Germany: Lambert Press, 2016), 31.

29. *Freedom in the World 2018: Transnistria*, https://freedomhouse.org/report/freedom-world/2018/transnistria, Accessed March 19, 2009.

30. *Freedom in the World 2018: Transnistria*, Accessed March 19, 2019.

31. Brezianu, *Historical Dictionary of Moldova*, 360.

32. "Russia's Humanitarian Assistance is a Planned Propagandist Action, Chişinău Claims," *Politicom.moldova.org*, March 23, 2006, https://www.moldova.org/en/russias-humanitarian-assistance-is-a-planned-propagandist-action-chisinau-claims-11365-eng/, Accessed December 15, 2019.

33. Joshua Kucera, "Russian Troops in Transniestria Squeezed by Ukraine and Moldova," *Eursianet*, May 25, 2015, https://eurasianet.org/node/73586, Accessed June 12, 2018.

34. *Freedom in the World 2017 Transnistria: Profile Freedom House*, 2017, https://freedomhouse.org/report/freedom-world/2017/transnistria, Accessed March 24, 2019.

35. Nick Middleton, *An Atlas of Countries that Don't Exist: A Compendium of Fifty Unrecognized and Largely Unnoticed States* (San Francisco, CA: Chronicle Books, 2015), 58.

36. Papoutsi, *Frozen Conflict Zones*, 31.

37. "The Black Hole that Ate Moldova," *Economist*, 2007, May 3, 2007.

38. This is based on varied reports from the press. As of 2018, there was still widespread suspicion of illegal arms and other contraband. The opening of Transnitria to the Europe Union markets in 2014, has reduced the incentive and need for illegal trade.

39. De Wall, "Uncertain Ground."

40. De Wall, "Uncertain Ground."

41. William H. Hill, "The Moldova-Transdniestria Dilemma: Local Politics and Conflict Resolution," *Carnegie Moscow Center*, January 24, 2018, https://carnegie.ru/commentary/75329, Accessed March 22, 2019.

42. Anton Polyakov, Anya Galatonova, and Chloe Coleman, "In this Unrecognized Republic, It's not a matter of if the Children Leave, it's When," *Washington Post*, March 7, 2018.

43. Isachenko, *The Making of Informal States*, 64.

44. De Wall, "Uncertain Ground."

45. Natalia Cojocaru, "Nationalism and Identity in Transnistria," *Innovation: The European Journal of Social Science Research* 19, no. 3–4 (2006): 261–72.

46. Pal Kolsto and Helge Blakkisrud, "From Secessionist Conflict Toward a Functioning State: Processes of State- and Nation-Building in Transnistria," *Post-Soviet Affairs* 27, no. 2 (May 2013): 178–220.

47. Pal Kosto, "Biting the Hands that Feed Them," *Journal of Post-Soviet Affairs* 36, no. 2 (December 2019): 140–58, https://www.tandfonline.com/doi/full/10.1080/1060586X.2020.1712987.

Chapter 5

Born of Ethnic Cleansing
Kosovo

Few people have heard of Nagorno Karabakh, Abkhazia, South Ossetia, or Transnistria, but most have heard of Kosovo. The crisis that gave birth to it as a nation drew international attention and resulted in the intervention of the North Atlantic Treaty Organization (NATO). It also has a much larger population than the other de facto states we have discussed, about 2 million, and is less remotely located from the major nations of the West. And unlike the others, it has substantial international recognition, including by the United States and the European Union (EU). The state formally declared its independence in 2008. As of early 2020, 98 of the 193 United Nations (UN) members had given it diplomatic recognition. It is, in fact, far closer to being an accepted member of the community of sovereign states. Yet, it remains excluded from the UN and many international organizations by Russia's and China's veto and by Serbia's insistence that Kosovo is in fact part of Serbia. In this respect it is like the other de facto states we have discussed—it broke away from another state that still claims it as part of its sovereign territory and that claim has enough international support to block its acceptance into the community of recognized countries.

Kosovo has an area of about 10,000 square kilometers (4,000 square miles) or the size of Connecticut. A landlocked country, it borders Albania to the southwest, Macedonia to the southeast, Serbia to the north and west, and has a short border with Montenegro to the west. It is mostly a flat plain ringed with mountains which are never far away. The highest peak rises 2,656 meters (8,714 feet). It has two major flat areas, the Metohija basin in the west, and the Plain of Kosovo in the east. About two fifths of the country are covered with forests and about half with agricultural land, both farms and pastures. The largest city is the capital Pristina in the center of the country with about two hundred thousand people. Other important urban centers are the historical city of Prizren in the southwest which is only slightly smaller, and the city of Pec in the west and Ferizai in the south, both having around 100,000 people.[1]

The people of Kosovo are called Kosovars. Most Kosovars are Muslim and speak Albanian, although there is a small Serbian minority. The name Kosovo is derived from "blackbird field," and it is the name of a plain in the eastern part of the country where a historic battle was fought in 1389. The Battle of Kosovo Field is important to understanding Kosovo, so we will get to that battle soon. Albanian speakers also refer to the country as Dardania, the name of a Roman province located in the area but mostly Kosovars refer to their country as Kosovo.

ALBANIANS AND SERBS

One day this author was on a bus filled with Serbs leaving a Serbian town in Kosovo for the city of Nish in Serbia. A fellow passenger struck up a conversation. When a comment was made at how pretty the Kosovo countryside we were passing through was, the friendly man became agitated and stated, "This isn't Kosovo, there is no Kosovo, this is Serbia!" And this is the problem. Kosovo's place in diplomatic limbo is due to Serbia's insistence that it is part of Serbia. This is a land that two different ethnic groups lay claim to. The people are overwhelmingly Albanian, but the Serbs have a strong emotional attachment to it.

The Serbs, a Slavic-speaking people, are linguistically and ethnically related to Russians, Ukrainians, Poles, Czechs, Slovaks, and Bulgarians. Serbs speak Serbian, which is mutually intelligible with Croatian. But Croatian is written in Latin script and Serbian in Cyrillic. The last fact is significant since the Serbs, unlike Croats, Slovenes, Czechs, or Poles, are Orthodox Christians. Thus, in religion at least they share an affinity with the Russians, Ukrainians, and Bulgarians as well as the Romance-speaking Romanians. Partly because of this, Serbs have often leaned politically and diplomatically more toward Russia than the West. This fact has been of world-shaking importance. In the early twentieth century the Serbs had a dispute over Bosnia with the Catholic, Western-oriented Austro-Hungarian Empire. When Austria-Hungary threatened to send its troops into Serbia in the summer of 1914 Russia came to Serbia's support and thus World War I started. Those ties to Russia have been seen in recent years when Russia supported Serbia's claim that Kosovo is a Serbian province.

Unlike the Slavic Serbs, Albanians speak a language believed to be the last surviving one from the ancient Illyrian languages once spoken in the region. Besides differences in language what separates the Albanians from the Serbs was their conversion to Islam under Turkish rule and their adoption of many Turkish customs. For some Serbs they were not only later migrants into their homeland but opportunists who abandoned Christianity and joined the religion of the oppressor of the Serbs. From the late eighteenth century, the Serbs waged an ultimately successful struggle to throw off Turkish rule. Albanians by contrast cooperated with the Turks, did well under the Ottoman Empire often rising to high office. Albanian national consciousness came much later. But by the late nineteenth century, Albanian were ready to form their own nation-state. And although Albania became an independent state in 1912 many Albanians found themselves outside of it. Some lived in northern Greece which still has several hundred thousand Albanians, a larger number in Kosovo came under Serbian rule.

LONG HISTORIES AND LONG MEMORIES

As with so much of the Balkan region Kosovo is land of people whose identities have been shaped by ancient histories and by different versions of those histories. As in the Caucasus, there is the dispute over who came first. Albanian Kosovars naturally regard themselves as having a prior claim to the region. They draw on the fact that their language is derived from the ancient Illyrians who are the first people in the area that appear in written records. Based on this fact they insist they are the original inhabitants Kosovo. However, it is not certain who the original inhabitants of the region were. We can say that Albanian is an Indo-European language and Indo-European speakers only entered Europe four to five thousand years ago, a long time, but not enough to call then "the original inhabitants" since people, including farming villages, flourished long before then. The region was part of the Roman province of Illyrium after 59 BCE then later transferred to the Roman province of Moesia Superior. The ruins of the Roman city of Ulpiana are just being excavated today. With the decline of the Roman Empire in the fourth century it was raided by various "barbarian" peoples. The most important of these were the Slavs who mostly peacefully migrated and settled in Kosovo as they did in most of the Balkans in the sixth and seventh centuries. Slavic peoples most likely mixed with earlier settlers rather than displaced them, but their language dominated.

During most of the Middle Ages what later became known as Kosovo seems to have been a predominantly Slavic land, although before the thirteenth century our knowledge is very limited. Kosovo was part of the Slavic-speaking Bulgarian Empire after 850 and then after 1018 part of the Byzantine Empire. Around 1200 it was part of Serbian kingdom. In the 1300s, Serbia experienced a golden age when it was large and prosperous, and left many beautiful monasteries. Kosovo at that time was part of the heartland of the Serbian state and an important center of Serbian culture. The Serbian archbishop, the head of the Serbian Orthodox Church, presided from Pec (Preja) for a while and later from Prizren. Kosovo is still dotted with Serbian monasteries and fortresses from this period. Four Serbian churches and monasteries in Kosovo are part of Medieval Monuments of Kosovo UNESCO World Heritage Site.[2]

If there is a single event in the history of Kosovo that can explain the powerful emotional appeal of the land to modern Serbs it is the legendary battle took place at Kosovo Polje (Field of Blackbrids) near modern Pristina in 1389. Serbian Prince Lazar met the Ottomans forces under Sultan Murad IV and suffered a defeat that ended Serbia as an independent state. The Serb commander was killed. After the battle Murad was assassinated by the Serb Milosh Oblic. At least that's how Serbians remember it. In fact, the battle was a draw. It took decades more for the Ottomans to conquer the Serbians, an effort that was not completed until 1459. Nonetheless, the battle has become the subject of epic poetry and has been a key event in the memory of Serbs—the most tragic event of their history.[3] Albanians too remember this battle, but in their version some of the main participants were ethnically Albanian. For example, the Serb Milosh Obilic who assassinated Sultan Murad IV was in their telling really an Albanian named Millosh Kopiliqi from the Drenica Valley, later a hotbed of Albanian nationalism.[4] But it is the Serbian version that has been more historically significant. Modern Serbian nationalism has dwelled on this defeat as marking the end of their time of glory, reversing its outcome was a sacred, national mission.

From the fifteenth century to the nineteenth century, Kosovo as well as most of the rest of the Balkan region was under Ottoman Turkish rule. The Serbs remained strongly attached to the Serbian Orthodox Church, to their language and to their culture, and consequently they remained a subject people. The Albanians on the other hand often converted to Islam and actively participated in the Ottoman government. Mainly a people of the mountains Albanians never had their own kingdom, they remained a clan-based society, often feuding and fighting among themselves. Nor did they have their own national church. In fact, Christianity did not seem to penetrate as deeply in their society as it did among the Serbs.[5] As a result many Albanians, eventually most, converted to Islam and were often recruited as soldiers and administrators by the Ottomans. Some rose to high office in the empire. Serbs tended to view the Albanians as cooperating with their Turkish oppressors, of actively participating and benefiting from Ottoman rule, while as administrators they were involved in the suppression of the Serbian Christians. Reality was more complex. Many Albanians did serve in the Ottoman Empire. Yet, Albanians too often resented being ruled from Istanbul and frequently rose up in rebellion. And despite the opportunities that were afforded to some of them to advance in the empire most were poor tenant farmers working the land of rich Albanian warlords.

During the Ottoman period, Kosovo went from being majority Serb to majority Albanian but it is not clear how and when this happened. One explanation is that this occurred when in 1689, the Austrian army invaded the area and the Serbs rose up; when the Austrians retreated many Serbs left with them.[6] This is only a partial explanation. According to some historians, the Serbs, for a variety of reasons, migrated northward and as they did Albanians settled into the farmland they left behind. But there are other interpretations. According to Serbian geographer and ethnologist Jovan Cvijic while some Albanians in Kosovo were descended from Albanians who came down from the mountains of Albania and settled in the Kosovo plain, the majority were Serbians who converted to Islam and assimilated into Albanian culture.[7] It also possible that there have always been many Albanians they just weren't politically and cultural dominant, new immigrants added to that population to become a majority. In other words, Kosovo may have always had a mixed population. As Serbs migrated north, the Albanians stayed becoming the majority.

In the nineteenth century emerging nationalist sentiment in Europe influenced the Christian subjects of the Ottoman Empire. In 1804, the Serbs rose in rebellion and briefly gained independence. After a second uprising, the Ottomans in 1815 gave much, but not all, of Serbia autonomy within the empire. In this autonomous region the people were ruled their own Serbian princes in Belgrade. The Turks kept a military garrison in the capital to keep an eye on things but largely left the Serbs to govern themselves. Serbs, however, wanted to be totally free from the Ottomans. When in 1876 Russia went to war with Turkey, the Serbs joined and in 1878 Serbia became completely independent. It was also larger expanding to include the area around Nish bordering Kosovo. Many Albanians living in that area fearing Christian persecution fled to Kosovo adding to its Albanian and Muslim composition. An estimated 60,000–70,000 Albanian Muslims took refuge there.[8]

Russia's defeat of the Ottomans in 1878 saw Serbia, Bulgaria, Montenegro, and as we have seen, Romania become fully sovereign states. Albanians now feared losing their lands to their Christian neighbors—Serbs to the north and the newly independent Bulgarians to the south. In 1878, Albanian leaders met at the town of Prizren to deal with the situation. They were not united, some wanted to preserve their Albanian and Muslim traditions; others sought not to defend the past but to create new modern Albania as a fully autonomous state within the Ottoman Empire. The latter had a vision of Albania that included all the predominantly Albanian lands including Kosovo as well was the western regions that would become the state of Albania. To that end they created the League of Prizren and began to govern themselves in what was, all but in name, an independent state until the Ottomans intervened and crushed it in 1881.[9]

While the winds of change were blowing throughout the region Kosovo remained a conservative, traditional society. Western European visitors found Kosovo an "alien Muslim and medieval land."[10] However, the short-lived League of Prizren was a turning point giving birth to modern Albanian nationalism. This nationalism went beyond religion or tribe to a common ethnic Albanian identity that would include even the Catholic and Orthodox Christian minorities, and it would embrace the northern Gheg and southern Tosk tribes that had previously been antagonistic. This new identity was summed up by the Albanian poet Pashko Vasa who declared "the religion of Albanians is Albanianism."[11]

KOSOVO IN THE TWENTIETH CENTURY

The twentieth century saw constant rounds of ethnic violence and turmoil that eventually gave birth to the Kosovo state. The first major upheaval took place in 1912, during the First Balkan War. Greece, Serbia, Romania, and Bulgaria attacked the Ottomans who lost all their European territories except a small area near Istanbul, still Turkey's toehold in Europe. Half of the Albanian lands became an independent state of Albania. Serbia, however, was determined to regain all its medieval homelands including Kosovo which it succeeded in doing so at the battle of Kumanovo in Macedonia in October 1912. For Serbs this military victory was a satisfying revenge for the Battle of Kosovo. Having won control of it they would hold on to Kosovo to the end of the twentieth century.[12]

With the annexation of Kosovo the Serbians began a series of expulsions of ethnic Albanians that lasted throughout the twentieth century. They constituted an overall project of ethnically cleansing Kosovo to make it majority Serbian; in the long run this proved unsuccessful. In 1912 and 1913, when the Serbs conquered the area, they killed an estimated 20,000–25,000 Albanians although the numbers are not clear.[13] While the Serb population may have grown following the annexation, it was still only about a third of the population of Kosovo in 1914. Between 1912 and 1915 tens of thousands of Albanians fled Kosovo and neighboring Macedonia as a result of Serb campaigns in the Balkan Wars and World War I. One study suggests 100,000–120,000 Albanians were driven out of Kosovo.[14] During World War I, Serbia was an Allied power fighting the Axis powers Austria-Hungary and Bulgaria.[15] Many ethnic Albanians hoping to rid themselves of Serbian rule joined the Axis. Serbs formed *komitadji* militia that attacked Albanians perpetuating the cycle of animosity between the two ethnic communities.

During the war the Axis powers overran much of Serbia including Kosovo. The Albanian majority was briefly freed from Serbian rule. But only briefly. In 1918, with the collapse of the Central Power the Serbs returned and many took revenge on Albanians massacring Albanian Kosovars. Ethnic Albanians formed a Committee for the National Defense of Kosovo that supported guerillas called *Kachak*s who fought with arms smuggled in from Albania. The *Kachak*s, who combined banditry with freedom fighting were largely subdued by the mid-1920s, although some bands continued to operate until the 1930s.

Following the end of World War I, the Serbian king became the ruler of the Kingdom of Serbs, Croats, and Slovenes—this awkward name was replaced in 1929 by the simpler Yugoslavia—"land of the South Slavs." Although now the dominate group in a new multiethnic state, the Serbs continued their efforts to make Kosovo more Serbian. When a repatriation agreement was worked out with Kingdom of Yugoslavia and Turkey after World War I, thousands of Albanians were reclassified by Serb authorities as Turks and repatriated to Turkey. This was part of the larger post–World War I Wilsonian project to make the political boundaries of Europe coincide with ethnic-national identities. But doing so proved hard because many communities were ethnically mixed, and blocs of different ethnic groups were often scattered in discontinuous patches. One solution was to carry out exchanges of populations. This was done between Turkey and some of its Balkan neighbors with ethnically Turkish people in Bulgaria and Serbia being sent to Turkey. Albanians weren't Turks but since most were Muslims, the Serbs classified them as Turks and expelled them. When the new communist Yugoslavia revived this agreement in 1953 thousands more Albanians were again classified as Turks and encouraged to leave.[16]

Under the Yugoslav kingdom some 70,000 Serb colonists were settled in Kosovo. Displaced Albanians were supposed to have been compensated for their lost lands but seldom were.[17] In 1939, Mussolini, the Italian fascist leader, invaded Albania setting up an Italian puppet state. In 1941, Germany invaded and dismembered Yugoslavia and gave Kosovo to the Italian controlled Albania. Kosovars who had hope to unite with their fellow Albanians in Albania, got their wish but not their freedom. The Serbian part of Yugoslavia was under German occupation. During World War II many Serbs and other Yugoslavia joined the communist partisans. They proved to be effective resistance fighters and in 1944 liberated the country largely without outside help. After World War II Yugoslavia became a communist state.

This new communist Yugoslavia, under its charismatic leader Tito, became a federated state of several republics, sort of a miniature version of the Soviet Union. The states were Serbia, the biggest of them, Croatia, Bosnia, Slovenia, Macedonia, Montenegro, and later Bosnia. Unlike many of the other peoples of Yugoslavia, the Albanian Kosovars did not embrace the communist movement which they associated with Serbs. Instead of seeking their own autonomous republic, many continued to seek union with an independent Albania. But the new communist state of Albania that emerged in 1944 under Enver Hoxha had no wish to annex Kosovo since it focused on carrying out its socialist revolution at home and wanted to maintain good ties with its new communist neighbors. Despite this wish, in 1948, relations between Enver Hoxha's government in Albania and the Yugoslavia government under its leader Marshal Tito worsened. The border between the two countries was closed and most contacts ended. As a result, Albanian Kosovars were largely isolated from Albania. And Albania was isolated from almost everybody; it was the most repressive and reclusive state in Eastern Europe, a sort of European North Korea. So, Kosovo became part of the Serbian federal republic within the communist state of Yugoslavia.[18]

AN UNHAPPY MEMBER OF YUGOSLAVIA

As part of Yugoslavia, Kosovo was effectively under the domination of the Serbs. In theory it had some regional autonomy but not in practice it was firmly controlled by Serbian Republic within Yugoslavia. Part of the reason was that Yugoslavia was a one-party communist state and communist party officials controlled almost all institutions. Since few Kosovars were active in the Communist Party, they were effectively excluded from most decision making. However, during the years of communist Yugoslavia Kosovo became more Albanian and less Serb. The Albanian population grew whereas the Serbian minority shrank from 27 percent in 1948 to 11 percent in 1991.[19] Partly this was because Albanians had a higher birthrate. It was also because few Serbs were attracted to Kosovo which was the poorest region of Yugoslavia, a place with only modest economic opportunities. In addition, Serb migration out of the region increased in the 1980s as unrest took place in Kosovo.[20]

Kosovars leaders worked toward greater recognition as a separate culture from the Serbs and greater autonomy from Belgrade. They got both. In 1968, they changed the province's name from Kosovo-Metohija to simply Kosovo. The name Metohija is derived from the Greek word for monastery and thus loosely means monastic land—a reference to the strong presence of the Serbian Orthodox Church and its many monasteries. This name reinforced Serbia's historic claim to the area. A year later Belgrade allowed Kosovars to fly the Albanian national flag as a symbol ethnic identity. Albania was permitted to supply teachers and textbooks for Albanian instruction.[21] The Albanian language University of Pristina created in 1969 was important in fostering the region's cultural identity. Then in a further concession, the government in Belgrade gave the region some political autonomy in 1974.[22]

But the measures were enough to satisfy many in Kosovo. In 1971, the Bosnian region was given its own federal republic and the Kosovars wanted the same. In 1981, they carried out protests over the status of Kosovo, some demanding a separate republic of Yugoslavia, a reasonable enough demand since the Albanian population was the only major group not to have one. Others however, called for Kosovo's succession from Yugoslavia and its union with Albania shouting, "We are Albanians not Yugoslavs."[23] The government responded harshly to calls for succession resulting in a number of deaths, how many was never reported. It then reduced the rights the Albanians already had such as use the use of Albanian language textbooks in the schools. All this led to a rise in ethnic violence between Serb and Albanian Kosovar residents that continued throughout the 1980s. Many Serbs left because of the unrest making Kosovo only more ethnic Albanian. Meanwhile, a few radical Kosovars formed the People's Movement for the Republic of Kosova with the aim of making Kosovo (or Kosova as it is also called) its own republic within Yugoslavia. The oppressive nature of the Yugoslavian state limited the activities of this group.[24]

THE END OF YUGOSLAVIA AND THE RESURGENCE OF SERBIAN AND KOSOVAR NATIONALISM

The call for greater autonomy by Albanians was part of a larger revival of ethnic-national identity in Yugoslavia. Just as the seventy-year experiment in creating a Soviet national identity that would override ethnic ones failed in the Soviet Union, so did communist Yugoslavia's attempt to create Yugoslav identity. Unfortunately for the Kosovars with the wave of greater freedom that swept Eastern Europe in the late 1980s Serbian nationalism was allowed full expression. In 1986, the ultra-nationalist Slobodan Milosevic came into power in Serbia and sought to promote Serbian language and identity at the expense of non-ethnic Serbs. The traditional claims by Serbs that Kosovo was their homeland was heightened by the discovery in Kosovo of what were thought to be the bones of their medieval hero Stefan Dushan. In 1989, Milosevic took away the Kosovo's regional autonomy. A Serbian curriculum was imposed on the schools, the media was taken over by Serbs.[25]

With the collapse of communism regime in Yugoslavia in1990 Slovenia, Croatia, Macedonia, and Bosnia-Hercegovina withdrew from Yugoslavia declaring themselves independent states in 1991. The breakup was accompanied by violent conflicts. Each of the new states created a national identity based on ethnicity but the boundaries of the Yugoslav republics did not coincide neatly with ethnic boundaries. Particularly fierce fighting took place between Serbs and Croats. In January 1992, Serbia and Croatia ceased fighting and in May 1992 Croatia, Slovenia, and Bosnia were recognized by the international community and were admitted to the United Nations. Macedonia also had declared its independence and was admitted to the UN the following year. A new Yugoslavia Republic was established in 1992 from what remained of the old one: Serbia and tiny Montenegro. This new Yugoslavia contained only 45 percent of the population and 40 percent of the territory of the old. The Serbian dominated government in Belgrade was determined to not to lose any more territory and at the same time promote a kind of greater Serbia that would encompass as many people as possible.

The result of this was a Serbian move to take over all the ethnically dominated parts of the new nation of Bosnia—leading to the horrible Bosnian conflict. Serbian ethnic militias in that country backed by Belgrade carried out ethnic cleansing campaigns that shocked much of Europe and the world in their brutality. Their goal was to terrorize and drive always Muslim Bosniaks from parts of Bosnia and make it Serbian. In 1994, NATO intervened and began bombing the Bosnian Serb forces; in the following year negotiations began between the Serbs, Bosnians, and Croats that resulted in the Dayton Agreement. Bosnia's boundaries were recognized by all parties and the Serbs within Bosnia were granted autonomy.

VIOLENT BIRTH OF THE KOSOVO STATE

Meanwhile, in July 1990 the Kosovo Albanians proclaimed a Republic of Kosova (with an "a"). And in September 1992 they declared it to be an independent sovereign state. Ibrahim Rugova who was emerging as the leader of the independence movement was elected president in an election that was ignored by the Serbian minority. Only Albania recognized the new state. The proclamation of Kosova was a protest gesture, Serbia was still firmly in charge. Rugova was an advocate of nonviolence and had no desire for his people to participate in the bloodletting that was going in the region. Kosovars, therefore, for the most part just watched events in Bosnia unfold hoping that a Serbian setback there would lead to international pressure for Belgrade give up control. However, when in November 1995 the Dayton Agreement to bring the wars that accompanied the breakup of Yugoslavia to end was signed, the issue of who ruled Kosovo was left untouched. In fact, it left the hyper-nationalist government of Serbia more determined than ever to hang on to as much as possible, it was in no mood to accommodate Kosovar desires for greater autonomy or independence. The failure to deal with Kosovo encouraged Kosovars to take more active measures to free themselves from Serb rule. Frustrated with Rugova's nonviolent campaign for separation which seemed to get little recognition by the outside world and made little headway achieving freedom from Serbian rule, some formed a Kosovo Liberation Army (KLA). Unlike Rugova, the KLA was willing to use violence to achieve the separation of Kosovo from Serbia. Thus, the Dayton Agreement ended the war in Bosnia but contributed to a new one in Kosovo.

The KLA began military operations in 1996. At first these were isolated attacks on Serb police and paramilitary forces. But in early 1998 the KLA escalated their effort into what was becoming a civil war. Belgrade brought more troops in and carried out some brutal reprisals targeting KLA leaders and their families. Like many Kosovars the KLA goal at first was the eventual unification of Kosovo with Albania, with independence at best a temporary measure until that could be arranged. But the post-communist government of Albania seeking to join the EU and NATO and to pull itself out of poverty was not interested.[26] So most Kosovars opted for independence.

Serbian forces responded without restraint to these attacks. One Serbian operation was on the family compound of Kosovo Liberation Army commander Adem Jashari. Jashari is considered by many as the "father of the KLA." He came from a line of Kosovo guerillas who had fought Serbs for generations. In 1991, the thirty-six-year-old had gone to Albania to train with fellow Albanian Kosovars. He was briefly arrested by the authorities there. Returning to Serbia he was involved in violent attacks on Serbian police. In early March 1998, Serbian forces surrounded his home village of Prekaz killing Adem Jashari and fifty-seven members of his family. The massacre made Jashari a hero.[27] His bullet riddled home has become a kind of Kosovo nationalist shrine and the international airport at Pristina is named for him. Following the massacre many Kosovars joined the KLA to seek revenge. Fighting now began in a large scale.

Diplomatic talks began in France in February 1999 to work out a peaceful solution, but these were undermined by reports of ever increasing Serbian attacks on Albanian communities. The United States and its European allies decided to put pressure on Serbia and began air strikes on Serbian military targets in March. The Serbians responded by driving out all of Kosovo's Albanian population—ethnically cleansing the entire province. They carried it out with horrifying speed. Out of the less than 2 million Albanians, 900,000 fled to Albania, Macedonia and Montenegro while another 500,000 were internally displaced. That is, in a matter of weeks over three quarters were homeless. Had the campaign continued Kosovo would have been a largely depopulated land with only the small Serbian minority remaining. NATO continued the air strikes until June of that year, targeting not only Serbian forces in Kosovo but also the Serbian capital of Belgrade. Almost all NATO members were involved. It was a major NATO operation involving 1,000 aircraft and 38,000 missions.[28] Milosevic encouraged by the strong anti-NATO rhetoric coming from Moscow hoped for Russian support. When it was clear that this was not coming, he in gave in. On June 10, 1999, Milosevic agreed to withdraw his forces from Kosovo and the war ended.

The Serbian forces left behind 11,000 dead, several thousand missing, and hundreds of thousands of displaced people.[29] When they withdrew, the Albanians returned home. Most of the Serbs and other non-Albanians in Kosovo were expelled. The Serbian attempt to ethnically cleanse Kosovo and replace the Albanian population with Serbs had resulted in most of the Serbs being ethnically cleansed. Some remained in isolated towns under NATO protection. An International Criminal Tribunal for the former Yugoslavia (ICTY) prosecuted crimes committed during the Kosovo War. Nine senior Yugoslav officials, including Milosevic, were indicted for crimes against humanity and war crimes between January and June 1999. Six of the defendants were convicted, one was acquitted, one died before his trial could commence; Milosevic also died before his trial could conclude.[30] Kosovars too were held accountable for their actions. Many KLA members were accused of crimes against humanity and war crimes by the ICTY.

KOSOVO BECOMES INDEPENDENT

From 1999 onwards Kosovo was governed as a UN-NATO protectorate under the administration of United Nations Interim Administration Mission in Kosovo (UNMIK). The EU also played an important role channeling aid to rebuild infrastructure and helping with relief. The EU Rule of Law Mission in Kosovo (EULEX) sought to establish an orderly stable legal and administrative system in accordance with European standards. In 2002, Kosovars elected a president. From that date it was fully autonomous but under UN supervision and technically it was recognized under international law as still part of the Republic of Serbia. Independence was delayed by the opposition to its independence from Serbia and Russia. In 2007, the UN Security Council proposed a "supervised independence" for the region which was still technically a province of Serbia.

Serbia, however, was adamantly opposed to independence no matter how qualified. Russia which had friendly relations with Serbia and was a permanent member of the UN Security Council with the power to veto any decision, made it clear it would not support any solution that was not acceptable to both Serbia and the Albanian Kosovars. Not wishing to inflame nationalist feelings in Serbia during a presidential election in that country in 2008, the United States and the most EU members while backing independence had the Kosovars hold off until after these elections were over. Western countries wanted to see pro-EU moderates win and felt approving Kosovo independence on the eve of these elections would only strengthen the hardline ultranationalists. The Kosovars held parliamentary elections in in 2007 which led a government by the Democratic Party of Kosovo headed by Hashim Thaci. The new government was committed to independence and on February 17, 2008, declared it. The international group that supervised the administration of the country left but the NATO-led force and the EU rule-of-law monitors remained. The Kosovo Force (KFOR) a NATO-led peacekeeping force was to maintain order.

Another the problem that had delayed independence was the treatment as status of the small Serbian minority. The end of the Kosovo War did not mark the end of violence in the country. Many Serbs fled in 1999 but those that remained behind, living in their own communities were harassed by Kosovars who had hoped they would leave. Having been rescued from ethnic cleansing by NATO, the embittered Albanian Kosovars were engaging in their own ethnic cleansing. Violence continued into 2001, mostly carried out by Albanian Kosovars against the remaining Serbian population. In 2004, violence broke out in the town of Mitrovica between the two ethnic groups. Nineteen people were killed, 600 homes burned, and twenty-nine monasteries and churches destroyed. The Serbian minority remained hostile to the idea of an independent Kosovo and boycotted the elections.[31]

Over the next several years, the United States, most EU members and all the states that border Kosovo except Serbia gave it diplomatic recognition. Serbia refused to recognize it and took its case to the International Court of Justice. The court in 2010 ruled that Kosovo's declaration of independence did not violate any international law.[32] Serbia was supported by Russia, China, and some other countries. By 2019, half the 193 UN members had formally recognized Kosovo as a member of the international community of sovereign states. But Serbian opposition and Russia's support of the Serbian position meant that Kosovo could not join the UN and so it had a somewhat ambiguous status in that international community. Recognized individually by the majority of the world's sovereign states, it was still blocked from the privileges of joining the UN organization. In 2015 its effort to join UNESCO fell short by three votes.[33] Kosovo was recognized by twenty-three of the twenty-eight members of the EU and was allowed to join some EU sports organization. It even became a candidate for eventual membership in the EU.

It was Serbia, and Russia and China's willingness to support Serbia, that kept Kosovo in de facto status. Kosovo and its supporters looked for change in Serbia. However, there were some promising signs that the Serbs might relent in the refusal to accept Kosovo. In 2003, Yugoslavia, reduced to Serbia and Montenegro, was dissolved and a new federation of Serbia and Montenegro was formed. But the Montenegrins wanted independence, so this state was in turn dissolved in 2006. Now Serbia's idea of being part of a greater state was finally dead; there was simply a Republic of Serbia. In 2008, a pro-Western political party eager to join the EU the Democratic Party of Serbia won 40 percent of the vote while the hardline ultra-nationalist Serbian Radical Party only 30 percent. In 2009, the Democratic Party was able to form a pro-EU, coalition. It was more open to cooperation with punishing Serb war criminals and carrying out more democratic reforms. All these developments promised a Serbian reconciliation or acceptance of the reality that Kosovo was now a separate state.

Yet for all the movement toward democratization, European integration and the abandonment of the idea of a greater Serbia, the issue of Kosovo remained a sore point. Most Serbs still saw Kosovo as part of their homeland and were outraged by Albanian Kosovar attacks on the small Serbian minority that still lived there. Travelers who visited Kosovo from a third country and then tried to enter Serbia were often denied entry since they "illegally" entered Serbia when they entered Kosovo without going through Serbian immigration first.[34] Furthermore, there was little sign that Russia's support of Serbia's contention that Kosovo is Serbian territory was weakening. The reason has to do with Russia's historic links to Serbia. The Russians were liberators of Serbia in the 1870s, allied with Serbia in both world wars. They share a common Orthodox Christian tradition. While almost all of Serbia's neighbors including recently the Montenegrins have switched to the Latin alphabet, the Serbians proudly use the same Cyrillic script used by Russia. Of course, there is more than historical traditions and sentiments that link the two countries. Russia saw Serbia as a country that it could still have a considerable influence in and had no interest in seeing either the EU or NATO expand further in its backyard. Consequently, it supported Serbia and used its veto power to block Kosovo entry into the United Nations. Thus, Kosovo remained a somewhat ambiguous status as a sovereign nation, a somewhat less than full member of the international community of nation-states.

TWO CONTRASTING HEROES

Kosovo's founding hero is Ibrahim Rugova. Rugova was born in 1944 at a time when Kosovo was unified with Albania and both were under Nazi Germany's control. While still an infant, the territory was placed back into Yugoslavia as part of the Yugoslav republic of Serbia. Earning a PhD in literature from the University of Paris he returned to his homeland to become a professor at the University of Pristina where he researched and taught Albanian literature. His interest in Albania's cultural traditions was linked with his desire to see an autonomous Albanian Kosovo. He helped establish the Democratic League of Kosovo for that purpose. Not a very charismatic figure he was chosen mainly as a compromise candidate.[35] He was a believer in nonviolence and when Serbia removed Kosovo's autonomy in 1989, he sought to oppose Serbian rule through passive resistance. In 1992 he was elected president of the self-proclaimed and mainly symbolic Republic of Kosova. Unfortunately, the failure of the Dayton Accords to even mention Kosovo was a blow to those who had hoped to achieve independence through nonviolence and diplomacy. After 1996 the more violent approach to independence of the Kosovo Liberation Army (KLA) prevailed.[36]

Under Rugova the Kosovo independence movement attempted with some success to take the moral high ground and win international sympathy; however, Hashim Thaci lost the first and somewhat weakened the second. Thaci was the political leader of the KLA. At its founding in the mid-1990s the KLA had only about two hundred members; in the late 1990s it grew into an organization numbering in the thousands. The Serbs labeled it a terrorist organization as did the United States. With the ethnic cleansing campaign carried out by Serbia the KLA became heroes to the Albanian Kosovars as they conducted guerilla warfare. As the political leader of KLA Hashim Thaci led the peace talks in 1999. By this time Rugova had been relegated to a secondary position in the independence movement. Ibrahim Rugova eventually regained his position as the country's great independence leader and was elected president when Kosovo held its first democratic elections in 2002. He died four years later. He remains the national hero. The main square in Pristina is named after him and his statue is at the center.

Hashim Thaci became prime minister in 2002 and was elected to the ceremonial role as president in 2016; however, he has a decided mixed legacy. Not just Hashim but the KLA suffered from a tarnished reputation. In fact, the word "tarnished" is an understatement. Members had links with drug traffickers. This was not surprising since at the time most of Europe's heroin trade was in the hands of Albanian Kosovars. It is not clear if Thaci or the KLA was directly involved in it, but they did receive most of the funds for arms and support from the heroin trade. The KLA's moral authority was further eroded by its ethnic cleansing campaigns terrorizing Serbs with the intent of driving them away. It was also accused of abusing prisoners, there was even an unsubstantiated rumor that they sold the organs of Serbian prisoners to raise money.[37] This might not have been true, but such was their reputation that it was at least suspected to be true by sober members of the international community. In 2016 he was elected president of Kosovo. In June 2020 Hashim Thaci then serving as president of Kosovo was charged by the Kosovo Specialist Chambers and Specialist Prosecutor's Office in the Hague for war crimes as leader of the KLA.

KOSOVO, THE DE FACTO STATE

There are about 2 million people in Kosovo. Estimates of the ethnic composition vary but a common guess is that 88 percent are Albanian, around 7 or 8 percent Serb. There are small numbers of Bosniaks, Turks, and Roma. Albanian and Serbian are both official languages. The majority of the population is Muslim, almost all ethnically Albanians are. Roughly speaking nine-tenths of Kosovars are at least nominally Muslim and one-tenth Christian. Kosovo is a secular state.

Kosovo's capital and largest city is Pristina. With its many mosques, its bazaar, and Great Hammam (Turkish style bathhouse) it has a strong Turkish flavor. But it is also a modern city which has experienced a postwar construction boom with EU and NATO money pouring in. The center is the modern Ibrahim Rugova Square. Kosovo's other main cities include Prizren the second city with about 200,000. It is a historically an important city with many old buildings from Ottoman times. Peja (also known by the Serbian name of Pec) is the third city of the country. While reminders of the long rule by Turkey are found so are its long history as part of Serbia. Although some have been destroyed, there are still many old, beautiful Serbian Orthodox churches and monasteries. One of the most impressive is the Gracanica Monastery built in 1321 by Serbian king Milutin.

Kosovo has a multiparty parliamentary government with an elected Assembly and a president. It also has an independent judiciary, and in general has a political structure that is democratic, based on the rule of law and meets most EU requirements to be a member. The president is head of state and serves for a five-year term and is elected by the parliament through a secret ballot with two-thirds of the votes cast. But real power is in the hands of the prime minister. The constitution stipulates that ten of the 120 Assembly seats must be set aside for Serbs and other minorities. While democratic, a major problem has been how to guarantee the rights and protection of the Serbian minority.

Kosovo is one of the poorest countries in Europe. It has Europe's youngest population with 70 percent under thirty-five years of age.[38] But it is a population that faces low wages, high unemployment, and an economy that has seen little growth despite large amounts of aid and money spent by NATO peacekeepers. Furthermore, Kosovo is isolated. Its ambiguous diplomatic status has made travel outside the country difficult. Even the countries that recognize it require a visa, but these are hard to obtain. So hard that in 2018 the prime minister was denied visas by the United States and the United Kingdom.[39] Kosovars are unable to look for work outside the country or even visit their neighboring countries.

Kosovo national identity has had to compete with its Albanian national identity. Somewhat like Nagorno Karabakh Armenians, Albanian Kosovars tended to see themselves more as Albanian than as members of a separate Kosovar nation. Many would still probably prefer to be part of a greater Albania. The Kosovo independence movement chose the Albanian flag as their national flag but when the country moved toward independence in 2008 it was required to adopt a different flag since two countries cannot have the same national flag. Today one sees both flags flying. One is the flag of the Kosovo state and the other is of their Albanian ethnic identity. Religion has been a basis of its identity, a major way that Albanian Kosovars are distinguished from the Orthodox Christian Serbs. And almost all Kosovar Albanians are Muslims. But not all Albanians are Muslims; Albania itself has a substantial minority of Orthodox and Catholic Christians. The world's most famous Albanian, Mother Teresa, was a Catholic nun. They also differ somewhat in language. Modern Albanian has two main dialects: Tosk spoken in southern Albania and Gheg spoken in northern Albania and in Kosovo. After World War II the Tosk dialect was made the basis for standard Albanian used in Albania. Not surprising since Enver Hoxha the dictator that dominated Albania from 1944 to his death in 1984 was a southern Albanian. So today the dialect used in Kosovo is a bit different from that of Albania.[40]

Kosovo's independence is constrained by the role the international community plays in its administration. The United Nations Mission in Kosovo have a role in police, justice, and civil administration. The EU has considerable authority to monitor and advise institutions through its representative in Pristina, helps guide its economic development. An International Civilian Authority created by a Group of twenty-five, mostly EU members, appoints an International Civilian representative who has enormous power to guide domestic administration and has been called a "shadow prime minister."[41] Furthermore, the presence of KFOR to protect the Serbian minority also places a limitation on the country's internal sovereignty.

THE SERBIAN MINORITY

A major problem Kosovo has faced is what to do about the Serbian minority of Kosovo. In 2020, the Serbian minority was estimated at about 120,000. They represented probably less than half the original number of Serbs in Kosovo at the time of the Kosovo War. During the fighting, about 1,000 Serbs were killed and many fled the country. The remaining Serbs live under protection of the United Nations Mission in Kosovo (UNMIK). There are almost no Serbs living within Albanian communities, all have fled the country or to the UNMIK protected enclaves. The enclaves include a number of towns and villages in the north and several outside the north including Gracanica not far from the capital in the center of the country. In 2008, they formed the

Community Assembly of Kosovo and Metohija. These Serbian communities are self-governing units not integrated with the rest of the country. The Serbs living in them for the most part have never accepted Kosovo's independence and consider that whole country part of Serbia.

Tensions between these little outposts of Serbian culture and the rest of the Kosovars are a major problem. Albanian Kosovars, who resent their presence, have carried acts of intimidation and harassment, hoping the Serbs will leave. Neither the UNMIK nor KFOR appeared to be capable of preventing abuses by them.[42] The European Union worked out the Brussels Agreement in 2013 that would allow the Serb minority in Kosovo to have its own police force and court of appeals. But it was not ratified by the Kosovo Parliament or by the Serbian Community Assembly. Small provocations continued between the two countries—Kosovo and Serbia. In one bizarre incident a train arrived at the border decked in the colors of the Serbian flag and with Orthodox Christian symbols and a sign stating: "Kosovo is Serbia."[43] Inside the country Albanian Kosovars sometime carry out activities to intimidate the Serbs, for example, driving through Serb towns waving Albanian flags.

Kosovo's future is linked then with its Serbian minority. As long tensions between the Serb enclaves and the Albanian Kosovars continued, Serbia's hostility to the Kosovo is likely to continue. Both sides share blame. The refusal of the Serbs in Kosovo to acknowledge the existence of an independent state infuriates the other Kosovars and makes reconciliation difficult. These autonomous communities are a reminder of the suffering Albanian Kosovars experienced at the hands of the Serbs while also acting as outposts of their former oppressor in the midst of their new small nation. At the same time the harassment of the Serbs lessens international sympathy for Kosovo's position and fans the flame of Serbian nationalist anger and resistance to the acceptance of the reality of Kosovo's independence.

HOW LONG BEFORE DE FACTO BECOMES DE JURE?

While most of our de facto states are also states with limited prospects for full membership in the international community of nations, this is not the case for Kosovo. The country in 2020 already had diplomatic relations with half the world's countries. The problem is the opposition of Serbia, compounded by the treatment of the small Serbian minority within the country. Serbia may drop its opposition to Kosovo's independence as a price for membership in the EU. In that case, Russia and China will probably recognize it and it will be able to join the UN and other international organizations. But then there is the problem of the Serbia minority. One possible solution is to partition the country giving the northern slice where most Serbs live to Serbia. That would still leave isolated minorities, and of course, Kosovo would be unhappy about losing territory.

There is the problem of Kosovo and Albania. Many Kosovars may still wish for a united Albanian nation. But that seems unlikely since Albania has developed its own institutions and identity and is struggling to integrate itself into Europe. It became a candidate for EU membership in the 2010s and has received considerable EU development aid. At one time Albania was the poorest country in Europe but it has made some progress in pulling itself out of poverty. Union with even poorer Kosovo would only complicate this. Then there is another problem. If Albania and Kosovo were to form a greater Albania, what about the Albanian minorities in Greece, North Macedonia, and Montenegro? North Macedonia, in particular, has a large Albanian minority that forms a majority in parts of that country. Would North Macedonia be partitioned so they could join as well?

Kosovars with their separate history may well be developing their own sense of nationhood. Recent global history has shown that once modern nation-states emerge, they are unlikely to unify as they develop their own identity and the population becomes attached to them. East and West Germany were an exception, but their division was imposed on them from the outside and was never accepted by most Germans. So, Kosovo is likely to remain a separate, small nation-state and as of 2021 seemed likely to eventually gain full recognition as a full member of the international community of sovereign states.

NOTES

1. "Kosovo," *Mundi Index*, https://www.indexmundi.com/kosovo/#Geography; Verena Kraus and Gail Warrander, "Updated by Bridget Nurre Jennions and Larissa Olenicoff," in *Kosovo the Bradt Travel Guide* (Guilford, CT: Bradt Travel Guides, 2017).

2. "Medieval Monuments in Kosovo," *UNESCO World Heritage List*, https://whc.unesco.org/en/list/724/, Accessed December 18, 2018.

3. Tim Judah, *Kosovo: War and Revenge* (New Haven, CT: Yale University Press, 2000).

4. Arben Qirezi, "Settling the Self-Determination Dispute in Kosovo," in Leandrit I Mehmeti and Branislav Radeljic, editors, *Kosovo and Serbia: Contested Options and Shared Consequences* (Pittsburgh, PA: University of Pittsburgh Press, 2016), 37–62, p. 44.

5. Judah, *Kosovo*, 8.

6. Judah, *Kosovo*, 9.

7. Qirezi, "Settling the Self-Determination," 47.

8. Noel Malcolm, *Kosovo* (New York, NY: New York University Press, 1998), 229.

9. Malcolm, *Kosovo*, 221–27.
10. Judah, *Kosovo*, 13.
11. Judah, *Kosovo*, 12.
12. Malcolm, *Kosovo*, 252.
13. Qirezi, "Settling the Self-Determination," 45–46.
14. Qirezi, "Settling the Self-Determination," 46.
15. Judah, *Kosovo*, 21.
16. Qirezi, "Settling the Self-Determination," 49–50.
17. Judah, *Kosovo*, 21–22.
18. Malcolm, *Kosovo*, 319–20.
19. Judah, *Kosovo*, 44.
20. Malcolm, *Kosovo*, 331–32; Veljko Vujacic, "Kosovo: A Case Study in the Unintended Consequences of Communist Nationality Policy, 1968–1986," in Leandrit I Mehmeti and Branislav Radeljic, editors, *Kosovo and Serbia: Contested Options and Shared Consequences* (Pittsburgh, PA: University of Pittsburgh Press, 2016), 14–36, p. 19.
21. Vujacic, "Kosovo," 20–21.
22. Malcolm, *Kosovo*, 326–27.
23. Vujacic, "Kosovo," 15.
24. Judah, *Kosovo*, 35–36. Small underground movement wanted union with Albania in early years of Yugoslavia.
25. Judah, *Kosovo*, 62.
26. Judah, *Kosovo*, 96.
27. Judah, *Kosovo*, 99–102.
28. "Facts &Figures: War in Europe," *PBS Frontline*, 2014, https://www.pbs.org/wgbh/pages/frontline/shows/kosovo/etc/facts.html, Accessed September 3, 2019.
29. "Kosovo War: Thousands Killed as Serbian Forces Tried to Keep Control of Province," *Daily Telegraph*, March 31, 2009, elegraph.co.uk/news/worldnews/europe/kosovo/5084374/Kosovo-War-Thousands-killed-as-Serb-forces-tried-to-keep-control-of-province.html, Accessed September 3, 2019.
30. *Global Policy Forum*, March 12, 2006, https://www.globalpolicy.org/component/content/article/163/29359.html, Accessed September 3, 2019.
31. Gent Cakaj and Gezim Krasniqi, "The Role of Minorities in the Serbo-Albanian Political Quagmire," in Leandrit I. Mehmeti and Branislav Radeljic, editors, *Kosovo and Serbia: Contested Options and Shared Consequences* (Pittsburgh, PA: University of Pittsburgh Press, 2016), 149–66, pp. 160–61.
32. *International Court of Justice*, July 22, 2010, https://www.icj-cij.org/files/case-related/141/141-20100722-ADV-01-00-EN.pdf, Accessed September 3, 2019.
33. "Kosovo Fails UNESCO Membership Bid," *The Guardian*, November 9, 2015, https://www.theguardian.com/world/2015/nov/09/kosovo-fails-in-unesco-membership-bid, Accessed September 3, 2019.
34. This was a problem for the author in July 2017 who had to first enter Serbia via Montenegro then go to Kosovo.
35. Judah, *Kosovo*, 66–67.
36. Howard Clark, *Civil Resistance in Kosovo* (London: Pluto Press, 2000).

37. "Kosovo PM is Head of Human Organ and Arms Ring, Council of Europe Reports," *The Guardian*, December 14, 2010, https://www.theguardian.com/world/2010/dec/14/kosovo-prime-minister-llike-mafia-boss, Accessed December 12, 2018.

38. "Kosovo Finds Little to Celebrate after Ten Years of Independence," *New York Times*, February 16, 2018.

39. "Kosovo's Haradinaj Cancels U.S. Visit After 'Failing To Get Visa'," *Radio Free Europe/Radio Liberty*, January 8, 2018, https://www.rferl.org/a/kosovo-haradinaj-cancels-us-visit-refused-visa/28963498.html, Accessed September 4, 2019.

40. "Tosk Language," *Britannica.com*, https://www.britannica.com›topic›Tosk-language; "Tosk and Gheg: Dialect Still Divides Kosovo," *CaféBable*, May 18, 2008, https://cafebabel.com/en/article/gheg-or-tosk-ialect-still-divides-kosovo-5ae006aff723b35a145e1031/, Accessed August 18, 2019.

41. Gergana Noutcheva, "Contested Statehood and EU Actorness in Kosovo, Abkhazia and Western Sahara," *Journal of Geopolitics* 25, no. 2 (December 2018): 449–71.

42. Leandrit I. Mehmeti and Branislav Radeljic, "Introduction," in Leandrit I. Mehmeti and Branislav Radeljic, editors, *Kosovo and Serbia: Contested Options and Shared Consequences* (Pittsburgh, PA: University of Pittsburgh Press, 2016), 8.

43. "Serbian Train Sparks Escalation of Tensions with Kosovo," *BBC News*, January 17, 2017, https://www.bbc.com/news/world-europe-38625872, Accessed September 3, 2019.

Chapter 6

Divided Island

Turkish Republic of Northern Cyprus

One of the curiosities of the beautiful island of Cyprus is that it is politically divided. There is the Republic of Cyprus, then there is another Cyprus on the northern part of the island, one that does not appear on many maps but is clearly a separate state. Northern Cyprus or as it is officially known—the Turkish Republic of Northern Cyprus (TRNC)—is a self-declared state occupying the northeastern portion of the island, a state recognized only by Turkey. A buffer zone under the control of the United Nations (UN) divides it from the Greek-speaking Republic of Cyprus. The buffer zone passes through the island's largest city Nicosia, which is the capital of both republics. The basis for the TRNC took place in 1974 when Turkey invaded the island to prevent Greece from annexing it. Following Turkey's invasion, the island was effectively divided. Thousands of Greek Cypriots fled south and Turkish Cypriots north. In 1983, the Turkish Cypriots unilaterally declared independence. Lacking international recognition, the TRNC remains heavily dependent on Turkey for economic, political, and military support. Turkey maintains troops in the breakaway republic.

So today although Cyprus appears as one country on the map and the international community recognizes it as one sovereign state, it is really two separate states. The ethnically Greek state has about 850,000 people, almost all Greek speakers. The TRNC has about 310,000 people who almost all speak Turkish as their first language, 99 percent being Muslim. At one time, the population of Northern Cyprus was very mixed, but the vast majority of Greeks have left and only a few hundred remain. An island that once was the home of two communities, who lived together and socially mixed, is now sharply divided into two ethnically based halves. Sadly, the birth of the TRNC, like that of Nagorno Karabakh, Abkhazia, and Kosovo, was accompanied by refugees fleeing homes and the violent separation of peoples that once peacefully lived together.

DIVIDED ISLAND

With 9,224 square kilometers (3,565 square miles), the island of Cyprus is the third largest in the Mediterranean in both area and population, after Sicily and Sardinia; it is a little smaller than the state of Connecticut (which has become our standard unit of comparative measurement). Cyprus stretches 240 kilometers (149 miles) from east to west and 100 kilometers (62 miles) north to south at its widest. It has been historically associated with Greece but it is closer to the Middle East—just 75 kilometers (47 miles) from Turkey, 104 kilometers (65 miles) from Syria, 107 kilometers (67 miles) from Lebanon, 200 kilometers (124 miles) from Israel, and 379 kilometers (236 miles) from Egypt. The nearest Greek island is 273 kilometers (170 miles) from but the Greek mainland is 800 kilometers (497 miles) distant. Much of the southern and western half of the island is covered by the Troodos Mountains whose highest peak Mount Olympus (not the one in Greece) is 1,952 meters (6,404 feet) high. The smaller Kyrenia Range occupies part of the north. The climate is Mediterranean with mild winters and hot dry summers. It has abundant sunshine which, along with its warm weather and beaches, has made it a popular European tourist destination. The mountains limit the amount of land for agriculture and all that sunshine limits the amount of water. Cyprus suffers from chronic water shortages.

The TRNC occupies the northern 34 percent and the Republic of Cyprus the rest. The two halves are divided by the Green Line, which is a barrier stretching across the island. This division is based on ethnicity, politics, and history, not on any geographical logic. The TRNC has an area of 3,355 square kilometers (1,295 square miles) about one-third of the island. This makes it a little smaller in area than most of our nine states with limited recognition, although its 3000,000 strong population is larger than any of the three in the Caucasus and just a little smaller than Malta, the least populous of member of the EU. The narrow Kyrenia mountain range which runs along the north reaches just over 1,024 meters (3, 360 feet) with Mount Selvili. The coast contains two bays: Morphou Bay and Famagusta Bay. About 56 percent of the land is suitable for agriculture; wheat and barley are planted as winter crops, as the summer is too hot and dry. Winters are cool and rainy with 60 percent of rainfall in December-February. Snow sometimes falls on the higher mountains. The plain is especially hot in summer. Northern Cypriots speak a distinct local dialect of Turkish and are overwhelmingly Sunni Muslims. They mostly practice a moderate form of Islamic belief and are rather secular in outlook.

THE ISLAND OF COPPER

How the island became divided is, of course, a story rooted in its long history. Humans have lived on the island of Cyprus for more than ten thousand years. Curiously, a cat found buried with a person around 7500 BCE is the first-known human-feline association predating the earliest in Egypt where they are thought to have been first domesticated. It is possible that Cyprus is the origin of cat domestication. In ancient times, Cyprus was an important center for trade, noted for the export of copper. In fact, the name Cyprus comes from the Latin word for copper, *cuprum*.[1]

While all of this is interesting enough, the origins of the two ethnic communities began with the arrival of the Greek-speaking people. They first settled on the island after 1100 BCE and most Cypriots have been culturally and linguistically Greek ever since. The strategically located island was under the control of many states including the Roman Empire and the Byzantine Empire; the latter ruled it during most of the Middle Ages. It was also on the frontline between the clash between Christian Europe and the Muslim World; one could argue it still is. Muslim pirates and rulers frequently raided it. Cyprus was taken by the English king Richard I (the Lion-Hearted) in 1191 and was used by the Crusaders as a supply base for the campaigns against the Saracens. Later it passed to the ownership of the Republic of Venice and was periodically attacked by the Ottoman Turks which finally gained control of it in 1570.

Under Ottoman rule, it was an impoverished land of Turkish-speaking Muslims who made up about a third of the population, and Greek Orthodox Christians who were about two-thirds. There was also a small Armenian community. Under their system called the *millet* the Ottomans who ruled a vast multiethnic empire allowed non-Muslims to govern themselves under their own community leaders. In Cyprus, the Greeks were under the supervision of the Church of Cyprus which attended to both spiritual and civil affairs. The church carried out education and some government functions such as tax collection. Church officials then turned tax revenues over to the Ottoman authorities.[2] This meant most of the Christian populations had little direct contact with Ottoman Turkish authorities.

In 1878, the British took over the administration of Cyprus, although it was nominally under Ottoman rule. Shortly after, in 1881, a census found that there were 185,000 people on the island, 74 percent Greek Orthodox, and 25 percent Muslim.[3] In 1914, at the start of World War I, when Britain and the Ottoman Empire found themselves on opposite sides of the conflict, the British formally annexed it. In 1923, the Republic of Turkey, the successor to the Ottoman Empire, renounced all claims to the island.[4] For the British the island was primarily important as a strategic naval base guarding the Suez Canal and the eastern Mediterranean, but after World War II the British became less of a world power, and their great empire began dissolving. As part of the movement toward decolonization and reducing their overseas commitments, the British prepared withdrawing from the island. During most of colonial rule, both the ethnically Greeks and the Turks were loyal to the British. Many Cypriots from both communities fought with the British in World War II. In the 1950s the situation changed.

TOWARD INDEPENDENCE

By the 1950s, it was becoming clear that colonial rule would be coming to an end. The issue was—what would the status of Cyprus be? Many, if not most, Greek Cypriots who made up according to the 1960 census 78 percent of the population wanted *enosis* (union) with Greece.[5] This prospect, however, was threatening to the Turkish minority. Not without reason. In 1912, the island of Crete, which had been part of the Ottoman Empire, was given to Greece. When this happened, the Greeks forced the entire Turkish minority to leave the island.[6] In fact, the Greek Cypriots felt themselves to be Cypriots with a strong attachment to their island home but also identified with a larger Hellenic culture that was centered in Greece. It seemed that Greek Cypriots were not sure whether they were Greek or Cypriot first. Both union with Greece and having a separated independent Cyprus state had its supporters.

The idea of *enosis* was not new, rather it can be traced to the nineteenth century. The mainland of Greece had long been under Ottoman rule but in the early nineteenth century a Greek nationalist movement emerged. In the 1820s, a Greek uprising on the mainland took place. Supported by many Europeans who had romantic ideas of restoring the glory of ancient Hellas, Greece gained independence from the Ottoman Empire in 1829. The capital of the new Kingdom of Greece was the sleepy village of Athens, chosen because it represented the glorious Greek cultural heritage. For many Greeks, however, the new state was not enough; they held what they called the *Megali Idea* (great idea), according to which all the lands that had once been part of Greece should be reunited. Gradually some Greek lands such as the island of Crete were annexed. There were a few Cypriot champions of the *Megali idea*, but it was only in the 1950s that many on the island began to actively support the idea that Cyprus should be united with Greece.[7]

Union with Greece, however, was as threatening to the Turkish minority as union with Romania was to the Russian-speaking minority in Moldova. The Turkish Cypriots were about 18 percent of the population in 1960.[8] Although the two communities mostly lived peacefully together, there was some resentment of the Turks by Greek Cypriots who regarded their Muslim neighbors as newcomers, although they had lived on the island for four centuries. Under Ottoman rule, the Turkish Cypriots as Muslims enjoyed special privileges denied to the Christians. They were taxed less heavily and were able to participate in government. It was a situation not unlike that between Muslim Albanians and their Christian Serb neighbors in Kosovo. Like the Greek Cypriots, the Turkish Cypriots were divided between those seeing themselves as Turks living in Cyprus or Cypriots that happened to be Turkish. Many may have felt a combination of both. However, few sought union with Turkey. Many Turkish Cypriots supported the idea of an independent Cyprus in which both communities would share power. Virtually all opposed union with Greece.

In the 1950s, those who called for union with Greece were encouraged by the change in attitudes in Greece itself. The government in Athens had not shown much enthusiasm for annexing Cyprus and had even turned down an offer to take possession of the island in 1915. Both governments changed their positions after World War II. The British were no longer interested in giving Cyprus to Greece, but Greece became interested in acquiring it. However, Athens needed Britain's political and economic support so did not push for it. This changed in 1954 when Greece decided to put the matter before the UN; however, the UN declined to deal with the proposal. At about this time, Greeks Cypriots formed a militia called the EOKA (National Organization of Cypriot Fighters) to fight for independence. Some individuals in Greece began to support the idea of a Greek rebellion against the British. The chief instigator of these intrigues was George Grivas, a Cypriot-born retired colonel in the Greek army.[9] They began to supply arms to EOKA. Meanwhile, when EOKA fought the British, the alarmed Turkish Cypriots responded with a call for *taksim* (partition).

The leader of the Greek Cypriot community, who did not advocate violence, was the charismatic Archbishop Makarios. It might seem strange that the political leader of Cyprus was also an Orthodox priest, the head of the Greek Orthodox Church in Cyprus. Yet from Ottoman times, the Cyprus Church had taken on a sort of political role, administering and protecting the Greek community. The growth of a secular government under the British undermined this somewhat but the Church leaders were still very influential and saw themselves as the representatives of Greek Cypriot culture and identity.

In the summer of 1955, EOKA led an uprising. It was unsuccessful but guerilla warfare continued. Some Turkish Cypriots in response formed an underground militia group called Volkan.[10] In 1957, members of the Turkish community established another more open organization, the Turkish Resistance Organization (*Turk Muksavemet Teskilati*, TMT) under the leadership of Rauf Denktash. Rauf Dentash emerged as the counterpart to Archbishop Makarios, the leader of his community. A British trained lawyer, he served as a British prosecutor after returning to Cyprus, serving in that role while secretly helping to organize resistance to the Greek Cypriots who advocated *enosis*.[11] Armed clashes took place in 1957 and 1958. Turks began quitting organizations with Greek members so that the two became increasingly separate communities.[12]

In 1959, the British invited the governments of Greece and Turkey and the leaders of the Greek and Turkish Cypriot leaders to discuss the situation in Cyprus. The inclusion of Turkey infuriated Greek Cypriot leaders who resented and feared Turkish involvement in Cypriot affairs. The memory of the long domination by the Turkish Ottomans was still alive. It also became clear that the union of Cyprus and Greece was unacceptable to Turkey, an important NATO ally of both Britain and the United States. By the late 1950s, as fighting on the island continued, Greek Cypriots realized that with the Turkish Cypriots armed, with Turkey alarmed at the idea and the British not supportive, union with Greece was not possible. Facing this reality Makarios came out in support of independence.[13] All parties, the United Kingdom, Greece, Turkey, and the Greek and Turkish Cypriot leaders then came to an agreement, the London-Zurich Accords. Under this agreement, a power-sharing constitution was arranged between the two communities on the island. Turkey, Greece, and Britain would be guarantors of this new independent republic. On August 16, 1960, the Republic of Cyprus was proclaimed. Makarios was elected president.

POWER SHARING FAILS

Under the power-sharing agreement, positions in the civil service were divided 70 percent for Greeks and 30 for Turks; in the army the split was 60–40 percent. As in Abkhazia, a compromise was worked out, with a group that feared it would be a small discriminated minority given a larger share in governance than their population represented to allay those fears. Greek Cypriots were unhappy with this arrangement since the Turks made up only 18 percent of the population. Furthermore, they tended to see Turks as a minority rather than a co-equal community with which they shared power.[14] Yet both sides, Greek and Turkish Cypriots agreed to being governed under a constitution which apportioned cabinet posts, parliamentary seats, and civil service jobs on an agreed a fixed ratio between the two ethnic groups.

This new power-sharing agreement did not last long. Within three years tensions between Greek and Turkish Cypriots grew over disputes over taxation, the autonomy of the separate communities, and other matters. This created deadlock in government. President Makarios in 1963 facing this government paralysis proposed a series of amendments to the constitution which reduced the role of the Turks in the government. Turkish Cypriots responded by withdrawing from most of their administrative posts. They felt it would remove the constitutional protections and demote them from one of the co-founding communities of the state to a discriminated minority. Turkey also objected to the changes. The Turkish Cypriots filed a lawsuit against the Greek-dominated government and won when the Supreme Constitutional Court of Cyprus found the amendments to be illegal.[15]

Greek Cypriot leaders refused to accept that they needed to share power with their Turkish fellow islanders. When the constitutional court ruled against the changes, Makarios ignored its ruling, instead abolishing the constitutional court by merging it with another court. He then had the amendments passed. That year, 1963, the Greeks in the government created the Akritas plan outlining a policy for removing Turkish Cypriots from the government. The goal was to create a series of steps that would eventually lead to the unification of the island with Greece. Tensions mounted when on December 21, 1963, police fired on a crowd of Turkish Cypriots and killed two. This set off a wave of communal violence as Greek Cypriot paramilitary attacked Turkish Cypriots in Nicosia and Larnaca. Fighting took place between the armed Turks and Greeks. Most of the victims in the subsequent violence were Turks. In one incident, 700 Turkish Cypriots including children were taken as hostages from their homes in the northern suburbs of Nicosia. By 1964, 364 Turks and 174 Greeks had been killed in violent incidents. The chief victims were the Turks. Their villages were looted and over 500 of their homes destroyed. Some 20,000 Turks fled to enclaves in the north where they depended on Turkish supplies for survival. Thousands of Turkish Cypriots left the country for Britain, Australia, and Turkey.[16] The government was now completely in the hand of the Greeks. On December 28, 1967, the Cypriot Turks established the Cypriot Provisional Administration and created paramilitary groups to defend themselves.[17] At this point the island was divided into two hostile camps.

THE TURKS INVADE

Many Greeks on the island and the mainland were enthusiastic about the union, but not all; some worried that it would bring about a conflict with Turkey. Both the United States and Britain wanted to avoid a potentially disastrous war between two strategically located NATO allies and placed pressure on Athens to avoid any provocative action that would bring this about. But a Greek military junta that came to power in 1967 was sympathetic to *enosis*. On July 15, 1974, the Greek military junta backed a Greek Cypriot military coup d'etat in Cyprus. Pro-*enosis* Nikos Sampson replaced President

Makarios who had been critical of the Greek government's involvement. The coup leaders proclaimed the establishment of the "Hellenic Republic of Cyprus." Turkey responded to this by invading Cyprus on July 20, 1974. The coup collapsed and the talks began between the two sides. The Turkish Cypriots insisted on immediate acceptance of a federated state with an autonomous Turkish region. The Greek Cypriot delegates delayed while deciding whether to accept this. Turkey then decided to force things by launching a second invasion on August 14th that occupied most of Northern Cyprus. An issue was the legality of Turkey's invasion. Greece and Turkey had earlier signed the Treaty of Guarantee that guaranteed the protection of the two communities on the island. Under this treaty Turkey's intervention in July was a legal action. Furthermore, Turkey, as required under the agreement, informed Britain of its actions beforehand. However, most experts in international law regard the second invasion as illegal.[18]

Legal or not, Turkish forces took over 36 percent of the island. On August 2, 1975, Rauf Denktash, a leader of the Turkish community, and Greek Cypriot leader Glaicos Clerides signed an agreement under the auspices of the UN to carry out a massive population exchange. What occurred was a striking case of ethnic cleansing. Almost immediately 142,000 Greek Cypriots moved to the south, with another 20,000 leaving over the next two years. By that time, only 500 were left in the North.[19] Meanwhile, 42,000 Turkish Cypriots headed to the North. The area still controlled by the Republic of Cyprus was now 99 percent Greek, the north was 99 percent Turkish. An island where the two communities had long lived side by side was now divided into two ethnically homogenous halves. Turks in the north created the autonomous Turkish Cypriot Administration meaning there were in effect two states. However, the Turkish Cypriots were not fully committed to creating their own state. In 1975, the Turkish Cypriots declared the Turkish Federated State of Cyprus as the first step toward a future proposed federated state.[20] Neither the Republic of Cyprus nor the UN accepted this proposal.

BIRTH OF THE TRNC

The UN attempted to broker a settlement but without success. Then on November 15, 1983, the Turkish Cypriot administration took everyone by surprise by declaring itself an independent TRNC. After eight years of failed negotiations with the leadership of the Greek Cypriot community, the north unilaterally declared its independence. This declaration of independence was universally condemned. A few days later, the UN Security Council passed Resolution 541, which stated that the declaration of independence was illegal and should be immediately withdrawn. Furthermore, the UN called on all members to support the sovereignty and territorial integrity of the Republic of Cyprus.[21] No member except Turkey recognized the new state at the time, and none did so over the next several decades.

One of the tragic reminders of the division was the "Green Line." This had its origins in 1964 as a kind of buffer zone established by the UN between the two communities following the violence in the early 1960s. With the Turkish invasion in July 1974, it became a barrier dividing the island. It consisted of barricaded roads, walls, and other obstacles that blocked travel between the two halves. Northern Cypriots were unable to go south of it and Greek Cypriots were unable to go north of it. The name incidentally is derived from a green line drawn on a map as it was being created—it was not painted green. In 2003, responding to pressure from Turkey the TRNC government under Denktash agreed to allow travel across the line. On April 23, it opened the border and about 5,000 people crossed it. Soon the word spread among a skeptical population that it was really open and thousands of people mostly Greeks from the south crossed, cars were backed up for 8 miles. A quarter of the island's population passed through the line. Many were Greek Cypriots who wanted to see the homes and villages that they had been driven from. Contrary to predictions it all went peacefully, and Greeks and Turks mingled without bloody confrontations.[22] It gave hope to some that the division between the two communities could be bridged and Cyprus could become unified again. However, this did not happen.

Since 1983, the people of Northern Cyprus have not given up on the idea of forming some sort of federation with the south. This became a more attractive prospect when the EU, in 2000, decided to accept Cyprus as a member even if the island was divided. Partly this was due to the belief that the TRNC leader Rauf Denktash was the main obstacle to reconciliation. Another reason was pressure from Greece. The European Union (EU) was planning to expand to include a number of former communist countries in Eastern Europe, but under EU rules to become a new member required unanimous approval by existing members and Greece threaten to vote against the new membership unless Cyprus was allowed to join.[23] Meanwhile Turkey was applying for EU membership and wanted to solve the Cyprus situation.

Therefore, finding some sort of solution to the problem of a divided Cyprus was in the interest of most parties involved: Greece, Turkey, the EU, NATO, and the UN. And one appeared to be at hand when the UN General Secretary Kofi Annan provided a plan to create a bi-communal federation. The parliament would have a chamber of deputies based proportionally on population, and an upper house evenly divided between Turks and Greeks. Each part of Northern Cyprus and the Greek part of the island would have a great deal of autonomy; in fact, they would be like two states that acted together in foreign affairs and in some domestic matters. In 2004, the UN brokered a peace settlement and a referendum on the plan was held. However, the hopes for peace and unity were dashed. While 65 percent of Turkish Cypriots voted in favor of it, 76 percent of the Greek islanders rejected it. One reason the Greeks Cypriots opposed it was that the agreement had called on Turkey as its guarantor, which many Greeks feared allowed Turkey to interfere in their affairs. This was not the only reason. Many Greek Cypriots were unsatisfied with the property provisions that did not fully compensate them for their lost homes in the north.[24] For the Turkish Cypriots it was a setback. Their commitment to independence was not as strong as the attraction of membership in the EU.[25] If TRNC was a separate state it was due as much to Greek Cypriot intransigence as it was to a desire for independent nationhood.

Despite the rejection of the plan, Cyprus was admitted to the EU anyway in 2004. But it was a rather strange EU member since the northern third of island did not share the benefits of membership. The EU regards Northern Cyprus as part of the Greek led state of the Republic of Cyprus but beyond its control. Therefore, the laws of the EU are "temporarily" suspended. Since the TRNC is considered part of the Republic of Cyprus its citizens are allowed to vote in EU elections if they hold a Cypriot passport. They can vote but as long as they reside in the TRNC they enjoy no benefits of being part of the EU. Both the Cyprus president Tassos Papdopoulos and Rauf Denktash opposed the referendum. Denktash who lost popularity because of the North's isolation, resigned after the vote. His successor was the pro-settlement Mehmet Ali Talat. Frustrated TRNC voters supported the pro-independence candidates in the 2009 general elections and voted for pro-independence former prime minister Dervis Eroglu in presidential elections the following year.[26] Eroglu's National Unity Party, despite its name, favored independence rather than reunification with the Republic of Cyprus. Yet the advantages of reunification which meant the end of isolation and the opportunity to enjoy the full benefits of EU membership was such that he still negotiated with the Greek Cypriot side on reunification. In 2015 he was succeeded by Mustafa Akinci of the more left-leaning pro-unification Republican Turkish Party which won a plurality of seats in the Assembly.

NORTHERN CYPRUS AS AN INDEPENDENT STATE

Since 1983, the TRNC has carried out most of the normal functions of government. It created a semi-presidential system. The state is divided into six districts. The president is elected for a five-year term. The Assembly of the Republic has fifty members and is elected by proportional representation from five electoral districts. Its general elections are mostly free and the TRNC is a democratic state; although there have been some restrictions of press freedom. The main human rights issue has been the restrictions on the freedom of movement caused by the partition. In 2019, Reporters Without Borders rated it 76th out of 180 countries for press freedom.[27] That year, Freedom House ranked it as "free," noting freedom of the press, and free elections but with a problem of nepotism, cronyism, and other forms of corruption.[28]

Yet for all this normalcy, no nation other than Turkey recognizes Northern Cyprus. The UN considers it a territory of the Republic of Cyprus under Turkish occupation. Pakistan and Bangladesh initially recognized it but withdrew their recognition as a result of US pressure. The UN regards its declaration of independence legally invalid. Several resolutions in the UN have reiterated that stance. In 2004 the Organization of Islamic Co-operation upgraded the delegation of the Turkish Cypriot Muslim community from "observer community" to that of a constituent state designating it the "Turkish Cypriot State," making it an observer member of the organization. That same year the Parliamentary Assembly of the Council of Europe gave it an observer status without voting rights. These, however, are rather minor acknowledgments of its existence. Scorned by the international community and cut off from the rest of Cyprus, the people of the TRNC were initially isolated. This became less so over the years. By the end of the 2010s there were border crossing along the "green line." Still their passports are not valid for international travel. Ironically, as a result of this, TRNC citizens use Cypriot passports to travel.

A feature of a sovereign state is that it has its own armed forces. Northern Cyprus maintains an 8,000 strong security force made of conscripts and it has about 26,000 reserves. However, this was dwarfed by the Turkish military presence. Turkey maintains the Cyprus Turkish Peace Force of 30,000–40,000 troops equipped with tanks and artillery. It is deployed principally along the Green Line and in locations where hostile amphibious landings might take place. Thus, like Abkhazia and Transnistria, which relies on a Russian military presence, and Nagorno Karabakh, which relies on Armenian bases and support, the TRNC is well-armed but still depends on a foreign military protector. The Turkish military presence is opposed by Cyprus, Greece, the EU, and by almost all parties other than the Turks. Several UN Security Council resolutions have called for the withdrawal of Turkish forces. The EU regards it as under Turkish occupation and has exempted it from EU legislation until a settlement is reached. The status of Northern Cyprus has been an issue in Turkey's application process for EU membership; the presence of Turkish troops has been a stumbling block.

An international embargo hinders the TRNC's economic development. Since the Republic of Cyprus as the international recognized authority has declared its ports and airports not under effective control, UN member states (except Turkey) honor this and do not use them. In this way, it resembles Nagorno Karabakh and Transnistria in its isolation.

To be economically viable it depends on Turkey. Symbolic of this link is a pipeline the Turks built that brought water from southern Turkey to the dry TRNC. Running under the Mediterranean it was completed in 2015. Since it is not part of the international banking system, it relies on money transfers from Turkey. It uses the Turkish lira linking its economy to Turkey; the Republic of Cyprus uses the Euro. Exports and imports have to transit through Turkey. International telephone calls are routed via Turkey since the TRNC does not have its own country code or internet domain. Mail must be addressed via Mersin 10, TURKEY, as the Universal Postal Union does not recognize it. Its only direct air connections are with Turkey. Its universities are part of the Turkish university system.[29] And of course, some thirty thousand Turkish troops defend. The opening of Green Line in 2003 gave them an alternative route to the outside world but it still relied on Turkey which in 2018 supplied two-thirds of the government budget.[30]

A symbol of its isolation is the Ercan International Airport. Opened after the division of the island, Ercan was an international orphan much like the international airport in Nagorno Karabakh. International flights from it are banned by all governments but Turkey, and the only flights in and out of it must touch down in Turkey first before arriving or when leaving. Since the TRNC Cyprus is so dependent on tourism this is an enormous inconvenience. It has tried to negotiate the use of charter flights. But talks with the United Kingdom after 2006 failed. The large number of European tourists who come every year fly in from airports south of the Green Line.

Yet TRNC is not poverty-stricken; rather, it enjoys a moderately prosperous economy based on tourism. It has some of Cyprus's best beaches. In 2012 1.1 million visitors came to the country mostly for those beaches which have a reputation for being unspoiled. Many come to Kyrenia (Girne in Turkish), which has become a major tourist resort. Kyrenia has numerous hotels, entertainment facilities, nightlife, and shopping centers.[31] Many Europeans have bought summer homes there. Casinos and sex tourism aimed primarily at Turkish visitors are also important, although there have been reports of sexual abuse. As a result of the tourist boom, it has seen real economic growth in the 2000s and 2010s with the GDP per capita nearly tripling. Still the country's lack of recognition makes it a challenge to attract foreign investment. Companies that do open face legal challenges since they are operating in the Republic of Cyprus illegally by international law. Some companies such as HSBC and Gloria Jean's Coffee have overcome the challenges and accepted the legal risks and have opened branches.[32] But they are the exceptions. Another form of business has been higher education. Several universities actively pursue foreign students; in 2018 20,000 were studying in the state.[33]

There are other problems with being linked to the Turkish state besides the fear that it will be swallowed up by Turkey which few Cypriot Turks want. There have been concerns that the increasingly Islamic nature of Turkey will lead to the Islamicization of the TRNC. Turkish money has financed the building of mosques that promote a more conservative Islam.[34] While Europeans worry about the spread of militant Islam, there is a concern among Turkish Cypriots that Islamic groups will tie the country closer to Turkey and widen the gap with the Greek Cypriot south making future reconciliation more difficult.

TURKISH PUPPET STATE?

Is TRNC a real country? Or is it a Turkish puppet state? Many observers see it as the latter. It is heavily dependent on Turkey. TRNC uses the Turkish lira. Turkey exercises considerable influence over its politics. The Turkish army stations troops there to protect it. Its communications with the outside world are often via Turkey, and it uses the Turkish lira as its currency. Yet the state has its own elected government that can be at times critical of the government of Turkey. Turkish Cypriots, who have their own distinct dialect and traditions, see themselves as different from Turks on the mainland of Turkey. For example, in April 2017 when Igit Bulut, a Turkish presidential advisor, called Northern Cyprus "an overseas province of Turkey," he was heavily criticized by officials, legislators, and the press. Facing this avalanche of criticism, Bulut was forced to state that he only meant to express how close the relationships between the two countries are.[35] In 2019, TRNC president Akinci became increasingly critical of the Turkish government's involvement in Syria, stating it should focus on mending relations with the EU. TRNC leaders consider themselves a sovereign state and Turkish Cypriots are at times uncomfortable with the degree of Turkish influence in their country. They have not shown much interest in being part of Turkey. Meanwhile, the politics of the democratic TRNC became divided between pro-EU moderate parties and more parties that were more influenced by Turkish nationalism and are protective of the country's autonomy from the Republic of Cyprus.[36]

DIVIDED COUNTRIES

Cyprus's situation and prospects for the future can be clarified by placing it in global perspective. World history since 1945 has seen a number of divided countries. In almost all cases, they have been the products of collapsing empires. At the end of World War II Germany was divided. At first it was divided into four Allied occupation zones: Soviet, American, British, and French. In 1949, the American, British, and French zone became the Federal Republic of Germany (West Germany) and the Soviet zone became the German Democratic Republic (East Germany). The first was capitalist, democratic, and allied with the West; the second, communist allied with the Soviet Union. In 1989, the smaller, poorer, and rather repressive East German regime collapsed and was united with West Germany the following year. The Soviet Union and the United States partitioned Korea at the end of World War II. In 1948, a separate Democratic People's Republic of Korea (North Korea) was created by the Soviet Union as a communist state, and a non-communist Republic of Korea (South Korea) was established with the assistance of the United States. Unlike Germany, Korea has remained divided and evolved into two very different societies, although most Koreans hope for unity someday.

But Germany and Korea were divided by outsiders and almost all Germans and Koreans felt themselves one people and wished for eventual unity. Other partitions were the result of conflicting visions of nations. The most massive was the partition of British India in 1947 into an Islamic Pakistan and a majority Hindu India. Another British colony, Palestine, was divided into Israel and Jordan in 1948. Less well known is the case of Yemen. Yemen became independent with the fall of the Ottoman Empire after World War I but the southern coastal region was acquired by the British in 1874 who were interested in the strategic port of Aden. In 1967, as the British dismantled their empire their section of Yemen became the People's Democratic Republic of Yemen commonly called South Yemen. There was no ethnic or linguistic difference between the peoples of the two Yemens, and the two states peacefully unified in 1990. However, with the political turmoil and civil war that began in Yemen in 2010s, a movement to restore an independent South Yemen began. Another famous case of divided countries, and one that was like Cyprus an island was Ireland, divided in 1922 into the Republic of Ireland and Northern Ireland which remained part of the United Kingdom. Here differences were based on religion—the Catholic republic and the majority Protestant north, and by the different visions of what kind of society a united Ireland would be. All these cases are different, yet they have one thing in common with Cyprus, the divisions remained tense or unstable.

THE UNCERTAIN STATUS OF THE TRNC

As of 2020, it appeared possible, even likely, that the TRNC would continue for many more years as a de facto but unrecognized independent state. The old fear that Cyprus would become part of Greece, and they would be a tiny discriminated minority became less realistic. The *enosis* with Greece was highly unlikely. It would be too provocative and could lead to war with Turkey. More than that, Greek Cypriots, by-and-large, are no longer interested in being part of Greece. After nearly six decades of independence, they have come to identify with their Cypriot state and have little interest in being a province of Greece. As an independent state and member of the EU they have an independent voice in European affairs, their own seat at international and European forums. This would be lost if they were no longer a separate state.

But if the Greeks in the Republic of Cyprus had become too used to being their own sovereign state to wish to be part of Greece, the TRNC has grown too far apart, and Turkish Cypriots are too used to managing their own affairs to consider being part of a unified Cyprus other than some sort of federation that allowed a high degree of autonomy. Nearly four decades after declaring their independence the partition of the island, although not recognized by the EU, the United States, or the international community, the TRNC appeared a permanent reality. The question was: Would it be annexed by Turkey? This did not seem to be impossible but there were obstacles. Annexing what was still considered part of the sovereign territory of an independent state and EU member would likely cause an international crisis. It would badly damage Turkey's relations with its European allies. Annexation would probably be condemned internationally as well. A cautionary example is the outcry and sanctions that resulted from Russia's 2014 annexation of Crimea. However, Turkey under the increasingly authoritarian regime of President Tayyip Erdogan become more aggressive, less cooperative with the United States and the EU and more assertively nationalistic. Therefore, annexation was not impossible.

One way the TRNC differed from Kosovo, Transnistria, or the de facto states in the Caucasus was the degree its creation was due to the intervention by an outside power. Turkey's invasion set its political boundaries and fostered the establishment of a separate administration. Thus, it has been seen as an extension of Turkey. But few people in the TRNC wanted to be part of Turkey. Their identity as Cypriots was too strong. Most Turkish Cypriots belong to families that have lived on the island for generations and identify themselves as Cypriots. Furthermore, Turkish Cypriots no more want to be relegated to a minor province of Turkey than most Greek Cypriots want to become a province of Greece. However, with the large number of Turkish settlers in the country that might have been changing. About three quarters of the population in 2020 were Turkish Cypriots and about a quarter are Turkish immigrants. The immigrants from the Turkish mainland often see themselves as Turks, that is, see Turkey as their nation not Cyprus. Still opinion polls showed that the most Turkish Cypriots wanted their own independent state.[37]

Perhaps some kind of federation or association with Turkey might be acceptable but most would probably prefer independence.

Yet internationally recognized independence thirty-seven years after its formal declaration seemed hard to achieve. No one other than Turkey would likely support it. It was unlikely to gain backing in the UN since Britain and France would likely oppose it. Few if any in the EU felt comfortable with having one of its members lose permanent sovereignty over its territory since it could set a precedent for Basque, Catalan, and all kinds of separatist movements. China and Russia on principle look down on the secessionist movements since they have potential secessionist movements of their own. Russia has supported breakaway movements in Georgia and Ukraine, but these were very different circumstances. There would be no advantage for Moscow to support a breakaway state in a country that it has good relations with.

It was possible that over time the TRNC could gain recognition from a few more countries, especially if it could somehow move out of the shadow of Turkey. Perhaps it could garner support from Muslim states, although Northern Cypriot society is quite secular. As of 2021, it looks most likely that the present situation will continue, and the TRNC will remain in that strange limbo or de facto but not de jure states.

NOTES

1. James Ker-Lindsay, *The Cyprus Problem: What Everybody Needs to Know* (Oxford, UK: Oxford University Press, 2011), 2.
2. Michaelis Stavrou Michael, *Resolving the Cyprus Conflict: Negotiating History* (New York, NY: Palgrave Macmillan, 2009), 11.
3. Tufan Ekici, *The Political and Economic History of North Cyprus A Discordant Polity* (New York, NY: PalgraveMacmillan, 2019), 18.
4. Ekici, *The Political and Economic History*, 19.
5. Ker-Lindsay, *The Cyprus Problem*, 2.
6. Isachenko, *The Making of Informal States*, 38.
7. Ker-Lindsay, *The Cyprus Problem*, 15.
8. Ker-Lindsay, *The Cyprus Problem*, 5.
9. Ker-Lindsay, *The Cyprus Problem*, 21.
10. Ekici, *The Political and Economic History*, 20.
11. Ker-Lindsay, *The Cyprus Problem*, 19.
12. Isachenko, *The Making of Informal States*, 39.
13. Ker-Lindsay, *The Cyprus Problem*, 24–25.
14. Isachenko, *The Making of Informal States*, 40.
15. Ekici, *The Political and Economic History*, 22–23.
16. Pierre Oberling, *The Road to Bellapais* (Ann Arbor, MI: Social Science Monographs, 1982), 120.
17. Isachenko, *The Making of Informal States*, 42.

18. Ker-Lindsay, *The Cyprus Problem*, 45.
19. Van Coufoudakis, *Cyprus: Contemporary Problem in Historical Perspective* (Minneapolis, MN: University of Minnesota Press, 2006), 87–88.
20. Ekici, *The Political and Economic History*, 30–31.
21. Ker-Lindsay, *The Cyprus Problem*, 51–52.
22. Ker-Lindsay, *The Cyprus Problem*, 61–62.
23. George Christou, *The European Union and Enlargement: The Case of Cyprus* (New York, NY: Palgrave Macmillan, 2004).
24. Ker-Lindsay, *The Cyprus Problem*, 67–71.
25. George Kyris, *The Europeanisation of Contested Statehood: The EU in Northern Cyprus* (London: Routledge, 2015), 67.
26. "Eroglu Elected President of Northern Cyprus," *Euronews*, April 18, 2010, https://www.euronews.com/2010/04/18/eroglu-elected-president-of-northern-cyprus.
27. "Doctors San Frontiers," *2019 Report*, https://rsf.org/en/northern-cyprus, Accessed July 26, 2019.
28. Freedom House, "Freedom in the World 2019," 2019, https://freedomhouse.org/report/freedom-world/2019/northern-cyprus, Accessed July 26, 2019.
29. De Wall, "Uncertain Ground," Accessed June 8, 2018.
30. De Wall, "Uncertain Ground."
31. *Hurriyet Daily*, February 13, 2017, http://www.hurriyetdailynews.com/northern-cypru, Accessed July 9, 2018.
32. De Wall, "Uncertain Ground."
33. De Wall, "Uncertain Ground."
34. De Wall, "Uncertain Ground."
35. "Turkish Cypriots Slam Erdoğan's Advisor for Calling Turkish Cyprus an 'Overseas Province'," *Hurriyet Daily News*, April 26, 2017, http://www.hurriyetdailynews.com/turkish-cypriots-slam-erdogans-advisor-for-calling-turkish-cyprus-an-overseas-province-112474, Retrieved June 10, 2018.
36. Kyris, *The Europeanisation*, 80–91.
37. Ker-Lindsay, *The Cyprus Problem*, 2.

Chapter 7

State in Waiting
Sahrawi Arab Democratic Republic

The Sahrawi Arab Democratic Republic (SADR), unlike our previous de facto states, is shown on many maps, but usually labeled "Western Sahara." Even stranger, it is often not labeled at all but appears as an empty space between Morocco, Mauretania, and Algeria. All of its territory is claimed by Morocco which occupies most of it. Territorially, it is the largest of the de facto states, that is, if all the territory the SADR claims is considered. In many other ways, it is different from most of our other de facto republics. The others were secessionist states in which all, most, or, in the case of Kosovo, some powerful members of the international community back the parent state's continued claim of sovereignty over it. However, in 2021, forty-two countries and the African Union gave diplomatic recognition to the SADR. No United Nations member except the U.S. in 2020 recognized it as part of Morocco. Many states and organizations, including the UN, and the European Union (EU), recognize neither Moroccan territorial claims nor the SADR. Oddly enough, the UN and many member states recognize Spain as the governing authority although Spain abandoned its former colony in 1976. Moroccan maps show it as a long southern continuation of the country. Most maps published elsewhere do not show it as part of Morocco, but as a separate territory.

The SADR, or Western Sahara as it is better known to the outside world, is a disputed and partially occupied territory bordered on the north by Morocco, on the northeast by Algeria, to the southeast and south by Mauretania, and by the Atlantic on the west. It covers 266,000 square kilometers (103,000 square miles), roughly the size of Italy or Colorado, but most of it is, as the name implies, desert. Apart from the frozen lands of the Arctic, it is one of the world's most sparsely populated territories. It has been described as a "vast, desolate area."[1] Only about a half a million people inhabit it. Forty percent of these live in Laayoune, the largest city. Very arid, mostly flat, it is where the Sahara reaches the Atlantic but not the Sahara of endless sand dunes but a barren, stony desert that forms a rather monotonous landscape. The coast is low in elevation, and the interior has some small mountains rising to about 600 meters (2,000 ft) in the north. It has no permanent rivers or streams. It experiences extremely hot summers with temperatures averages 43–45 degrees Celsius (109–113 degrees F). In winter it is only about 25–30 degrees Celsius (77–86 degrees F) but can drop to near freezing at night especially in the north.

About four-fifths of the territory is under the control of Morocco; the remainder is under the control of the SADR, which functions as a self-governing, independent state. The indigenous people sometimes call themselves Ahel es-Sahel, literally "the people of the west," referring to the littoral of the desert. The term, which originally referred to inhabitants of the fishing villages on the coast, now applies to all the people of the interior as well. More commonly they are called Sahrawis (also spelled Saharawis, the two forms Sahrawi and Saharawi are both widely used).[2] It is from the Arabic for Saharan referring the Bedouin nomads of the desert but in recent times has come to mean the indigenous peoples of the former Spanish territory of the Western Sahara.[3]

WESTERN SAHARA BEFORE THE SPANISH ARRIVED

Our earliest sources on the region date from Roman times when Berber tribes are recorded in the area. Although today the region is Arab-speaking and as the name of the state implies, the inhabitants consider themselves Arab, earlier it was the home of Berber-speaking people. This Berber heritage is still evident in the place names and the names of local tribes. Unrelated Serer peoples who now live much further south in Senegal may also have lived there. During the Middle Ages, Arab tribes moved into the region, intermarried with the local Berber peoples and Arabic replaced Berber as the principal language. Islam also arrived in the region. Today it is almost 100 percent Muslim. The dry, infertile conditions meant that nomad groups were small and forced to migrate over great areas. As a result, there were no larger political organizations. The people themselves were primarily camel herders who were also traders selling their camels in markets. Their loyalties were to their scattered tribes and extended families not to rulers or states. The tribes were organized into hierarchies of free tribes and those that had to pay protection money to the free tribes. Mobile and dependent on hunting to supplement their diet, they were fierce fighters, skilled in firearms.[4]

The historical basis for Morocco's claims to the area rest in good part on the fact that it briefly fell under the hegemony of the Sa'dian dynasty of Morocco in the sixteenth century; however, from the seventeenth century there was little Moroccan interest or involvement in the region.[5] Whatever vague claims Moroccan rulers might have had over it, Western Sahara was a land of independent tribal groups. In fact, in March 1799 the Moroccan king Moulay Sliman signed an accord with the king of Spain in which he conceded that Saguia el-Hamra, the northern part of what became Western Sahara, was beyond his control.[6]

BERBERS AND ARABS

Just who are the Sahrawis? They are Arabic-speaking peoples of mixed Berber-Arab descent. The Berbers, or as they call themselves the Amazigh (plural is Imazighen), refer to the peoples who lived in North Africa before the arrival of the Arabs during the Middle Ages. They speak a number of closely related languages. Originally, they made up most of the peoples of what is now Morocco, Algeria, Tunisia, and Libya. Between the seventh and fifteenth century, Arabic replaced the Berber languages as the main language of the region. Many Arabs settled in and intermarried with Berber people, and Berber people adopted Arab language and culture along with Islam. However, there are still between 20 and 30 million people who speak a Berber language in North Africa as well as throughout much of the Sahara and parts of West Africa. The largest numbers are in Morocco. Today about a third of Morocco's population speaks one of three Berber languages, and another third identify as Berber, but nearly everyone speaks Arabic. While many people in the region think of themselves as both Berber and Arab, the Sahrawis identify themselves as Arab. Sahrawis claim descent from the Beni Hassan, an Arab tribe that migrated across the desert in the eleventh century. Their origins, however, are more likely to be the Berber peoples of the area. Their lifestyle, in fact, is similar to the famous Berber-speaking Tuareg peoples of the Sahara. Like almost all people in the region, they are Sunni Muslims.

Sahrawis cannot be distinguished from their neighbors by language—they have the same Arabic dialect spoken in much of Mauretania. Their traditional culture was hardly different from their desert-dwelling neighbors. There are no obvious geographical features that separate Western Sahara from the vast stretches of desert that cover most of their neighboring countries. It has not been a distinct cultural or political region in the past. Instead, Western Sahara was a product of arbitrary boundaries created in the desert by European powers in the late nineteenth century. This is suggested by its borders—mostly straight lines across remote emptiness. Sahrawis differ from their neighbors in that they wound up under Spanish rule and thus were exposed to Spanish culture. This contrasted with the people surrounding them who ended up living under French colonial rule.

ARRIVAL OF THE SPANISH

The region is sparsely populated, uninviting, and thus attracted little attention from outsiders. Spanish slave ships made use of ports; from at least the eighteenth century, Spanish fishermen operated off the coast. But real Spanish interest began only when in 1884 the major European powers met at the Berlin Conference. There, during the so-called scramble for Africa, the colonial powers established rules for setting up spheres of influence. Spain lost no time and declared a protectorate over the African coast from Cape Blanc to Cape Bojador in December 1884. Shortly thereafter, the Spanish government began having an actual presence in the territory by setting up trading and military posts. To legitimize their claim, Spain signed a treaty with the Emirate of Adrar in what is now Mauretania in which the emirate ceded the territory, which it never really possessed, to Spain. This gave the Spanish the pretense of legality, but it was all rather phony since in truth the sparse population was independent, not part of anyone's state to give away. In 1886, the Spanish Society of Commercial Geography sent Julio Cervera Baviera, Felipe Rizzo, and Francisco Quiroga on a scientific expenditure to survey this largely unknown (to Europeans) region. In 1900, as the Spanish expanded south an agreement was made with France, which had become involved in Mauretania setting the southern border. Further agreements with France marked the northern border of their Saharan territory.[7]

All the lands around this Spanish territory, Morocco, Algeria, and what is today Mauretania, became part of the great French colonial empire in Africa. Morocco's case is a little complicated, in the early twentieth century France and Spanish carved up Morocco with the Spanish gaining possession of the arid south, the southern port of Ifni, and a strip in the north opposite Spain. These separated segments became Spanish Morocco; the lion's share of the kingdom became French Morocco.

Spanish rule in Western Sahara was confined to the coast although they occasionally made military forays into the interior. Spain's attempt to control the desert and scrub inland met with stiff resistance from the nomadic people not accustomed to any authority beyond their clans and tribes. In 1904, a rebellion arose led by the powerful Smara-based marabout (religious teacher) Shaykh Ma al Aynayn. Known as the "Blue Sultan" Ma al Aynayn and his son el-Hiba effectively controlled much of the territory. His palace and "Great Mosque" can be seen today. Smara itself was founded by the Blue Sultan in 1898 becoming and remaining the only Western Saharan city not founded by the Spanish.[8] Ma al Aynayn was defeated by a French military contingent out of Algeria, but various uprisings continued.[9] Not until the 1930s did Spain gained effective control over the hinterland. Ma al Aynayn has become a hero to modern Sahrawis as the first anti-colonial leader. His capital Smara holds a place of significance as a purely Sahrawi city and a symbol of independence.

In 1924, Spain created two colonies out of the territory: Rio de Oro and Saguia el-Hamra. Rio de Oro, literally "river of gold," seems an odd name for a territory with no rivers or gold; it was based on the Portuguese description of a bay they mistook for the mouth of a river. It was the larger and less populated territory and had its capital at Villa Cisneros (renamed al-Dakhla by the Moroccans). Most of the Spanish lived in the fishing post of Villa Cisneros, which was a Spanish town; in fact, only Spanish colonists and those working for them were allowed to reside there. The modest economy of Rio de Oro was based on fishing. Saguia el-Hamra was named after a *wadi* (a mostly dry riverbed that occasionally after rains becomes a river). Its economy was based on phosphate. In the 1930s the Spanish built a new town Laayoune near the main phosphate mine at Bou Craa El Aaiun along the *wadi*. The other main town was Smara the Blue Sultan's home. These two colonies were administered separately from the southern section of Spanish Morocco, which bordered Western Sahara to the north.[10]

In 1958, Spain, in response to the rising anti-colonial sentiment, rearranged the administration of its territories. It unified Rio de Oro and Saguia el-Hamra to form the overseas province of Spanish Sahara, while ceding a strip of territory at Cape Juby to Morocco. Technically, Western Sahara along with Spanish Morocco was part of Spain, not a colony. This was a legal fiction so that Spain could avoid being a colonial power, and it reflected a hope that these territories could at some point be integrated into Spain. Spain ceded its territory in northern part of Spanish Morocco to the newly independent Moroccan state in 1956 and the southern section two years later. In 1969 it returned the small territory of Ifni on the southern coast of Morocco to the government in Rabat. The government of Morocco insisted that it turn Western Sahara over as well.[11]

However, Morocco's claim to Western Sahara was a rather dubious one. It derived from the fact that the Moroccan sultans during the peak of the power in the sixteenth and seventeenth century regarded the region as under their sovereignty. While some tribal leaders had, in the past, given their allegiance to the sultan of Morocco, the premodern Moroccan state never effectively ruled the territory. The Moroccans no more controlled the territory than did the Spanish before the 1930s. It also became linked with Morocco in another curious and complicated way. When Spain administered Western Sahara, they did so through the administration in Spanish Morocco. Local tribal leaders would approve and pay respects to the Spanish governors appointed by Spanish Morocco and during the annual celebration of Muhammad's birth would pay respect to the Moroccan monarchs who claimed to be caliphs. Thus, there was a kind of vague allegiance to the Moroccan monarch at the time as a sort of suzerain, at least in a religious sense. Of course, Moroccan kings themselves did not possess any real political authority. Still this ceremony was later used by Morocco to bolster its claim to the territory.[12]

Meanwhile, the Sahrawi found themselves surrounded by newly independent former colonies: Morocco to the north, the Mauretania to the south, and Algeria to the east. Inspired by their neighbors Sahrawi nationalism emerged. In 1967, Sahrawis established the Movement for the Liberation of the Sahara; three years later in 1970, with the secret help of Moroccan government, Sahrawis staged an organized protest in Laayoune against Spanish rule. The Spanish government, still under the Franco dictatorship which did not tolerate political protests, brutally suppressed it. The incident known as the Zemla Intifada resulted in the Spanish killing some Sahrawis. Spain outlawed the movement. As often happens in the case of political repression, the opposition itself became more militant and violent. In 1973, Sahrawis organized the *Frente Popular de Liberación de Saguía el Hamra y Río de Oro*, which is mercifully known by its acronym Polisario. Polisario began a guerilla campaign to gain independence from Spain.

By the early 1960s, most of the European colonies in Africa, Asia, the Pacific, and the Caribbean were gone; in fact, these former colonies now made up the majority of the United Nations membership. Eager to see the rest of the remaining colonies gain sovereignty, UN members drew a list of them in 1963, which included Western Sahara. In 1965, the UN General Assembly adopted a resolution asking Spain to decolonize it. In 1966, it passed another resolution requesting Spain to hold a referendum on the future status of the territory. Spain, which had only a couple of colonies in Africa (the other was Spanish Guinea, now Equatorial Guinea in West Africa), like its Iberian neighbor Portugal, resisted the trend toward decolonization. Yet bowing to international pressure, the government in Madrid promised a referendum on independence in Western Sahara. At the same time the UN was pressuring Spain to give independence to the colony, Morocco and Mauretania began pressing their claims to Western Sahara. Algeria, which bordered it and had a rivalry with Morocco, treated these claims with skepticism. The Algerian government under Houari Boumedienne in 1975 decided to support the Polisario.

INSTANT BUT INTENSE: THE ORIGINS OF SAHRAWI NATIONALISM

Nationalist sentiment emerged among the Sahrawi surprisingly recently, remarkably rapidly and powerfully. Sahrawi nationalism was the product of the identification with the territory of Spanish Sahara by its inhabitants. But this territory was a rather arbitrary patch of land that did not correspond to any ethnic group but was inhabited by tribes and clans who did not differ in their Arabic dialect and culture with the peoples living in adjacent regions of Mauretania and Algeria; that is, it is difficult to point to anything like a distinctive Sahrawi culture, ethnicity or identity. They identified with family and clan not as an ethnic group, and certainly not as a nation. The only thing that had in common was they were within the boundaries of Spanish territory. But the Spanish colonial administration did not have much impact on them at first. The Spanish were unable to pacify the interior until 1934.[13] Even then, there was not much involvement with the nomadic peoples. In fact, the Spanish had little presence at all in the territory, and their contact with the local people was limited. As of 1952, there were only 200 civilian employees. So limited was the impact of Spain that the entire territory at that time had only 354 school children in the two colonies that made up Western Sahara; moreover, most were children of those Spanish employees, with only nineteen being Sahrawis.[14]

Spain's involvement in Western Sahara changed in the 1960s when it became interested in developing its potential mineral wealth. It began serious efforts at oil exploration and development of the phosphate mines. The number of Spanish working in there jumped from the hundreds in the 1950s to 9,000 in 1967 and 20,000 in 1974.[15] Madrid poured money into infrastructure, and the small settlements grew into small cities. Thousands of Sahrawis abandoned their flocks and came to the towns to work. Many used their trading skills to become shopkeepers. In just a short period, from the early 1960s to the mid-1970s, the population became majority urban. Many learned Spanish, sent the children to modern schools, and some went to Morocco or Algeria for schooling.[16]

At the same time another revolution was taking place among the Sahrawis they were being connected to the outside world. Besides their increasing contacts with the Spanish they became more aware of the developments in the world around them. A contributing factor was the flood of cheap transistor radios from the Canary Islands. By the early 1970s, almost every family had one, and being Arabic speakers they listened to the Arab radio stations from Morocco, Algeria, Mauretania, and Egypt.[17] As they became informed about the world, Sahrawis became excited by the nationalist movements around them. A sense of what it meant to be a nation based on identification with the territory took root.

It was, however, as often the case, the modernized educated people that took the lead in organizing the national independence movement. An example was Mohammad Bassiri. Educated in Middle Eastern universities he became an early advocate for an independent Sahrawi state. Another example was El-Ouali Mutapha Sayed, one of the founders of the Polisario. He was only twenty-seven when he became the secretary-general of the organization. Sayed was born in the desert, although it is not known exactly where. His family moved into town and sent him to school in Morocco. There as a young student he became exposed to nationalist political activity and joined the Rabat-based organization Frente de Liberacion del Sahara.[18] There were now people like Bassiri and Sayed, mostly young, emerging to organize, and lead an independence movement. But they needed a mass movement to lead. This movement came in the spring of 1975. A UN mission of inquiry on May 12, 1975, came to investigate the situation as part of the effort of the UN to press for the end of Spanish colonial rule there. Thousands of Sahrawis from different tribes took to the street to support Polisario; it was the first collective activity by the Sahrawi in the cause of independence.[19]

THE SPANISH EXIT AND THE MOROCCANS ENTER

As important as this demonstration was, the key event in the recent history of the Western Sahara was the Moroccan invasion. The UN sent another visiting mission to the territory in late 1975. While acknowledging that both Morocco and Mauretania had some historical claims, the UN position was that the people of the territory had the right of self-determination. This stance was supported by the International Court of Justice, which had reviewed Morocco's historic claims and was not impressed by them. The UN added its authority to a growing call for a popular referendum on independence. Spain reluctantly agreed to carry out one. This was alarming to Morocco since it was clear that the majority, probably the overwhelming majority of Sahrawis, would vote for independence. Moroccan king Hassan II had made regaining the "lost" territories of his country a major rallying cry; now this would be a setback. Wasting little time, the king organized the "Green March." The name came for the green color of Islam. This curious event was to be a mass march of unarmed civilians into the territory intended to force Madrid into negotiations. The assumption was Spain would not want to fire on unarmed civilians, a move that would inflame public opinion in Morocco and could lead to war.[20] Some 350,000 Moroccan civilians gathered in a town in southern Morocco. The mass march never occurred. After hasty arrangements with Spain, a small number symbolically walked a short way into Western Sahara. Three days later, the king called them back. He had made his point.[21]

A few days later, delegates from Mauretania and Morocco met with Spanish representatives in Madrid to discuss the situation. In the Madrid Agreement, Spain, Morocco, and Mauretania would begin a three-nation transitional administration until the Spanish had time to leave at the end of February 1976. The Spanish did leave, including all its civilians. As they left, the Spanish took as much with them as they could, even digging up graves of Spanish and bringing them back to Spain along with the animals from the zoo.[22] The Madrid Agreement also secretly gave Spain fishing rights and a continued share of the phosphate production. In April 1976, Morocco and Mauretania drew up their line of partition in Western Sahara. Mauretania agreed to divide the territory—two-thirds would go to Morocco and one to Mauretania. Spain never agreed to this partition and annexation; its only aim was to withdraw which it did on February 1976, effectively relinquishing administrative control of the territory to Morocco and Mauretania, which immediately took over. Polisario responded by proclaiming the independent SADR on February 27, 1976. Tindouf in Algeria became the headquarters of the SADR government-in-exile. The UN supported the Polisario as the legitimate representative of the Sahrawi people. In any case no UN member state recognized either Morocco's or Mauretania's claims to the territory.

The Polisario Front with Algerian support began to wage a guerilla war against the two occupiers with surprising effectiveness. The guerillas had a few things going for them. They were familiar with the terrain, had a tradition of fighting, and operated in a vast open area that was difficult for foreign troops to control. Their tactics were derived from the traditional practice of *ghazi* raids which involved quick assault and retreats from different directions, making it difficult for their opponent to prepare or anticipate. They were also aided by the fact that some Sahrawis who had served in the Spanish colonial forces defected to the Polisario and that some of the retreating Spanish troops provided them with weapons.[23] Libya and Algeria gave them material support, and Algeria provided training. The last was especially useful since the Algerians had considerable experience in using guerilla war against the French. A key advantage was the Polisario's ability to retreat to their base in the refugee camps in Algeria. Moroccan or Mauretanian forces could not pursue them as they retreated across the border without risking war with Algeria. It also could not, as many armies do in fighting insurgencies, retaliate against or hold the civilian population hostage because most of the Sahrawi population fled to Algeria and in any case, the Polisario did not depend on a local civilian population to support them.

The war went badly for Mauretania—a very poor country with small, ill-equipped armed forces. It proved unable to sustain the war. Polisario made the war effort more costly by attacking the rail line that brought its iron ore, Mauretania's principal export, to the port. Thus, they attacked the jugular vein of the country's economy.²⁴ Furthermore, the war was not very popular. Unlike Morocco, there never was a lot of enthusiasm for annexing the territory. Now that it was resulting in a costly conflict, there was even less enthusiasm. Morale was low since most of the Mauretanian soldiers were blacks conscripted from the south of the country who had no interest at all in fighting the Arab Sahrawis for an Arab-dominated Mauretanian government. When in 1978, the government was overthrown, the new administration signed an agreement with the Polisario in the summer of 1979 secretly handing over its portion of the territory to the Sahrawis forces and withdrew. The Mauretanian government held on to only a small piece of the territory, which it still holds. Morocco moved in and took over Mauretania's portion.²⁵

Meanwhile, the hit and run attacks of the Polisario proved very effective. They repeatedly won engagements with larger Moroccan forces. A highpoint in their campaign was the 1979 Battle of Smara, the city of an earlier anti-colonial resistance, in which the Polisario inflicted heavy losses on Moroccan forces, briefly taking the city. When they retreated, about 7,000 civilians joined them and moved to the Polisario-controlled refugee camps.²⁶ Polisario forces launched raids into Morocco and in March 1980 defeated Moroccan forces at Jebel Ouarkziz.²⁷ These humiliating setbacks convinced the Moroccan government that it had to switch tactics. It built a wall.

Morocco never established control over all of the vast desert but held all the towns along the coast. From 1978, Rabat received generous military aid from France and the United States and financial support from Saudi Arabia. French supplied warplanes, and helicopter gunships were very helpful. Although the Carter administration was somewhat reluctant to help Morocco, the new Reagan administration in 1981 was much more willing to do so. The United States supplied a ground sensor system that also proved effective. Americans helped train Moroccan forces in counter-insurgency methods and worked closely in supplying intelligence. Other countries supported Morocco, including South Africa.²⁸

The single most important turning point in the war was the building of an extensive sand-berm in the desert known as the Border Wall or Moroccan Wall. Construction began in 1981 with American help. The wall was 3 to 6 feet high, with landmines planted on the Polisario-controlled side. By the late 1980s, it had effectively excluded the guerillas from about 80 percent of the territory leaving the remainder beyond the barrier to the SADR. By that time the wall was 2,400 kilometers (1,500 miles) in length, the largest functional military barrier in the world.²⁹ It became an extraordinary barrier eventually stretching some 2,700 kilometers (1,700 miles) across the Sahara just 400 kilometers (250 miles) less than President Trump's proposed wall along Mexico.³⁰ It is the second longest wall in the world, after the Great Wall, but unlike the famous one in China it is fully intact and functional. It is topped with barbed wire, an elaborate system of electronic sensors to warn mobile Moroccan units of a possible breach. Any attempt to cross it would counter a continuous field of land mines, estimated at 7 million, one of the most anywhere.[31]

In 1988, both sides accepted a UN proposal for a referendum on independence, at least in principle. The UN in 1991 negotiated a ceasefire overseen by the United Nations Mission for the Referendum in Western Sahara, known as MINURSO after its initials in French and Spanish.[32] Under the UN peace settlement plan, there was to be a referendum scheduled for 1992, giving the local opposition the option of voting for independence or integration with Morocco. Little progress was made toward carrying it out. The main dispute was over who could vote in the referendum. The original inhabitants or the thousands of Moroccans who have settled there. The Polisario insisted that only those living there at the time of the 1974 Spanish census could participate in it. Morocco insisted that this excluded tribes who fled the territory when the Spanish occupied it in the nineteenth century and then settled in Morocco. By 1999, the UN had identified about 85,000 voters, about half in the Moroccan-controlled part of Western Sahara or southern Morocco and the rest in the Tindouf refugee camps, in Mauretania or elsewhere. Polisario accepted this list, but not Morocco. Rabat instead insisted that each applicant for voting be individually scrutinized, effectively putting the voting registration procedure on hold.[33]

In 2000, former US secretary of state James Baker acting as a UN envoy presented the Baker Plan. This called for an autonomous Western Sahara Authority that would be followed after five years by a referendum. Everyone present in the territory would be allowed to vote, regardless of birthplace and with no regard to the Spanish census. Although initially derived from a Moroccan proposal it was rejected by Morocco and by the Polisario. The Polisario objected to the fact that it would allow tens of thousands of immigrants from Morocco proper to vote even though these were colonizers in their eyes. Furthermore, there were three options: independence, an unspecified "autonomy" within Morocco, and integration with Morocco. Polisario feared an option between independence and autonomy was intended to divide the Sahrawi vote. Morocco was also allowed to keep its army in the territory potentially intimidating voters. In 2003, a new version of the plan was made official with some additions spelling out the powers of the Western Saharan Authority with details making it harder to subvert the elections. Called Baker II, it was accepted by the Polisario as the "basis of negotiations," a change from their previous insistence that only those in the 1974 Spanish census could vote. It was unanimously supported by the UN Security Council. Morocco was not interested and did not accept the plan. Moroccan king Mohammad VI refused to accept any referendum stating, "We shall not give up one inch of our beloved Sahara, not a grain of its sand."[34]

Mohammad VI proposed instead a self-governing Royal Advisory Council for Saharan Affairs that would make it an autonomous community within Morocco. This was not acceptable at all to most Sahrawis, so negotiations came to a virtual standstill. Violence flared up from time to time between the Polisario and Moroccan forces. Morocco supported by France and at times the United States tried to arrange bilateral talks between Rabat and Algiers over the status of Western Sahara. Such talks would define the degree of autonomy in the territory in exchange for recognition of Moroccan sovereignty over it. Algeria has refused, arguing that it does not have the right to negotiate for the Polisario Front. Demonstrations broke out in the Moroccan held territory in 2005 with Sahrawis calling for independence or for a referendum. Some, including the Polisario, had termed these the "independence intifada." In April 2007, Morocco under international pressure issued its "Initiative for Negotiating an Autonomy Status for the Sahara."[35] This seemed a compromise, but it was only an offer to negotiate on some sort of autonomous status. The Sahrawis doubted the sincerity and in any case wanted full independence, not some sort of autonomy. Polisario at the time came up with its own offer to Moroccan settlers to join the Sahrawis and together become citizens of an independent SADR.[36]

Sahrawis continued protests. In October 2010, they set up a camp Gadaym Izik, near Laayoune, as a protest about the living conditions. By autumn it had become home to 12,000. Then Moroccan security forces came in the middle of the night, using helicopters and water cannon forcing the protesters to leave. Protesters in Laayoune set fire to tires and vehicles and burned a TV station. The situation in the territory remained tense throughout the 2010s. In 2016, the European Union declared that "Western Sahara is not part of Moroccan territory." That year UN secretary-general Ban Ki-moon called Morocco's annexation of Western Sahara an "occupation." Rabat responded by expelling 70 UN civilian staffers with MINURSO.[37] It also responded by accusing Spain and the foreign media of giving distorted information and banning all members of the foreign journalists from entering the area.

WHY WAS MOROCCO SO DETERMINED TO RULE WESTERN SAHARA?

Why is Morocco so determined to rule Western Sahara? Some have viewed it as just a grab for the territory's resources. It does have phosphate deposits, but in 1975, Morocco was already the world's largest phosphate producer with huge deposits. It might have oil, but there are no proven worthwhile fields. There are some rich fisheries, yet these resources hardly justified the enormous coast of a military occupation. Rather Morocco was determined to annex the region because it was part of its "Greater Morocco" agenda. When the Moroccan nationalist movement emerged as a powerful force, many nationalists envisioned the reconstruction of the nation as including all of what they felt was part of historical Morocco. This included all of the French colony which became independent in 1956 and the smaller Spanish portion of Morocco which Spain gave up in 1958. This was not enough for some nationalists. They went back to the height of the Moroccan sultanate in the sixteenth century choosing this point as "the historical Morocco," even though it represented only a brief period in the long history of the country. One group the Istiqlal (Independence Party) of Allal al-Fassi, an independence leader in the 1950s, drew up a map claiming Western Sahara, most of Mauretania, northern Mali, and a large area of the Algerian Sahara region as part of the historic homeland.[38] He declared, "So long as Tangier is not liberated from its international statute, so long as the Spanish deserts of the south . . . are not liberated from their trusteeship, our independence will remain incomplete."[39] In 1958, Mohammad V who received Tarfaya strip, the Spanish territory just north of the Western Sahara, pledged "to continue to do everything in our power to recover our Sahara and all that which, by historical evidence and by the will of its inhabitants, belongs to our kingdom."[40]

When Hassan II became king, he did not have the legitimacy of his father had when led the independence movement. He inherited a poor country where wealth was concentrated in a few families and which was ruled in absolute fashion at a time when absolute monarchy had long gone out of fashion. There was radical socialist opposition, radical college students in the universities, and many disgruntled military officers who saw military-led republican regimes come to power in Egypt, Algeria, and Libya. He had real reason to be concerned. There was a military coup attempt against him in 1971, and in August 1972, air force officers attempted to shoot down his plane.

In order to secure his throne Hassan II played the Greater Morocco nationalist card, keeping alive the nationalist independence movement that had worked so well for his father.[41] First he became involved in border clashes with Algeria as soon as that country became independent in 1962. In September 1963 what was called the "Sand War" broke out. Hassan sent a large Moroccan force in the Tindouf area, which Greater Morocco nationalists laid claim to. The Algerians responded by invading the area around the Moroccan town of Figuig further north. At first Moroccans were victorious, then Egyptian leader Nasser rushed military aid to Algeria and the Organization of African Unity (OAU) stepped in. The OAU negotiated a peace restoring the prewar boundaries. An agreement on the border with

Algeria was reached in 1972.⁴² Morocco failed to gain anything and relations with its neighbor remained unfriendly.

Then there was Morocco's claim to Mauretania that became independent from France in 1960. For nearly a decade Morocco refused to recognize the state, but in 1969 it did so. There was still Western Sahara, which conveniently was a colonial territory much to the opposition of the international community. That became Hassan II's chief focus as he pursued the nationalist agenda. His decision to launch the Green March proved successful in gaining support. Moroccans identified with the cause of reclaiming their lost national territory. With state encouragement, many settled in Western Sahara. The fighting and sacrifices that followed annexation only bound the people to the cause. When Hassan II died in 1999, his son and successor Mohammed VI was more politically reform minded and the country's economy grew. Yet he too found it useful to wave the nationalist flag in Western Sahara.

ALGERIA'S SUPPORT FOR POLISARIO

That there is any Western Sahara state at all, even if confined to patches of desert making up less than a fifth of the area it claims to represent, is due to its support by Algeria. The question is, why does Algeria support the Polisario? At first it didn't. The regime in Algiers had no special fondness for Polisario radicals and expelled some of them from its territory after the organization was formed. This changed in 1975. The Algerian government of President Boumedienne had hoped to make his country a leader of the Non-Aligned Movement, and a regional leader in Africa and the Middle East. Morocco, with which it had tense relations since the border war of 1963, was a potential rival and threat to those aspirations. Algeria seemed particularly upset when Morocco and Mauretania agreed to partition the country without its Algiers approval. The Green March and Morocco's military occupation were unacceptable, and Algeria reversed course and started actively backing the Polisario. It recognized the SADR that the Polisario had proclaimed as an independent state.⁴³ For Algeria it was a chance to drain Morocco of its resources, gain support from other African and Arab states who generally backed Western Saharan independence, and to promote its efforts to be a regional leader.

THE TENTED STATE

The conflict has resulted in the displacement of tens of thousands of Sahrawis and the expulsion of tens of thousands more. It has left the Western Sahara a divided territory, with a landscape dotted with *sangar* (fortresses). In a strange way the barrier wall the Moroccans built acted as a fixed and permanent border. It kept the Polisario out, and in practice it ceded the remaining part of the territory to the SADR. On their side of the border, the Polisario forces number only a few thousand but are well-armed with underground military fortresses. The SADR controlled portion is home to only 30,000 nomads. Most of the people under the government of the SADR live in refugee camps in in the Tindouf area of Algeria. It has become what one author calls a "tented state."[44]

Half of all Sahrawis live in the refugee settlement in Tindouf, while the other half live in their homeland under Moroccan occupation. Settlement in Tindouf began in the fall of 1975 when the Spanish began to withdraw, and Moroccan soldiers began to enter Western Sahara. Thousands of Sahrawis fled into the interior settlements of Guelta Aemmr and Oum Dreyga where Moroccan forces dropped napalm bombs on them. Some 9,000 fled across the Algerian border to the Tindouf area. This is a section of flat, barren desert that forms a short border with Western Sahara. It is an inhospitable land that gets little rainfall, some years almost none, and has temperatures that routinely soar to 50 degrees Celsius in the day and can drop to zero on winter nights. But people live there because the Algerians offered the refugees safe haven and supplied tents, food, and basic necessities. Later the UN High Commission for Refugees (UNHCR) came in along with other international aid groups to support the camps. By mid-1976, there were 60,000 refugees in the Tindouf area; that number grew to 165,000 in the 2010s.[45]

There are several major camps in the area. They are named after Sahrawi cities: Smara, El Aiun, Dakhla, and Ans Awserd. The camps are like small cities with houses made of clay often covered in fabric for protection and having a permanent look to them.[46] There is also a February 27 Camp that serves as an education center. The original camp was at a settlement called Rabouni which is today the seat of the Sahrawi government. It has been described as a chaotic jumble of low-rise administrative buildings, warehouses, and trucks. There are no permanent residents in the "capital"; workers commute from the residential camps.[47] Much of the aid and other supplies arrives there and is then redistributed to the other nearby camps. Algeria has given the Sahrawis considerable autonomy to run this corner of their country. Therefore, the Tindouf refugee camps are unusual in that unlike most refugee camps that are administered by the UNHCR in conjunction with the host nation, these are administered by the Polisario. The Sahrawis control the access to the camps,[48] although Algeria monitors the movement in and out of the camps and between them closely.[49] The government of the SADR is inseparable from the Polisario organization. Within the Polisario there is some openness and debate, but for all practical purposes it is a one-party state. It runs the camps, including possessing its own police and prison, and for most the people in the camps it is the only government with which they have direct contact.[50]

Education in refugee camp SADR is universal, and outside observers have been generally impressed by the high levels of literacy. Many young Sahrawis from the camps have been able to go abroad for higher education. About 5,000 have received university degrees in Cuba.[51] As a result, the SADR has created one of the most educated peoples on the African continent. Another achievement has been the role of women in the administration of the "tented government." Sahrawi women have always been freer in society than women in most Arab and African societies but the Polisario have further promoted the active participation of women in society. The main vehicle for doing is the National Union of Sahrawi Women, which was established in 1994. Educating everyone and getting women involved in the cause has been a part of a strategy to foster a strong sense of Sahrawi national consciousness and sense of social cohesion among the population. It has been successful—the Sahwaris trapped in a remote patch of hostile desert have become a highly educated, cosmopolitan, mostly bilingual (Arab and Spanish), and often multilingual modern people with what one observer in 2018 described as "powerful reality of Sahrawi nationalism."[52] But the SADR is far from democratic. It is controlled by one political organization, and there have been reports of human rights abuses among the civilian population in the SADR and of mistreatment of Moroccan prisoners.[53]

Morocco's portion of the Western Sahara has an economy based almost entirely on fishing and phosphate mining. The phosphate mines have not brought much income, and while there may be offshore oil deposits they have not been discovered. It imports almost all its food from Morocco and is heavily dependent on Morocco for economic support. It is said to be an economic burden on the country. An example of the cost of controlling the territory is water. Laayoune gets its water from desalinization plants. These are very costly, but the costs are paid by the state. Overall, the territory is a drain on the Moroccan economy, which subsidizes its costs, supports a large military presence, and offers tax incentives for settlers.

It is unclear just how many of Sahrawis there are. In 2004, there were 267,405 people in the Moroccan-controlled territory plus 160,000 Moroccan military personnel. A 1974 Spanish census showed 74,000 Sahrawis and 20,000 Spanish living in the territory. Although the majority of the Sahrawis were urbanized in 1974, there were still many nomads who were probably undercounted. In 1999, the UN identified 86,000 eligible voters, Sahrawis over 18.

As of 2021, the population of the Tindouf camps was according to the Polisario 155,000. A number that Morocco disputes, claiming it to be much smaller. But at any one time the actual number was much smaller since so many Sahrawis go to Europe, mostly Spain and Italy to work and then return home. Others probably have permanently settled abroad but the number of these is not clear. Then there are the many students at study in Spain or spend homestays there or in other countries. As a result, the UN estimates that there were only 90,000 year-round refugees living in the camps. Then there were the 30,000 Sahrawis, mostly the last of the nomadic population that live in the 20 percent of Western Sahara beyond the Moroccan berm, territory directly controlled by the Polisario. Most survived in this harsh dry land by trading in Mauretania and in the Tindouf area. How many Sahrawis live in Moroccan-controlled Western Sahara is not known since the government in Rabat has no interest in revealing information that may undermine its claims to the area and wants to minimize the number of eligible Sahrawi votes should the referendum on the status of the territory ever take place. However, it appears they make up less than half of all Sahrawis and by the late 2010s were outnumbered by Moroccan immigrants.[54]

The Sahrawis who have become a minority in their own country have shown a fierce resistance to Moroccan rule. One example was of this resistance within the Moroccan-controlled territory was the most remarkable leader was Aminatou Haidar. She became active in the nationalist movement when she was only twenty and by the early 2000s became its most prominent leader. An advocate of nonviolent resistance, she has been called the "Sahrawi Gandhi." In 2008, she was nominated for the Nobel Peace Prize. Arrested and tortured by Moroccan authorities on more than one occasion, she was barred from re-entering the country in 2009 after traveling abroad to seek support for the Sahrawi cause. Haidar responded to the ban on her return to her homeland by going on a hunger strike so intense that it damaged her bones and vertebrae.[55]

The Sahrawis as an ethnic-national group are in good part a product of European colonialism. That is, the rule by Spain and wide use of Spanish language sets them apart from their neighbors in Mauretania, southern Morocco, and Algeria who were under French rule. And although the Spanish left more than four decades ago, the Spanish connection is still important due to various education exchanges and host programs for Sahrawi children in Spain and Cuba. One is the Vacaciones en Paz, an annual holiday program created in 1988 organized by the Union of Sahrawi Youth, in collaboration with 300 associations throughout Spain. Each year 7,000–10,000 children between ages of eight and twelve spend the summer in Spain. Some return to the same household each year while forging strong bonds.[56] Sahrawis differ from many Arab-speaking people in another way—the strong role women play in society. Marriage has been monogamous.

All indications are that most Sahrawis have developed a strong sense of national identity. In fact, it was the Mauretanian and Moroccan invasion that solidified a sense of national consciousness and much of the population fled into refugee camps. There all tribes and families lived and struggled together. Cut off from their traditional homes, they bonded together in the common effort to win their independence and regain their homes.

WESTERN SAHARA MOSTLY UNDER MOROCCAN RULE

In the past, the situation was too dangerous for travelers to explore the region. But by the late 2010s things calmed down enough for tourists to visit the Moroccan-controlled Western Sahara, as long as they are not journalists and writers, those will be quickly sent packing. Most of the territory is a long drive from the nearest Moroccan city. The drive is along the rocky, empty *hamada* as the stony desert of the Sahara is called, there are a few areas of sand dunes but it is mostly rather a bleak landscape. The cities look new, which they are, since most of the construction has been done since the Moroccans took over. The government has poured an enormous amount of resources in settling and developing the region, especially impressive for a relatively poor country. Rabat's policy of absorbing the region by encouraging Moroccans to settle there, offering them tax breaks and jobs has succeeded enough that Moroccans outnumber Sahrawis. Laayoune, the dusty former Spanish capital, is now a new modern city with wide streets, great for holding military parades. And there is a lot of military to parade. Visitors report that it seems there are more soldiers than civilians in the city. The new city is a contrast to the "lower town," the small older Spanish section. The second city Dakhla has become a center for kitesurfing, so it has a bit of a tourist trade. More importantly it serves as the home of Morocco's largest fishing fleet.

Most Moroccans fervently believe Western Sahara is part of their national homeland and have little sympathy for the Sahrawi desire for independence. The dispute has remained stalemated. Morocco is committed to its annexation and development of the region. Algeria with its own border disputes with Morocco is committed to support the SADR directly or indirectly. Spain, France, and the United States all have interests in resolving the dispute. Their ideal solution is, if not independence which seems increasingly unlikely, some sort of autonomy for Western Sahara.[57] Meanwhile tension has often been high between the Sahrawis who have remained in the territory or returned and the Moroccan immigrants. This occasionally flared up. Violence between the two communities broke out in Dakhla in 2011 and in Laayoune in 2014.

HOW DE FACTO IS THE SADR?

The SADR became more of what one writer has called "a state in waiting."[58] But it may be a long wait. As of 2021 it is hard to envision the SADR ever controlling more than the few patches of desert it has now. Morocco is unlikely to be persuaded to give up the territory especially after the U.S. under President Trump recognized its claim to it in 2020. It has dragged out any peace process, believing the longer it waits the more the region it controls will be absorbed into the country. This has already happened—Western Sahara has become majority Moroccan, integrated into the country's national economy. In fact, it is possible if Algeria were to decide to stop supporting it, the SADR could cease to exist as anything resembling a state. That could happen if Algeria reached an agreement with Morocco in which it abandoned its support for the SADR in return for a favorable settlement on the border disputes it has with that country. Yet it is not impossible that the SADR or some version of Western Sahara could emerge as an independent country in the future, but forty-four years after it proclaimed its independence that did not appear likely to be soon if at all.

Western Saharans have become a nation in search of their own nation-state. They are organized, have shown an impressive resilient in the face of repression and a determination to obtain their complete independence. But they hardly represent a de facto state since the government operates out of a refugee camp in another country and controls only small bits of nearly uninhabited desert. So why include it in our list at all? Partly because for more than a generation it has controlled a territory with stable boundaries. It does have a government that effectively controls the population within that territory, and it is able to enter in relations with other states, many of whom recognize it. And yet the territory is does control it only a small part of the homeland in claims and does not include a single major city. The locus of government is in another sovereign state as is most of the population it controls. It is as much a potential state as a de facto one. The outline of a state is there; it even appears on many maps. However, with the mass settlement of Moroccans in their territory the Sahrawis are no longer the majority in their own land. In contrast to most of our nine political entities, the international community is sympathetic and would probably support an independent state, but as more and more Moroccans settle into its heartland Western Sahara's chance of becoming a fully sovereign state seemed to be receding.

NOTES

1. Erik Jenson, *Western Sahara: Anatomy of a Stalemate?* (Boulder, CO: Lynne Rienner, 2012), 9.

2. Anthony G. Pazzanita, *Historical Dictionary of Western Sahara*, 3rd Edition (Lanham, MD: Scarecrow Press, 2006), 5.

3. Stephen Zunes and Jacob Mundy, *Western Sahara: War, Nationalism, and Conflict Irresolution* (New York, NY: Syracuse University Press, 2010), 92–93.

4. Tony Hodges, "The Origins of Sahrawi Nationalism," in Richard Lawless and Laila Monahan, editors, *War and Refugees: The Western Sahara Conflict* (London: Pinter Publishers, 1987), 31–62, 31–32.

5. Zunes and Mundy, *Western Sahara*, 98.

6. Osama Abi-Mershed and Adam Farrar, "A History of the Conflict in Western Sahara," in Anouar Boukhars and Jacques Rousellier, editors, *Perspective on Western Sahara: Myths, Nationalism, and Geopolitics* (Lanham, MD: Rowman & Littlefield, 2014), 3–27, p. 10.

7. Zunes and Mundy, *Western Sahara*, 100.

8. Pazzanita, *Historical Dictionary*, 392; Manuel Herz, editor, *From Camp to City: Refugee Camps of the Western Sahara* (Zurich, Switzerland: Lars Uller Publishers, 2013), 84.

9. Abi-Mershed and Farrar, "A History of the Conflict," 12.

10. Zunes and Mundy, *Western Sahara*, 100.

11. Abi-Mershed and Farrar, "A History of the Conflict," 14–16.

12. Zunes and Mundy, *Western Sahara*, 104.

13. Hodges, "The Origins of Sahrawi Nationalism," 31.

14. Hodges, "The Origins of Sahrawi Nationalism," 19.

15. Hodges, "The Origins of Sahrawi Nationalism," 37.

16. Hodges, "The Origins of Sahrawi Nationalism," 38.

17. Hodges, "The Origins of Sahrawi Nationalism," 48.

18. Pazzanita, *Historical Dictionary*, 115; Toby Shelly, *Endgame in the Western Sahara: What Future for Africa's Last Colony?* (London: Zed Books, 2004), 169–70.

19. Hodges, "The Origins of Sahrawi Nationalism," 55.

20. Zunes and Mundy, *Western Sahara*, 5.

21. Zartman, "Morocco's Saharan Policy," 55–70 in Anouar Boukhars and Jacques Rousellier, *Perspective on Western Sahara: Myths, Nationalism, and Geopolitics* (Lanham, MD: Rowman & Littlefield, 2014), 55–70.

22. Jenson, *Western Sahara*, 18, 9–60.

23. Zunes and Mundy, *Western Sahara*, 9.

24. Zunes and Mundy, *Western Sahara*, 10.

25. Abi-Mershed and Farrar, "A History of the Conflict," 18.

26. Pazzanita, *Historical Dictionary*, 393.

27. Abi-Mershed and Farrar, "A History of the Conflict," 18–19.

28. Shelly, *Endgame in the Western Sahara*, 16.

29. Zunes and Mundy, *Western Sahara*, 21.

30. Ruth McLean, "Build a Wall Across the Sahara-That's Crazy But Someone Did It," *The Guardian*, September 22, 2018, https://www.theguardian.com/world/2018/sep/22/western-sahara-wall-morocco-trump, Accessed February 28, 2019.

31. Nicholas Niarchos, "Is One of African's Oldest Conflicts Finally at an End?" *The New Yorker*, December 29, 2018, https://www.newyorker.com/news/news-desk/is-one-of-africas-oldest-conflicts-finally-nearing-its-end, Accessed February 24, 2019.

32. (French: *Mission des Nations Unies pour l'Organisation d'un Référendum au Sahara Occidental*; Spanish: *Misión de las Naciones Unidas para la Organización de un Referéndum en el Sáhara Occidental*).
33. Abi-Mershed and Farrar, "A History of the Conflict," 20–22.
34. Zunes and Mundy, *Western Sahara*, 23.
35. Zartman, "Morocco's Saharan Policy," 67.
36. Zunes and Mundy, *Western Sahara*, 265.
37. Zunes and Mundy, *Western Sahara*, 24.
38. Zunes and Mundy, *Western Sahara*, 36.
39. Jenson, *Western Sahara*, 13.
40. Zunes and Mundy, *Western Sahara*, 33.
41. Hodges, "The Origins of Sahrawi Nationalism," 40.
42. Laurence Aida Ammour, "The Algerian Foreign Policy on Western Sahara," in Anouar Boukhars and Jacques Rousellier, editors, *Perspective on Western Sahara: Myths, Nationalism, and Geopolitics* (Lanham, MD: Rowman & Littlefield, 2014), 91–117, p. 96.
43. Ammour, "The Algerian Foreign Policy," 96–97.
44. Konsantina Isidoros, *Nomads and Nation-Building I the Western Sahara: Gender, Politics and the Sahrawi* (London: I.B. Taurus, 2018), 247.
45. Manuel Herz, editor, *From Camp to City: Refugee Camps of the Western Sahara* (Zurich, Switzerland: Lars Uller Publishers, 2013), 88.
46. Herz, *From Camp to City*, 88, 90–91.
47. Herz, *From Camp to City*, 102.
48. Herz, *From Camp to City*, 92, 188; Aomar Boum, "Refugees, Humanitarian Aid, and the Displace Impasse in Sahrawi Camps, 261–75, 70," in Anouar Boukhars and Jacques Rousellier, editors, *Perspective on Western Sahara: Myths, Nationalism, and Geopolitics* (Lanham, MD: Rowman & Littlefield, 2014), 261–75, pp. 266–67.
49. Boum, "Refugees, Humanitarian Aid," 267.
50. Elena Fiddian-Qasmiyeh, "The Pragmatics of Performance: Putting 'Faith in Aid in the Sahrawi Refugee Camps," *Journal of Refugee Studies* 24, no. 3 (2011): 533–47.
51. Boum, "Refugees, Humanitarian Aid," 269.
52. Isidoros, *Nomads and Nation-Building*, 225.
53. *Human Rights in the Tindouf Refugee Camps*, October 18, 2014, https://www.hrw.org/report/2014/10/18/radar/human-rights-tindouf-refugee-camps, Accessed September 12, 2019.
54. Central Intelligence Agency, *The World Factbook: Western Sahara*, 2018, https://www.cia.gov/library/publications/the-world-factbook/geos/wi.html.
55. Niarchos, "Is One of African's Oldest Conflicts."
56. "Sahrawi Refugee Child in Spanish Host Program," *Forced Migration On Line*, December 2005, http://www.forcedmigration.org/research-resources/expert-guides/sahrawi-refugee-children-in-a-spanish-host-program/alldocuments, Accessed February 18, 2019; "Spain's Lie Hurts Western Sahara," *The Guardian*, November 17, 2010, https://www.theguardian.com/commentisfree/2010/nov/17/spain-lie-western-sahara, Accessed February 22, 2019.
57. Jenson, *Western Sahara*, 118.
58. Shelly, *Endgame in the Western Sahara*, 167.

Chapter 8

Not Being Somalia
Somaliland

INTRODUCTION

Everyone's heard of Somalia, the country sticking out of East Africa like an elbow into the Indian Ocean. Somalia is famous for anarchy, pirates, terrorists, famines, and fashion models. But how many have heard of Somaliland? The Republic of Somaliland is a self-declared state. It is not a tiny state; in fact, it is larger in area than England, South Korea, or Cuba. It has a population of over 4 million, larger than many United Nations members. Internationally, it is considered the northern part of Somalia; yet Somaliland has had a completely independent government since 1991. In many ways, it is the anti-Somalia, with no pirates, no terrorists, and no anarchy. Still it is not on the map—it remains unrecognized, ignored. Even well-informed businessmen, politicians, and travelers have not heard of it.

Somaliland lies in northwestern Somalia, on the southern coast of the Gulf of Aden. It is bordered by Somalia on the east, Djibouti on the northwest, and Ethiopia to the south and west. Compared to most de facto states it is on the large side, 137,000 square kilometers (53,000 square miles), with a population of 4 million. As of 2021, the government of Somalia still possessed little authority beyond the capital of Mogadishu, with much of the country being ruled by local warlords or thugs. Somaliland, by contrast, has a functional government that is in control of most of the country. No tourist in his or her right mind would think of traveling to Somalia; even intrepid journalists have described it as the most dangerous place in the world. Yet, travelers can safely visit Somaliland, although very few do.

The Republic of Somaliland was born on May 18, 1991, at a clan conference in the small Somali city of Burao (also known as Burco).[1] Since 1991, Somaliland has been for all practical purposes an independent state. It has all the characteristics of a modern sovereign state: a government that administers and controls the territory it claims, somewhat fixed and stable borders, a military, it is free from outside control, and has a flag, anthem, an educational system and a population that is mostly loyal to and identifies with the state. Yet not a single country recognizes it.

So how did this state come into being? The short answer is that before 1960 there were two Somalias: the larger Italian Somaliland and the somewhat smaller northern British Somaliland. There were really three, a very small French Somaliland that became the current country of Djibouti. The two biggest Somalias merged to become one independent Somali Republic (name change to Somali Democratic Republic in 1969). Then, in 1991, the government of Somalia centered in Mogadishu, the capital of the former Italian Somaliland, collapsed into anarchy. The north, the former British Somaliland, declared itself an independent state and local authorities carried out the functions of government while the rest of the country descended into chaos. The world has continued to insist that there is one Somalia, the one with its capital in Mogadishu. Somaliland and its struggles to build a viable nation have been almost totally ignored by the international community as well as by mapmakers.

Some of our de facto states are landlocked or isolated such as Nagorno Karabakh, Transnistria, and Kosovo. The Republic of Somaliland, by contrast, has a 740-kilometer (460-mile) coast on the busy Red Sea. The climate is a mixture of wet and dry conditions. Although much of the country is semi-desert, the Awdal, Sahil, and Maroodi Jeex regions are fertile. The Awdal region has some offshore islands, coral reefs, and mangroves. A scrub-covered semi-desert plain referred to as the Guban lies parallel to the Gulf of Aden littoral bisected by seasonal riverbeds. There are two mountain ranges: the Cal Madow range in the northern part of the country, which has the country's highest peak Shimbiris, 2,416 meters (7,927 ft), and the Karkaar Mountains. The northern mountain ranges give way to shallow plateaus and dry watercourses.

Over a quarter of the population, about 1.2 million, live in the capital and largest city, Hargeisa. With only one quasi embassy, Ethiopia's, it hardly seems like a capital city. Ethiopia does not formally recognize the state, no one does, but it does nevertheless have an informal embassy. Otherwise it is quite isolated. There are no international hotels, or banks, or McDonald's, or KFC, or Starbucks. The city feels remote, isolated, and provincial. One visitor described it as "a scruffy, sprawling town of cinderblock houses and potholed roads."[2] Yet it has a reputation for being one of the safest cities in Africa.[3] Hargeisa, whose name means "place where hide is sold," is an old town built around a reliable desert well.[4] But it has few buildings older than the 1990s since it was almost totally destroyed in the 1980s civil war. The city is located on a *wadi* riverbed that is dry most of the year called Maroodi Jeex ("Elephant Wadi"), a reminder of the day when wildlife was once abundant.[5] Other major towns include Berbera, a port on the Red Sea. An old historic town, it served as the capital of British Somaliland. Burao is the second largest city in Somaliland located 100 kilometers east of Hargeisa with an estimated 300,000–400,000 inhabitants.

SOMALIA AND SOMALILAND AND SOMALIS

The people of Somaliland are, as the name implies, Somali, ethnically the same people as the rest of Somalia. Somalis live in Horn of Africa, which juts out of the east coast of Africa. On the north side of the Horn is the Gulf of Aden and along the southern side the open Indian Ocean. The region of the Somali consists of about 1 million square kilometers (400,000 square miles) of desert and dry grassland. It covers the Republic of Somalia (including Somaliland), the eastern region of Ethiopia, Djibouti, and parts of northern Kenya. Much of it is flat but there are mountains. Agriculture is limited to a few areas that catch enough rain for crops to grow or are near a river that can be used for irrigation. Most of the land is pastoral, home to seminomadic peoples grazing their sheep, goats, cattle, and camels. Rain is largely limited to two brief periods of monsoon rains—one from March to April and the second from June to July. The rains are not always reliable, and the region is subject to severe droughts.

While most African countries are characterized by ethnic, linguistic, and tribal diversity making national unity a challenge, Somalia (including Somaliland) is ethnically and linguistically homogeneous. Nearly 90 percent of the entire population is Somali and speaks the Somali language. Nonetheless, that did not prevent the state from breaking apart when the northern region declared itself an independent state. Who are the Somalis? They are an ethnic group living in the Horn of Africa. Their language, Somali, is a member of the Cushitic branch of the Afro-Asiatic language family. This means it is distantly related to Arabic, Amharic, and Hebrew but its closer relatives are fellow Cushitic languages mostly spoken in Ethiopia and neighboring regions. It is written in the Latin alphabet. Almost all Somalis are Sunni Muslims. The homeland of the Somalis extends beyond Somalia to include eastern Ethiopia, Djibouti and parts of Kenya. There are (in 2020) around 12 million (perhaps a bit more) Somalis in Somalia, 4–5 million in Ethiopia, about 2.5 million in Kenya, and a half million in Djibouti. This is a significant fact. The boundaries of Somalia were colonial ones and did not encompass all the Somali people. Unlike most African countries Somalia is ethnically uniform, but like most of the states on the continent it is the product of arbitrary borders drawn up by the colonial powers with little regard to the interests or traditions or identities of the people within them.

Somali society is based on kinship groups. The largest kinship group is the clan. The majority of Somalis identify with five major ones. Clans are important in Somali society, since they, rather than a state, tend to be the prime object of allegiance for most people. Somalis clan structure is very complicated and confusing with many sub-clans. The dominant clan in Somaliland is the Isaaq clan. It is membership or loyalty to this clan that helps cement unity in the country. The Isaaq is divided into sub-clans including the Ara, Ayoup, Garhajis, Habar Awal, Habar Jeclo, and Tol Jecle. While Somalis are fiercely loyal to both their clans and sub-clan, affiliations are complicated by the fact the sub-clans inter-marry. Indeed, marriage often acts as a way different clan groups form alliances. Under colonial rule clan affiliation was a legal identity and clan organization was the principal way individual Somalis gained access to the state.[6]

A LONG BUT NOT WELL-UNDERSTOOD HISTORY

Little is known of the early history of this region. Somalia, especially the northern region, has been linked by trade and migration to the Red Sea basin lands of Arabia and Ethiopia since early times.[7] Islam arrived early, and it has been a deeply Muslim society for more than a thousand years. The Somali people themselves immigrated to the region from further north but it is not certain when this took place. The region was home to flourishing coastal cities during the Middle Ages, with those on the north coast trading with the Red Sea basin and those along the southern coast engaged in trade with the wider Indian Ocean.

In the fifteenth and sixteenth centuries, the Somalis were involved in a long drawn-out effort to spread Islam to the Christian and animist areas of what is now Ethiopia. At that time much of Somalia was part of the powerful Adal Sultanate that waged a long series of wars against the Christian kingdom of Ethiopia. Real power in Somalia has usually rested in clans, not states; the Adal Sultanate was an exception, but it was not a long-lasting one and disintegrated into competing clans. In the sixteenth century, the Ottomans arrived occupying the port of Berbera; outside the port area most of the land was effectively ruled by Somali clans who paid deference to no outside power. The Egyptians under Muhammad Ali had a presence in the area after 1821 but it was the British that gradually gained control. Starting in 1827 the British signed treaties of friendship with various local clans. Between 1884 and 1886, the British consolidated their position with a series of formal treaties that established a protectorate over the region that they called British

Somaliland.[8] For a while it was administered from British colony of Aden in southern Yemen as part of British India; it became a separate administrative unit under the Foreign Office in 1905. But British rule had little impact on most Somalis who were governed more by kinship and clan organizations than by formal governments.[9]

THE SCRAMBLE FOR AFRICA AND COLONIAL SOMALIA

The area, while poor in resources, was too strategic for the great powers to ignore during the heyday of imperialism in the late nineteenth century; therefore, it became part of the "Scramble for Africa," as the race among the European powers to carve up African is labeled. When the Europeans arrived, they found a country divided into clans but no effective state structure and a population that was majority nomadic. In an imperial landgrab, this region was effectively partitioned five ways. The largest part of Somalia was colonized by the Italians. Italy's arrival to the age of imperialism was late, by the 1880s when it began to seriously plan a colonial empire, most of the promising lands for colonial exploitation had been taken. One area that wasn't was the Horn of Africa. The Italians took possession of Eritrea in 1885, then from 1888 they began to acquire control over southern Somalia consolidating its holdings into the colony of Italian Somaliland in 1908. The big prize was Ethiopia but an Italian military expedition into that country was defeated by the Ethiopians in 1896. It was a humiliating setback for Italy, but at least it had Eritrea and a large chunk of Somalia.

British interest in the area was limited. Somalia had little in the way of resources or much economic potential. It was barren, sparsely populated, and poor. Still the region had its uses for the British and they acquired control over the northern region which they organized as British Somaliland. The new colony supplied food, particularly meat for the British outpost in Aden in southern Arabia and got the nickname "Aden's butcher shop."[10] British control over northern Somalia was also used to ensure order in the coastal areas and protect caravan routes to the interior. The British were also concerned with ending the slave trade in the region.[11] The French took the area around the strategically located port of Djibouti, a chunk of the west came under the rule of Ethiopia, and the southernmost area became part of the British colony of Kenya.

Lacking much in the way of natural resources and too poor to be a major market for their goods, the colonial rulers did not show an enormous interest in their new colonies nor did they invest much in the way of infrastructure. Most Somalis continued their life much as before, although some received modern education in colonial schools. British and Italian administration was mostly confined to the coast, with little penetration into the interior. Some Somalis resisted colonial occupation. Most famously the dervish leader Mohammed Abdullah Hassan fought the British in the north. He set up his own state and called on a holy war against the colonial rulers until the British in 1920, using aerial bombardment, defeated him.[12] The administration of the Italian and British Somalia differed. The Italian government encouraged Italians to settle there, and a few did, establishing fruit plantations. The Italians built schools, a few churches, and did more to develop their colony although still to only a modest extent. The British by contrast did not settle in the colony and devoted little to its development.[13] It was as two scholars of the region noted a "neglected part of the British Indian empire."[14]

Italy lost control over its colony during World War II when it was occupied by the British. After 1945, Italian Somaliland was returned to the Italians as a UN Trust Territory. This meant that Italy administered it under UN guidelines which included training personnel to prepare for eventual independence. Then in 1960 most of the European colonies became independent. The three colonies: Italian, British, and the small French Somaliland held referendums on their future. In British Somaliland and Italian Somaliland, the citizens voted to unite as one independent country, but those in French Somaliland did not. It became the separate small nation of Djibouti.

THE SHORTEST-LIVED STATE: INDEPENDENCE

Although British Somaliland joined Italian Somaliland to form the new Republic of Somalia it had a brief existence as an independent state. On June 26 the British colony became the Republic of Somaliland; this was just four days before Italian Somaliland's scheduled independence. The following day, on June 27, the Somaliland Legislative Assembly voted to unify the state of Somaliland with the Trust Territory of Somaliland (Italian Somaliland) when the latter became independent on the first of July.[15] The first Republic of Somaliland must have been one of the shortest-lived sovereign states in history. Still, during the four days of its existence, this first Somaliland was recognized by thirty-five states. That is thirty-five more than the current, second Somaliland had succeeded in gaining after three decades of existence.

Positions in the new unified Republic of Somalia were shared equally by officials from the two colonies. The president, for example, would be from the south and the prime minister from the north. However, it was, in reality, dominated by the residents of former Italian Somaliland. This was because the former Italian colony had the bigger population, it had the capital Mogadishu, and also because its officials as part of a UN Trusteeship requirements had more experience in administration. There were many problems integrating the two colonies. There were two different administrative languages, Italian and English, two different legal systems, the Italian and the British one based on the Indian Penal code. The educational system, limited as it was, differed as well.[16] Power, including seats in the National Assembly and cabinet positions, was shared roughly based on the population of the two former colonies.[17] However, the union didn't always go smoothly; there was friction between northern and southern officials. In a 1961 referendum formalizing the constitution arrangement, half the voters in the north rejected it. A year later northern officers led an abortive coup.[18] But overall the union seemed to be working. To the outside world Somalia appeared to be a unified, homogeneous country.

This began to change under the dictatorship of Siad Barre. For a short period, the country functioned as a democratic state. Then in 1969, the president of Somalia Addirashid Ali Shermarke from the south was assassinated by one of his bodyguards. At the time his prime minister was Muhammad Jaji Ibrahim Egal from the north who would later become the president of Somaliland. Following the assassination, the military staged a bloodless coup led by General Mohammed Siad Barre. The early civilian government came to an end. Siad Barre, who ruled as dictator for the next two decades, changed the country's name to the Somali Democratic Republic and politically oriented the country toward the Soviet Union. His government carried out large public works, implemented rural and urban literacy campaigns that made dramatic progress, and nationalized what little industry there was. Somalia became a one-party state under Barre's Somali Revolutionary Socialist Party. Its ideology was a vague mix of Islam and Marxist socialism, an odd combination for sure. His Marxism in turn was a mix of Soviet, Chinese, and North Korean influences plus a bit from the Gamal Nasser regime of Egypt.[19] Barre created his own cult of personality and tried to break the clan structure replacing it with a centralized, socialist state. He strengthened the country's links with the Arab world becoming a member of the Arab League in 1974 even though Somalia was not an Arab country. He also played an active role in the Organization of African Unity.

In 1977, Barre sought to win support from pan-Somali nationalists by invading the ethnically Somali Ethiopian region of Ogaden. By invading this region Barre would not only add both several million Somalis to the state, but would also incorporate some of its rich agricultural lands. Besides a land grab, it was an appeal to the greater Somali nationalism that sought to unify all the Somali people into one state. This resonated with many Somali nationalists who considered Ethiopia as another imperial power which like the Italians and British who invaded, subjugated, and divided the Somali people. The timing seemed opportune. In 1974, Ethiopia's ancient monarchy was overthrown and replaced by a communist government, the Derg. The upheaval that followed provided an opportunity to settle an old grievance by those Somali nationalists who saw Ogaden as rightfully part of Somalia. At first, Somalian forces were victorious, overrunning 90 percent of the territory, but the new leftist government of Ethiopia called upon support from the Soviet Union and its allies for assistance. Soviet military experts and weapons arrived, and 20,000 Cuban soldiers came and fought.

With Moscow and its allies abandoning him, Barre turned to the United States, which offered weaponry and aid. As a result, Somalia had the largest army in Africa. Somalia was, however, gradually pushed back out of Ogaden. By 1978, the Somali invasion had been a failure. The drain of this conflict as well as the corruption within the Barre administration began to weaken the regime. In the 1980s, the economy did poorly, and then with the winding down of the Cold War in the late 1980s the United States lost interest in Somalia which was no longer of great strategic importance. Economic hardships contributed to political unrest and the regime responded by cracking down on all dissent. Guerilla resistance movements emerged.

One of the centers of resistance to Barre's government was in the north. The main group was the Somali National Movement (SNM) under the leadership of Abdirahman Ahmed Ali Tuur. Barre carried out ruthless measures to crush the resistance, including bombing cities. Hargeisa, a resistance stronghold, was targeted in 1988 with Barre's son-in-law leading the bombardment. Between 1981 and 1991 the SNM fought the regime of Siad Barre. Disgust with the Siad Barre was compounded by the 1977–1978 war with Ethiopia. Many ethnic Somalis from Ethiopia fled to northern Somalia. Most of them came from the Darood clan and settled into land that the Isaaq regarded as theirs. Tensions with the Darood which tended to support the regime became linked to opposition to the regime itself.[20] The war escalated in 1988 when the SNM took control of Hargeisa and Burco, two major cities in the north. The Barre regime bombed the cities from the air retaking the cities.[21] Some clan militias fought with the Barre government. As they did the SNM became completely dominated by the Isaaq clan giving the conflict an element of clan warfare.[22]

Barre campaign targeted the members of Isaaq clan, killing not only the guerillas but civilians who supported them or were simply members of the clan. Estimations of the number of Isaaq civilians killed range from 50,000 to 200,000. Hundreds of thousands fled to Ethiopia and hundreds of thousands more were internally displaced. Hartisheik in Ethiopia became the world's biggest refugee camp with 250,000 northern Somalis.[23] A UN investigation found that the crime of genocide was "conceived, planned and perpetrated by the Somali Government against the Isaaq people."[24] Whether or not it fits the description of genocide, the campaign brought horrific death and hardship on the Isaaq people. At the fall of Siad Barre regime Hargeisa was in ruins, 70 percent had been destroyed, 5,000 people killed. Half a million people in the region were internally displaced.[25]

Siad Barre's opponents belonged to an array of organizations. Besides the Somali National Movment there was the Somali Patriotic Movement, the Somali Salvation Democratic Front, the Somali Democratic Movement, and others. For all their nationalist and democratic titles, most were based on traditional clans. The largest the United Somali Congress (USC) was largely drawn from the Hawiye Clan that lived in the region around Mogadishu. In early 1991, USC in alliance with other groups succeeded in driving Siad Barre from power. The regime collapsed when he fled the capital Mogadishu on January 17.[26] His regime had become corrupt, oppressive, and had left an already poor country poorer. However, his fall only made the situation worse as the country lapsed into famine, looting, and continual fighting among the various oppositional factions who now fought among themselves. An incredibly violent and chaotic struggle for control of the government took place among political factions based on clans and sub-clans. In Mogadishu two factions of the USC fought for control of the city.[27]

Violence became so severe that it created a humanitarian crisis within the country. International aid groups attempted to assist the desperate people in the capital Mogadishu that swelled with refugees, but most were forced to withdraw for the safety of their staff. Meanwhile, real power in the countryside fell to local warlords and to an Islamic terrorist organization al-Shabab. By 1992 there was no effective central government at all. Somalia was being pronounced as a "failed state." It became a region of anarchy, warring factions, lawlessness, and a suffering people often short of food, medicine, and other necessities.

THE BIRTH OF A NATION

As the Barre government in Mogadishu crumbled in early 1991 the Somali National Movement (SNM) got the upper hand and took effective control over the north. The SNM originally aimed at overthrowing the Barre administration but it moved toward separatism, seeking the succession of the north from the country.[28] In April and May 1991 it held a conference in Burco with various clan leaders meeting to discuss the establishment of an administration in the region that they now controlled.[29] On May 16, 1991, they declared the Republic of Somaliland. The declaration of independence was not part of a long-term plan, nor was it a goal of the SNM. The SNM was not initially in favor of succession. Rather its manifesto called on Somali unity. What seemed to have happened is that by 1991 rank and file members no longer wished to support the government, such as it was, in Mogadishu. In short, the decision to succeed was made during a time of chaos and crisis and was only reluctantly supported by much of the leadership in the region. Many of the SNM leaders had mixed feelings about it.[30]

SOMALILAND SINCE INDEPENDENCE

Many people in Somaliland continued to feel ambivalent about independence, including Abdirahman Ahmed Ali Tuur who served as the first president. Initially supporting secession in 1994 he changed and sought to rejoin his country with Somalia under a new federal republic that would give his region greater autonomy. But as often happens the longer the people of Somaliland became used to governing themselves, and the elites enjoyed the status of leaders of an autonomous state, the more support for independence strengthened. Tuur's successor, Muhammad Haji Ibrahim Egal, who served as president until his death in 2002 was more committed to independence. Under Egal the country improved its security situation and the state was consolidated. He was followed by Dahir Rivale Kahin, a former security officer in the Barre government who continued the commitment to building a separate nation.[31]

Somaliland claimed the entire area of the former British Somaliland. However, it did not control the entire region. In the 1990s, the government in the capital Hargeisa concentrated on securing order in the central part of the country leaving the peripheral areas to be governed by local elders and traditional kinship-based institutions.[32] As a result, the outer regions began to cease even acknowledging the authority of the central government. The northeastern Maakhir region declared itself a separate unrecognized autonomous state within Somalia. Somaliland also faced a rebellion in the Awdal region where local leaders briefly proclaimed an independent state of Awdalland before declaring it an autonomous state within a federal Somaliland. These threats were contained as the government gained control over the countryside.[33]

A bigger issue was its dispute with Puntland over its three eastern provinces. Puntland which occupies the extreme northeast of Somalia, covers about 200,000 square kilometers (80,000 square miles) of desert and scrubland and has about 2.5 million inhabitants. The area declared itself a separate autonomous State of Puntland in 1998, but autonomous within Somalia, not a separate sovereign state. The name, Punt incidentally is derived from the ancient land of Punt, mentioned in Egyptian sources. It is not sure where Punt was located but some historians believed it was in Somalia. In practice it has been largely free from any control from Mogadishu. What holds Puntland together is the Darood clan. In this way, Puntland, like Somaliland, is a state based on a common clan so that the dispute between the two has an element of a traditional clan rivalry.

Tensions with Puntland has centered over Somaliland's three provinces of Sool, Sanaag, and Ayn. Since these provinces were part of British Somaliland, the Somaliland government claims them as part of their state. However, since these provinces are dominated by the Dhulbahante, a sub-clan of the Darood Puntland claims then. Tensions with Puntland escalated into violence in October 2004, and in April and October 2007 the armed forces of the two clashed near the town of Las Anod, the capital of the Sool region. In October 2007 Somaliland forces took control over the town. Five years later the leaders from the three provinces declared themselves the state of Khatumo. They sought not independence but, like Puntland, autonomy from the central government in Mogadishu with the aim of creating a federal republic that would give Puntland and their region autonomy within a larger Somalia state.[34]

While the case of Khatumo is unclear, it is possible, if the government in Mogadishu continues to be weak and ineffective, that Puntland too could go its way but as of 2021 there was no indication that that would happen. Puntland, incidentally, has a less stellar record than Somaliland in exercising control over its territory. It became famous for pirate attacks launched from its coastal villages. From 2005 to 2012, these pirate raids, along with others from southern Somalia, posed a major threat to Indian Ocean shipping until suppressed by an international effort.

SOMALILAND THE DE FACTO STATE

Ethnically and linguistically Somaliland is a homogeneous country. Almost everyone speaks Somali which is the official language and the language of instruction in schools. Arabic and English are widely spoken as second languages. Arabic is a mandatory subject in school and is used in the mosques. English is also taught in the schools and has official status. Somali has in the past used several different scripts, most commonly the Arabic script, but since 1972 the Latin script has been official and is used today in Somaliland. Referred to as the Somali alphabet it does not use p, v, or z.

Almost the entire population is Sunni Muslim and adheres to the Shafi'i school of Islamic jurisprudence. Some practice Sufiism. Islam is central to Somali identity and is the basis for much of the society's social norms. There are some Wahhabi influences from Yemen and the Gulf states but, in general, Muslim extremism has not been an issue in the country. Still Somalis are mostly devout and strictly follow Islamic practices. Most Somali women wear a hijab when in public. Somalis abstain from pork and alcohol and attend Friday prayer. Islam is the state religion of Somaliland and under the constitution no laws may violate the principles of *Sharia*. The promotion of any other religion is illegal, and the state promotes Islamic tenets and discourages any behavior contrary to Islam. There are virtually no non-Muslims.

Somaliland's economy after a slow start began growing at an impressive rate. Between 2014 and 2019 it expanded between 8 and 11 percent a year, among the world's highest rates. This sounds, and is, impressive but since it was from such a low point it means that the country was still very poor. Climbing out of poverty in an isolated, resource poor society would be a challenge in any case, but lack of recognition makes it even harder. Lack of recognition means there are no international banks except for a Djibouti bank. Somaliland government and businesses thus do not have access to international financial markets and loans, and receiving economic assistance and conducting international trade are difficult. It hampers the receipt of foreign aid, and it makes its currency, the shilling, virtually worthless outside the countries. The chief source of revenue for the government has been remittances from the large Somali diaspora working in the Gulf states, Europe, and the United States. In the 2010s this amounted to hundreds of millions of US dollars a year, some estimated the figure as up to 1 billion dollars annually. A large sum for one of the world's poorest countries. Remittances were the chief source of this growth contributed to as much as half of the GDP. The diaspora has also been the major source of investment in the country for its first quarter century. This included some modern businesses and infrastructure projects such as a telecommunications system that is the best in the region. Internet connection, for example, is far better in Somaliland cities than in Somalia or even Ethiopia. The remittances of the diaspora have also created another major industry. Since the country was cut off from the international banking system, the cumbersome business of sending money to the country employs 4,000 Somalilanders.[35]

The economy is based on herding, and livestock provides its principal export. From its port of Berbera sheep, camels and cattle are shipped to Saudi Arabia and the Gulf States. So, it is again, as in the colonial period, a "butchershop" for lands across the strait. The country is not known to be rich in mineral wealth but does have some agricultural potential. Another source of possible income is tourism. Its chief attraction is the rock art and caves at Laas Geel on the outskirts of Hargeisa. Discovered by a French archaeological team in 2002, the ten caves date back 5,000 years. Visits to the site are restricted to protect the paintings. There is the historic town of Sheekh near Berbera. Berbera itself has some impressive Ottoman buildings as does another historic port, Zeila. Offshore, there are some coral reefs. Another possibility for economic growth is developing the port of Berbera that could be used by landlocked Ethiopia. There is an international airport at Hargeisa, but flights are mostly to Djibouti, Addis Ababa, Dubai, and Jeddah. Only two foreign carriers serve Somaliland: African Express Airways and Ethiopian Airlines. There is a local Daallo Airlines. Some NGOs, religious groups, and international governments have worked on development projects. But as mentioned its international isolation has often hindered the receipt of foreign aid. Somalilanders, for the most part, have had to rely on themselves to develop their economy.

MORE DEMOCRATIC THAN ITS NEIGHBORS

That Somaliland's economy functioned as well as it did is impressive. Impressive too is that it created one of the more stable and democratic governments in this region of the world. Somalilanders achieved this by integrating customary laws and traditions with modern state structures. Independence leaders created a parliament consisting of elected representatives and a House of Elders occupied with traditional clan leaders. Seats in the both houses of parliament were apportioned according the clan affiliation. Indeed, the government might be considered a coalition of different clans/sub-clans. Not all clans or sub-clans were satisfied with the formula for allotting them seats, but it worked well enough to bring some stability. In 2002, the state moved toward a multiparty democracy. The idea was to create a more national politics that identified with the state as a whole rather than with clans. Three parties were permitted to contest seats, each was designed to be based on ideology rather than clan loyalty. The government consists of a president and a vice president and a council of ministers who are nominated by the president and run the country. There is a bicameral parliament with an upper House of Elders (the Guurti) and a lower House of Representatives. Each has eighty-two members. Members of the House of Elders are elected to six-year terms in an indirect manner by local communities. Members of the House of Representative are directly elected to five-year terms. The highest court is the Constitutional Court. As of 2014, there were three political parties: The Peace, Unity and Development Party, the Justice and Development Party, and Wadani. Parties cannot be based on religion or clan. However, in reality clans and sub-clans do matter in politics.[36]

In the first freely contested presidential elections in 2003 the Peace, Unity and Development Party's Ahmed Mohamad Mohamad "Silanyo" was narrowly defeated by Dahir Riyale Kahin. He lost by eighty out of 675,000 votes. Silanyo, in a manner unfortunately not common in Africa, accepted defeat despite the narrow margin by which he lost. Then, in 2010, in a rematch, Silanyo defeated Kahin who then stepped down.[37] Thus, Somaliland has been able to accomplish what most African countries have had difficulty achieving, making politicians accountable to the electorate and having peaceful alternations of power. Not that it is a flawless democracy. While according to Freedom House elections have been "relatively free and fair," there have been long delays in holding them meaning officials serve beyond their allotted terms. There were also complaints about the effective exclusion of women from political participation and the domination of political meetings by clan elders.[38] The press is freer than most African or Islamic societies; however, journalists were often pressured to report favorably on the government, arbitrary detention was not uncommon, and minor clans were often marginalized from the governing process.[39] Freedom House in 2018 ranked the Somaliland government as only partly democratic.[40] But this was still higher than any other country in the region, even Ethiopia under its reform-minded president Abiy.

Somaliland has been able to create a modest but efficient military police force that has kept terrorists out and maintained order. The Ministry of Defense oversees both the national Police Force and other internal security forces as well as the Somaliland Armed Forces. The country's army is made up of twelve divisions mostly equipped with light weapons. It has a few armored vehicles and tanks left over from the Soviet Union and some aging Western vehicles and tanks, but little in the way of modern sophisticated weaponry. It has a tiny navy, consisting of a few coastal patrol boats. Despite its modest size and lack of weapons and equipment, this modest naval force has been able to suppress piracy and illegal fishing. In general, Somaliland has been a safe and stable place that has been free from Islamic extremism. An exception was a string of bombing in Hargeisa in 2008 that left thirty people dead, which was thought to be the work of al-Shabab the militant Islamic group based in southern Somalia.[41]

The country has made good progress in education. Literacy rates were low and became worse with the civil war in the 1980s. But starting in the 1990s, the government began to reconstruct a system of public education. Enrollment in public schools has grown considerably, but basic education is not yet universal. In 1999, Amoud University, the country's first university, opened its doors. By the 2010s, there were ten universities.

DROUGHT AND HUNGER

Somaliland is still very much a rural agricultural, pastoral society. Its food is similar to Ethiopia with a flatbread *laboh* (*injera*) served. Porridges are made from millet or cornmeal are staples as is pita bread; a popular dish is *maraq*, a vegetable soup. Meals include beans and of course lots of meat: goat, sheep, beef as well as camel meat. Somaliland, incidentally, claims to support the world's largest number of camels, about 6 million, which would mean there are more camels than people. Camels are not only used for transport and meat but also as a source of milk. Camel milk is lower in fat than cow's milk, stays fresh longer, and is rich in iron, potassium, and vitamins.[42] While the diet is a healthy one, the problem is there is often not enough to eat, especially in times of drought.

In fact, feeding its people is a major problem for Somaliland. Most of the time it is sunny and very dry. Rainfall is modest and falls seasonally. And it is not reliable. Sometimes during the two short rainy seasons, rains fall in heavy, torrential showers for a few days and then stops, too short and sudden for the ground to absorb it. Sometimes it hardly rains at all, even in the rainy seasons. An especially severe famine in 1984–1985 that impacted Ethiopia, all of Somalia, and Eritrea resulted in 1 million deaths in the Horn of Africa, despite a massive international relief effort. Drought again hit the region in 2009 and 2010. An El Nino caused drier conditions 2015–2016. In 2017, a drought was so bad that an estimated 3.2 million of the country's 4.4 million were in urgent need of assistance. International relief missions prevented mass deaths but did not prevent a cholera epidemic.[43] Added to the problem of unpredictable rainfalls is the high birthrate in the region, one of the highest in the world which means more people are placing pressure on a rather fragile environment.

So despite its progress, this combination of an exploding population, drought compounded by climate change, and of course its diplomatic isolation cast a shadow over its economic prospects. It has little industrial infrastructure and few proven mineral resources, and education is still not adequate for the needs of a modern economy. Its location on the busy Red Sea shipping lanes holds some promise, perhaps Berbera could become a major port, especially for populous, landlocked Ethiopia. As mentioned, it does have tourist potential. The coasts have fine beaches and pristine coral reefs, and the wild interior might attract the more adventurous visitors.[44] But as long as it remains diplomatically isolated it is unlikely that there will be much investment or interest in economic development in the country.

SOMALILAND AND THE INTERNATIONAL COMMUNITY

Somaliland has won many admirers among the small number of international experts that have studied it. It has been called a "beacon of success in a turbulent region."[45] Yet, despite its efforts the country has made little headway in gaining international recognition. It is a member of the Unrepresented Nations and Peoples Organization, an advocacy group, whose members consist of indigenous peoples, minorities, and unrecognized or occupied territories. This group, however, carries little weight in the international community. It did maintain political contacts with Ethiopia, Djibouti, South Africa, Sweden, and the United Kingdom. In 2007, the European Union sent a delegation for foreign affairs to discuss future cooperation. The African Union has also sent a foreign minister to discuss some sort of international acknowledgment of its de facto independence. But the African Union, contrary to the case of Western Sahara has not accepted Somaliland as a member. It has sought membership in the (British) Commonwealth, an organization of former British colonies. President Kahin showed up at the Commonwealth Heads of Government Meeting in Kampala Uganda in 2007. Kahin's appearance there gave some sort of hope that its status would be accepted. Yet, Somaliland was not invited to be a regular member. In Britain, only the fringe UK Independence Party supported full recognition.[46] The US State Department in 2010 announced it was sending aid workers to Somaliland and Puntland and suggested it was considering future development projects. However, it also stated that while the United States hoped to have more engagement in the country it had no intention of recognizing it as a sovereign state.[47]

If Somaliland has not achieved international recognition it is not for lack of trying. One of its most effective advocates is Edna Adan. She was born into a wealthy Somali family in what was then British Somaliland in 1937. Her father was a doctor who educated his sons but at that time there was no schooling for girls. She learned to read and write by looking over their shoulders while they were doing their lessons. Her parents seeing this eagerness for learning sent her to a school in French Somaliland. There was no secondary education for girls there, but she improved her English working as an interpreter for a British doctor and was able to go to the United Kingdom for education. She became the country's first mid-wife and the first woman to drive a car. She married Mohammad Egal, divorced him, and went to work for World Health Organization where she had a distinguished career. After retiring she returned to Somaliland where she found the country's first maternal hospital. There she has led a tireless anti-female genital mutilation campaign and worked for women's and childhood health. In a mostly unknown country, Adan was able to draw international attention to her work and used this to advocate for the country's independence, serving as foreign minister from 2003 to 2006.[48] Yet, even Adan could make only the most modest progress in gaining recognition for her country.

WHY IS THE INTERNATIONAL COMMUNITY NOT RECOGNIZING SOMALILAND?

The case for recognizing Somaliland is strong. The state has existed as de facto independent nation since 1991. It has a historical case for being a nation-state as a successor to the former British Somaliland. It created a stable government that controlled most of the territory, although not the eastern periphery. It developed a functioning democracy, a democracy with limits but one that was more democratic than any of the other countries in the region. It remained very poor, yet it managed its economy with a reasonable degree of competency. Unlike other de facto states we have discussed that have a foreign protector—Armenia, Russia, NATO, or Turkey—Somaliland has only itself to count on. Ethiopia is somewhat supportive, yet it cannot be called a protector. To a much greater degree than the other de facto states we have looked at, Somaliland has been a very self-created, self-supporting state.

Yet the international community continued to regard Somaliland as part of Somalia even though Somalia did not have a government that controls much beyond the capital in nearly three decades. Somalia, in fact, has for most of the time since 1991 hardly existed at all except on the maps. It has been a lawless place, mostly controlled by local warlords or by the al-Shabab Islamic organization, condemned internationally as a violent terrorist group. Somaliland by contrast has been a zone of stability which ironically is one reason why it has been ignored by the international media. It has not harbored terrorists or pirates and has not seen vast floods of refugees in neighboring countries. All this would appear to an argument for recognition. It is in many ways as a sovereign state, more real than the Republic of Somalia of which it is supposed to belong. Somaliland is viable as a state even if its borders are a bit uncertain.

Unfortunately for Somaliland, there was no reason for the international community to give it recognition. The African Union has from the days of its predecessor the Organization of African Unity, been committed to maintaining the territorial integrity of its members. There was a sensible reason for this policy. Most of the African states were based on arbitrarily drawn colonial boundaries with little regard for the interests and identities of the African people. Different ethnic groups that had never been a part of a common state or society found themselves under the same administrative structure, while ethnic groups like the Somali found themselves politically divided. For example, the Hausa peoples of northern Nigeria have little in common, ethnically, linguistically, and historically with the people of southern Nigeria but they share the same language and traditions with the Hausa who live across the border in Niger. They are the same people, divided by colonial boundaries and now national ones. So, the African states, in order to avoid the chaos of ethnic and tribal groups trying to politically unite or succeed from existing states, made the decision to stick with the colonial borders. Consequently, Somaliland's hope to legally join the international community has received little encouragement or sympathy from other African nations.

Still even by the standards of the African Union Somaliland falls in the category of conforming to colonial boundaries. Somaliland was a separate colony, briefly independent whose leaders in a wave of pan-Somali sentiment that prevailed among the educated elite at the time hastily established a union with the former Italian Somaliland. This was done without much consultation or legal niceties. Only after the fact was a referendum held. Almost from the beginning many northerners had second thoughts about their decision when they found themselves dominated by the larger clans of the south. President Kahin submitted an application for his country's entry into the African Union in 2005. A commission was then formed by the African Union to look into the application.[49] This commission questioned the very legality of the process which the former British unified with the larger former Italian colony to the south. A report it issued stated: "The fact that the union between Somaliland and Somalia was never ratified and also malfunctioned when it went into action from 1960 to 1990, makes Somaliland's search for recognition historically unique and self-justified in African political history." It then went to recommend "the AU should find a special method of dealing with this outstanding case."[50]

In fact, the formation of Somalia was the result of the merging of two former colonies. This generally has not worked out well. In 1958 the former British colony of Egypt and the former French colony of Syria formed the United Arab Republic but that fell apart when Syria withdrew in 1961. In 1990 South Yemen, a former British colony that became independent in 1967, merged with Yemen (North Yemen) which had been independent since the collapse of the Ottoman Empire at the end of World War I. The union worked reasonably well until the civil war in Yemen in the 2010s when a strong movement in the south to restore the independence of South Yemen emerged. A closer parallel is the merger of the former French colony of Senegal with the former British colony of Gambia in 1982 to form Senegambia, this too failed to work out with the smaller Gambia withdrawing from the union in 1989. Somalia/Somaliland too can be seen as another failed union of two former colonies with different histories. African leaders have been adamant on supporting the territorial integrity of Somalia least they encourage other secessionist movements. Yet despite the fears of African leader the recognition of Somaliland necessarily a threat to the stability of other nations. There have been only two cases in recent history of secessionist movements in Africa resulting in the creation of a new nation: Eritrea which became independent from Ethiopia in 1993 and South Sudan which won a decade-long effort to separate from Sudan in 2011. Both were recognized by the African Union and the international community. In neither case was there an uptick in secessionist movements elsewhere. Like Somaliland, each was a special case.

Somaliland does have some strategic significance. It is located along the Gulf of Aden near the entrance to the Bab al-Mandeb, a potential choke point along a sea lane through which one-third of the world's shipping passes. Its location attracted the attention of a Dubai firm that in 2018 announced it was planning to upgrade the port of Berbera. It is important for Ethiopia, the world's largest landlocked country as an outlet to the sea. It could function as an alternative or addition to Djibouti where France, Italy, Japan, the United States, and China all have military and security facilities.[51] It might well be in the interest of the international community to support a successful, stable state in the region.

Despite the strong case for recognition, the international community insists on adhering to the concept of a centralized, united state of Somalia long after that Somalia ceased to exist. Bronwyn Bruton, the director of programs and studies at the Africa Center at the Atlantic Council, has explained that there are two important reasons the international community will not recognize it. One is "apathy." There is no economic or vital strategic interest. It has no oil, no known major resources, no one has an economic stake in the country. Or as the Guardian newspaper put it, the "main obstacle is not the world's animosity, but its indifference."[52] The second reason is that recognizing an independent Somaliland runs counter to the international effort to construct a functioning central government in Somalia. Western countries have committed themselves to reconstituting the former centralized state based in Mogadishu that existed before the country became a lawless base for terrorists and pirates. As Bruton has put it, "Somaliland is effectively being held hostage to the chaos in southern Somalia, it is grossly unfair."[53]

Nor does the EU, the United States, or other major powers have an interest in creating a new nation. Few states feel comfortable with separatist movements. The Quebecois in Canada, the Catalans in Spain, and the Kurds in Iraq have received little international support. The general principle is to support the territorial claims of a state that is already accepted as a recognized sovereign entity. There are exceptions, such as if the people are suffering from persecution or threatened with ethnic cleansing as in Kosovo. As we have seen the Barre government did commit atrocities in northern Somalia, but this was not widely reported. It was largely overlooked as part of a confused civil war involving leaders, clans, and regions. Furthermore, and this is an important point, an independent Somaliland does not serve any great power's interest and seemed to just complicate the effort to put Somalia back together again. This was the main interest of the international community—to reconstruct a stable, functional Somalia that will no longer be a humanitarian crisis, no longer be a home to pirates and to terrorists.

Diplomatic recognition, if it were to come, would not be without problems. As a successor to the state of Somalia, it would be, under international law, subject to some responsibility for Somalia's debt. Siad Barre borrowed large sums of money that was never paid. Servicing these debts would be an added burden to a poor country. To gain African Union recognition it would have to assume the boundaries of the old British Somaliland since under the organization's rules countries must adhere to the colonial borders. But parts of British Somaliland are held by Puntland so this would be difficult. In addition, recognition would antagonize Somalia; should it ever establish an effective government it would most likely want to take back control of the region.

SOMALILAND, A TRULY DE FACTO STATE

Somaliland has all the characteristics of a real state. It is a self-created state with little outside support, with no real patron. As a result, it has made fewer compromises with its sovereignty than the other de facto states we have looked at. It has carried out all the functions of a state and except for some peripheral areas its government has achieved a high degree of internal legitimacy. We have examined the historical basis for the creation of Somaliland. It may be held together by a single, powerful clan organization but as a modern state it has its basis in a European colony. It still faces the problems of nation building in a region of the world where every internationally recognized country struggles to make a cohesive nation-state within boundaries that were arbitrarily drawn colonial powers, in places where kin, clan, and tribe compete with state for allegiance and identity. In this respect, it is much more a real country than any of its neighbors.

It seems almost tragic that Somaliland, where people have come together and created an island of stability in a violent, lawless area, should not be accepted by the international community. It is the most democratic society in the region, one that has kept out terrorists, prevented piracy, and in many ways has been a responsible member of the international community that refused to acknowledge the reality of its existence.

NOTES

1. Markus Virgil Hoehne, *Between Somaliland and Puntland: Marginalization, Militarization and Conflicting Political Visions* (London: Rift Valley Institute, 2015), 40.

2. "When is a Nation Not a Nation? Somaliland's Dream of Independence," *The Guardian*, July 20, 2018, https://www.theguardian.com/news/2018/jul/20/when-is-a-nation-not-a-nation-somalilands-dream-of-independence, Accessed February 28, 2019.

3. Philip Briggs, *Somaliland*, 2nd Edition (Guilford, CT: Bradt Travel Guides, 2019), 70.

4. Briggs, *Somaliland*, 71.
5. Briggs, *Somaliland*, 75.
6. Lidwien Kapteijns, *Clan Cleansing in Somalia: The Ruinous Legacy of 1991* (Philadelphia, PA: University of Pennsylvania Press, 2013).
7. Ioan M. Lewis, *A Modern History of the Somali: Nation and State in the Horn of Africa*, 4th Edition (Oxford, UK: James Currey, 2002), 20–21.
8. Rahpael Chijioke Njoku, *The History of Somalia* (Santa Barbara, CA: Greenwood, 2013), 56.
9. Alex de Waal, *The Real Politics of the Horn of Africa: Money, War and the Business of Power* (Cambridge, UK: Polity Press, 2015), 110.
10. Abdi Ismail Samatar, *The State and Rural Transformation in Northern Somalia, 1884–1986* (Madison, WI: University of Wisconsin Press, 1989), 31.
11. David Laitin and Said Samatra, *Somalia: Nation in Search of a State* (Boulder CO: Westview Press, 1987), 42.
12. Njoku, *The History of Somalia*, 73–74.
13. Ioan M. Lewis, *Understanding Somalia and Somaliland: Culture, History, Society* (Columbia, SC: New Columbia University Press, 2008), 31.
14. Laitin and Samatra, *Somalia*, 59.
15. Lewis, *Understanding Somalia and Somaliland*, 164.
16. James Crawford, *The Creation of States in International Law*, 2nd Edition (Oxford, UK: Oxford University Press, 2006), 413.
17. Lewis, *Understanding Somalia and Somaliland*, 34.
18. Lewis, *Understanding Somalia and Somaliland*, 35.
19. Lewis, *Understanding Somalia and Somaliland*, 39.
20. Hoehne, *Between Somaliland*, 41.
21. Hoehne, *Between Somaliland*, 40.
22. Rebecca Richards, *Understanding Statebuilding: Traditional Governance and the Modern State in Somaliland* (Burlington, VT: Ashgate Publishing Company, 2014), 96–97.
23. de Waal, *The Real Politics*, 32.
24. Chris Mburu, "Rights, United Nations Office of the High Commissioner for Human; Office, United Nations Development Programme Somalia Country (2002-01-01)," *Past Human Rights Abuses in Somalia: Report of a Preliminary Study Conducted for the United Nations (OHCHR/UNDP-Somalia)*, s.n. Accessed September 15, 2018.
25. World Bank Group, *Somaliland's Private Sector at a Crossroads: Political Economy and Policy Choices for Prosperity and Job Creation* (Washington, DC: World Bank, 2015), 7.
26. Njoku, *The History of Somalia*, 134.
27. Njoku, *The History of Somalia*, 138.
28. Njoku, *The History of Somalia*, 187.
29. Njoku, *The History of Somalia*, 140–41.
30. Hoehne, *Between Somaliland*, 44.
31. Lewis, *Understanding Somalia and Somaliland*, 97.
32. Hoehne, *Between Somaliland*, 49–50.

33. University of Pennsylvania, Africa Studies Center, *Awdal "Republic" Declaration of Independence*, http://www.africa.upenn.edu/Hornet/awdal.html, Accessed December 28, 2019.

34. "What is Khatumo?" *Somalia Report*, April 26, 2012.

35. UN Office for the High Representative for the Least Developed States, "The Role of Remittances in the Development of the Economy of Somaliland," *UN-OHRLLS 2019*, http://unohrlls.org/news/the-role-of-remittance-in-the-economic-development-of-somaliland/, Accessed September 29, 2018.

36. *Somaliland Government*, http://somalilandgov.com/the-administration/, Retrieved July 8, 2018; Briggs, *Somaliland*, 23.

37. de Waal, *The Real Politics*, 130.

38. Seth Kaplan, "The Remarkable Story of Somaliland," *Journal of Democracy* 19, no. 3 (July 2008): 143–57.

39. *Freedom House*, "Somaliland Report 2018-Freedom in the World," https://freedomhouse.org/report/freedom-world/freedom-world-2018, Accessed June 16, 2019.

40. *Freedom House*, "Somaliland Report 2018."

41. "5 Suicide Bombing Attacks Hit Somalia," *New York Times*, October 29, 2008, https://www.nytimes.com/2008/10/30/world/africa/30somalia.html, Accessed September 4, 2018.

42. Briggs, *Somaliland*, 91.

43. "Crisis in Somaliland: Drought and Famine Threaten Millions," *Euronews*, November 5, 2017, https://www.euronews.com/2017/05/11/crisis-in-somaliland-drought-and-famine-threaten-millions, Accessed July 17, 2019.

44. Briggs, *Somaliland*, 116.

45. Richards, *Understanding Statebuilding*, 20.

46. Unrepresentative Nations and Peoples Organization, "Somaliland: Surviving the Agonizing Process of International Recognition," *UNPO*, November 11, 2009, https://unpo.org/article/10322, Accessed July 18, 2019.

47. "U.S. Seeks Stronger Ties with Somaliland and Puntland," *BBC News*, September 25, 2010, https://www.bbc.com/news/world-africa-11410852, Accessed September 12, 2018.

48. "When is a Nation Not a Nation? Somaliland's Dream of Independence," *The Guardian*, July 20, 2018; Keating, *Invisible Countries*, 120–22; "Edna Adan: Half the Sky," *PBS Independent Lens*, https://www.pbs.org/independentlens/half-the-sky/edna-adan/, Accessed September 30, 2018.

49. *International Crisis Report*, "Somaliland: Time for African Union Leadership," May 23, 2006, https://www.crisisgroup.org/africa/horn-africa/somalia/somaliland-time-african-union-leadership, Accessed September 14, 2018.

50. Quoted in Peter Pham, "Somalia: When a State is Not a State," *The Fletcher Forum for World Affairs*, http://www.fletcherforum.org/home/2016/9/6/somalia-where-a-state-isnt-a-state?rq=somalia, Accessed September 14, 2018.

51. *Council of Foreign Relations*, "The Horn of Africa's Breakaway State," February 1, 2018, https://www.cfr.org/backgrounder/somaliland-horn-africas-breakaway-state, Accessed September 18, 2018.

52. "When is a Nation Not a Nation? Somaliland's Dream of Independence," *The Guardian*, July 20, 2018.

53. "Somaliland Want to Make One Thing Clear: It is Not Somalia," *National Public Radio*, May 30, 2017, https://www.npr.org/sections/goatsandsoda/2017/05/30/530703639/somaliland-wants-to-make-one-thing-clear-it-is-not-somali, Accessed September 16, 2018.

Chapter 9

One China, Two Countries
Taiwan

Most of our states with limited recognition are small, little known states. Not so with Taiwan or as it officially refers to itself, the Republic of China. With 23 million people, and a dynamic modern economy—home to Acer, Foxconn, and other international high-tech firms—Taiwan is by most measures an important country. It has one of the highest standards of living in Asia, in fact, in the world, and it is one of the few Asian societies to make a peaceful transition to democracy. It is hard not to see Taiwan as one of the Third World's success stories, a poor country that in two generations became a rich one. Yet, Taiwan is not recognized as an independent state by any major power; as of 2020 only fourteen countries, all small, formally recognized it. It has no seat in the United Nations nor in almost any international organization. Its athletes compete in the Olympics but only under the peculiar label of "Chinese Taipei." They cannot fly their flag or play their national anthem. How is it then that this successful, democratic state with a population and economy bigger than all but a few European countries does not officially exist at all?

Taiwan's problem is that the People's Republic of China regards it as one of its provinces and claims sovereignty over it. So strongly does Beijing feel about this that it will not have formal diplomatic relations with any country that recognizes Republic of China. It blocks Taiwan from membership of international organizations since this would imply it is a sovereign state. Since China has been the world's most populous nation, with more industrial output than any other country, with the globe's second or first largest economy in 2021 (depending how it is measured), it is too important for other countries not to have relations with it. Therefore, all but a handful of very small states, with lucrative ties to Taiwan, have had to accept this and pretend

Taiwan does not exist, at least as a separate state from China. It is only for this reason that the Republic of China is a de facto state.

ILHA FORMOSA: THE BEAUTIFUL ISLAND

Taiwan, or the Republic of China to use its official name, consists of one big island and some small ones, totaling some 36,193 square kilometers (13,974 square miles). It is about 230 kilometers long, north to south and 85 miles wide. The main island of Taiwan is 180 kilometers (110 miles) off the coast of southern China, separated by the mainland of China by the Taiwan Strait. All but around 300,000 of its 23 million people live on the island. It has been described as shaped like a tobacco leaf and like a sweet potato. In fact, the term "sweet potatoes" is a nickname given to the people of Taiwan by some of the neighbors in Fujian Province on the other side of the strait. The island straddles just above and below the Tropic of Cancer, and it has a mostly tropical climate, hot and humid much of the year with some chilly wet days in winter but never freezing cold. It is very rainy, with average rainfall of 250 cm (100 inches) of rain a year.

The older name for the island is Formosa, given by the Portuguese who called it Ilha Formosa, "beautiful island," which it is. Lush and green, it has high mountains and deep gorges. Mountains cover the eastern two-thirds of Taiwan dominated by the north-south Central Mountain Range. Fifty peaks are above 10,000 feet; Yu Shan (Jade Mountain) the highest is 3,952 meters (12,966 feet), the fourth highest mountain on any island in the world. Surprisingly for one of the world's most densely populated countries, 58 percent is covered by forests, mostly in the highlands.[1] It has an enormous diversity of flora and fauna, including the endemic Formosan macaque, the Formosan sambar (a kind of deer), and the endangered Formosan black bear. The Formosan clouded leopard is now believed to be extinct.[2] The country also possesses a chain of tiny islands called the Penghu or Pescadores by some Westerners, and the islands of Kinmen and Matsu just off the coast of China. Despite their small area, these islands have been important in Taiwan's history.

Most of the population lives on the western third of the island, along the Chiangnan Plain, a fertile land with rich volcanic soil that is highly productive. Ample rainfall contributes to the high yields of its farmland. Taiwan at one time was a major agricultural exporter; today it is an overwhelmingly urban, industrial nation. The largest city and capital is Taipei in the north; other cities include Taichung in the western center of the island, Tainan in the south and the ports of Keelung near Taipei and Kaohsiung in the south, all over more than 1 million inhabitants. Taiwan looks tiny compared to China; it has only 1/260 the area of its giant neighbor, but it is about the size of Holland and bigger than many UN members.³ Its population of 23 million makes it larger than 70 percent of UN members. Taiwan is among the world's most densely populated countries with most of the population packed into the western third. The birthrate, however, which in 1952 at 4.66 per 1,000 was among the highest in the world, has fallen dramatically over the past half-century and is now one of the lowest.⁴

Taiwanese are Chinese, but then what does this mean? China is far from being a homogeneous nation. The Chinese people speak a number of different languages and have strong regional and ethnic differences. Most Taiwan inhabitants are descended from the peoples of Fujian province across the strait and speak Taiwanese, a variant of the Hokkien (or Min) language native to that area. About 70 percent of the population speaks Taiwanese as their first language. About 14 percent speak another Chinese dialect Hakka, and most of the rest speak only Mandarin, that is standard Chinese, which every one else speaks as a second language.⁵ There is no difference in the written language among these groups—all writing is in standard Chinese. There is also a small aboriginal population that is not related to the Chinese at all. These aboriginal peoples have lived on the island for thousands of years, whereas the Chinese came to Taiwan only from the seventeenth century. Like Native Americans in the North America (and at about the same time), Chinese settlers landed and gradually pushed the aboriginal peoples into marginal lands. About 2.4 percent of the population is aboriginal but most of these have adopted Chinese culture and language. Only a small number can speak one of their twenty-six original languages.

TAIWAN: THE WILD FRONTIER LAND

People have lived in Taiwan for a long time. The first walked there, since until ten thousand years ago it was not an island at all. We know nothing about these earliest inhabitants. About six thousand years ago the direct ancestors of the aboriginal peoples of Taiwan settled in what was now an island and brought agriculture with them. They grew rice and other crops. All the languages of Taiwan belong to the Austronesian language family, meaning they are not even remotely related to Chinese but instead to the languages of the Philippines, of Indonesia, and Polynesia. In fact, some historians believe that it was from the people of Taiwan that all these other languages were derived. Thus, Taiwan may be the homeland of the languages and cultures of peoples from Madagascar to Hawaii. If so, the Taiwanese people were very important in shaping world history, but they were not literate so left no written records. They never formed states but remained, when Europeans and Chinese began writing about them four centuries ago, divided into tiny chiefdoms. For centuries these aboriginal peoples and their island of Taiwan were largely ignored by the rest of the world. Being so near China, near the South China Sea trade routes, and being a lush, and potentially prosperous, land this might seem strange. But it appears that the Native Taiwanese were an unfriendly group that discouraged traders from coming ashore, and the island did not possess anything—gold, silver, spices and so on—that was in great demand. In 1430, when the famed Chinese navigator Zheng He visited the island, he did not report of any Chinese living on there, nor did the Chinese show much interest in further ventures on Taiwan.[6]

In 1544, the Portuguese ship that sailed by christened the island Formosa, the name it was often referred to by Westerners until recent times.[7] The Portuguese just passed by, while the Dutch arrived in the early seventeenth century and established a fort on the Pescadores. Chased out by Ming Chinese authorities, they relocated to Taiwan where in 1624, they established Fort Zeelandia near the modern city of Tainan. From there they gained control of most of the western part of the island. Taiwan was still "on the outer edge of Chinese consciousness and activity."[8] That soon changed. In 1662, the Dutch were conquered by a Chinese pirate adventurer turned patriot Zheng Chenggong, better known to Westerners as Koxinga. At this time, the Manchus had captured control of most of China creating the Qing Dynasty in 1644. However, in the south of China loyalists to the old Ming dynasty fought a war of resistance. Zheng used Taiwan as a base in that effort. He also carved out his own domain declaring his own Kingdom of Tungning, with a government based on that of the Ming dynasty which was inherited by his son.[9] By 1683, the Qing had crushed all resistance on the mainland, but there was still the hostile state on Taiwan. That year the Qing forces captured Taiwan and incorporated it into the Chinese empire. Taiwan became Chinese as a result of a civil war in China. Interestingly, Taiwan's role as a stronghold of opposition to a new regime in mainland China would be repeated in the twentieth century.

TAIWAN BECOMES PART OF THE JAPANESE EMPIRE

For the next two centuries Taiwan was a prefecture of Fujian Province. During that time large numbers of Chinese emigrated from Fujian proper settling in the fertile eastern plain and forcing the indigenous Taiwanese to retreat to the mountains. For the Chinese settlers Taiwan was still a semi-wild frontier area, settled by pioneers that sought land and opportunity. By the late nineteenth century, the Qing government facing encroachment by Western imperial powers and threatened by a rising, modernizing Japan sought integrate this island frontier into the main empire. In 1887, Beijing made it a province, and it carried out modernizing projects including constructing one of China's first railroads.[10] But this proved a little too late; Japan which had annexed Okinawa to the north in 1874 took control over Taiwan in 1895 following its victory in the Sino-Japanese War, 1894–1895.

Local officials sought to thwart the Japanese takeover by declaring a Republic of Taiwan in 1895 before Japanese troops landed. But no one recognized their republic, and the Japanese forces quickly crushed it. Taiwanese Chinese did not surrender easily but kept up a resistance that lasted until 1903. It is estimated that more than 14,000 died in this resistance, about 5 percent of the population.[11] The indigenous people in the mountains resisted longer, and it was not until a major campaign in 1930 that they were fully brought under Japanese control.

The Japanese saw themselves as agents of modernization, and they were. They built a modern education system, modern roads, some industries and improved agriculture. The emphasis was making the island a supplier of rice and sugar for Japan. Output increased, and Taiwan became the world's seventh-largest producer of sugar. However, Taiwan's economy was directed at serving Japan's needs not that of the local population. While Taiwanese became better educated, healthier and developed many of the skills needed for the modern world, they remained a second class, subjected peoples. In the 1930s, the Japanese promoted the policy of *kominka*—essentially turning the Taiwanese into Japanese by discouraging the use of any language other than Japanese, requiring them to adopt the Shinto religion and change their names to Japanese. During World War II, many Taiwanese were enrolled into the Japanese armed forces and some women were conscripted as "comfort women," that is, prostitutes to serve the Japanese army.[12] Yet, Taiwanese were never assimilated into Japanese culture. Instead, Taiwanese, cut off from China, treated as second class citizens by Japan, sometimes saw themselves as "Asia's orphans."[13]

TAIWAN BECOMES PART OF CHINA AGAIN (BUT ONLY BRIEFLY)

After half a century under Japanese rule, Taiwan briefly rejoined China. At the Cairo Conference in 1943 the Allies agreed that Taiwan would eventually be returned to China. At the time China was officially called the Republic of China (ROC) and led by the Guomindang (Nationalist) Party which was determined to regain control of Taiwan. The Chinese leader, Chiang Kai-shek, in late 1945 sent one of his commanders, Chen Yi, to accept the Japanese surrender and take control over the island. The whole situation was rather confusing. First, the Allies had planned to place Taiwan under Allied military occupation as they did for Japan and its other major colony Korea. The United States, Britain, and the other Allied Powers never formally recognized the Chiang Kai-shek's occupation of the island, but they accepted the fact. Meanwhile, it was not certain who really ruled China since the government of the Guomindang centered in Nanjing was challenged by the Chinese Communist Party under Mao Zedong for control of the country. An all-out civil war took place between them from 1946 to 1949 with the United States supporting the Guomindang. Despite US military aid, the communists emerged as victors in 1949. On October 1, 1949, Mao Zedong proclaimed the People's Republic of China (PRC) in Beijing. The Guomindang's authority was crumbling everywhere and on December 7, 1949, Chiang Kai-shek moved the government to Taipei. Or to put it another way, the remnants of the army and government fled there.

SAVED BY A FLUKE

By 1950, the Republic of China (ROC) had contracted to one small island. The Guomindang regime was isolated; only South Korea transferred its embassy from Beijing to Taipei, other countries either recognized the PRC or like the United States and its allies just waited to see what would happen.[14] The United States had largely written the ROC off by then, and it was a matter of time before Taiwan too fell. In fact, in May 1950, PRC forces captured the island of Hainan and it seemed Taiwan would soon fall to them too. But then the ROC was saved by two invasions—one human and one non-human. Lacking a navy Mao Zedong planned to send troops to the island in a wave of small rafts. But the soldiers training along the muddy shores of Fujian were invaded by liver flukes found in the soil and became ill. Mao was forced to delay the invasion for a few weeks.[15] During this period Kim Il Sung, the North Korean dictator unintentionally came to Taiwan's rescue. On June 25, 1950, with the support of the Soviet Union and the blessing of Mao Zedong he invaded South Korea, launching the Korean War. President Truman responded almost immediately by ordering US troops to intervene and at the same time ordered the US 7th Fleet to sail into the Taiwan Strait and prevent the PRC from invading Taiwan. In this way Taiwan became effectively a separate state, ruled by a dictator and a loyal core of his supporters who fled there with him. It was as one writer calls it "an accidental state," a product of individual decisions and contingencies.[16]

THE GOVERNMENT-IN-EXILE STATE

Taiwan under the Guomindang was dominated by the 1.3 million mainlanders who came with Chiang, soldiers, government officials, business elites and their families. They ruled over 6 million Taiwanese Chinese who had grown up under Japanese rule. Many, if not most, longed for self-rule but what they got was rule by Mainland Chinese who did not speak their dialect or understand their culture. Few Taiwanese understood the standard Chinese used by the mainlanders. Furthermore, their hope to acquire Japanese businesses and properties were dashed when these were seized by the Guomindang government.[17] And the Guomindang government was brutal, corrupt and at first incompetent. Its rule of Taiwan started off badly. Chen Yi, who had been sent by Chiang to govern the island, quickly alienated the local people with his heavy-handed administration. On February 28, 1947, this led to what became known as the 2-28 Incident. Triggered by the arrest of a street vendor a mass uprising took place and Taiwanese briefly took over the island.[18] In response the Guomindang carried an even more violent repression in which 15,000–30,000 Taiwanese perished. For the next half a century, it was forbidden to even mention this incident, even uttering the numbers 2-28 (*er ershi-ba*) could result in imprisonment or worse. There were no public buses with that number.

Therefore, the arrival of Chiang's Guomindang loyalists in 1949 could have been hardly welcome; in fact, many Taiwanese were sympathetic to the Communists. Chiang reacted to his precarious situation on the island by declaring martial law in 1949, and it was not lifted for four decades. A forty-year period of repression commenced lasting to 1989. This was marked by White Terror, in which 140,000 Taiwanese were arrested and perhaps 4,000 executed for anti-regime activities or views. This included a large percentage of the country's intellectuals.

Welcomed or not by the local people, the Guomindang regarded itself as the sole legitimate government of all of China, the PRC was denounced as a bandit-regime, an illegitimate band of usurpers. Chiang and his government planned to use the island as a base for the eventual return to the mainland. Thus, in some respects the government in Taipei was a kind of government-in-exile, consisting of people for whom Taiwan was an alien land they hoped to leave. It differed from most governments-in-exile in that it controlled the place it was exiled in. One of the absurdities of the situation was since the ROC government claimed to be the government of all of China, Taiwan was theoretically one small province. The government was top heavy with bureaucrats who supposedly administered the mainland. This author remembers having an appointment near the office for Tibetan and Mongolian

Affairs. It was not clear what those in that office who were theoretically administering regions of China thousands of kilometers away could possibly have been doing.

On little Taiwan sat the National Assembly, the world's largest legislative body with 2,691 delegates. It was elected in 1947, fled to the island in 1949, and continued to exist without another election until 1991. New elections were to be held when the Guomindang retook the mainland. Taiwan was represented by just a few delegates, with the rest representing long-lost provinces on the mainland. As the aging delegates died, new ones were appointed in their place. In 1969 and 1972, Taiwan was given a few extra representatives, but they still only amounted to 4 percent of the total. Absurdly, 96 percent of the legislature still represented no one at all. All this didn't matter very much since the National Assembly was a rubber stamp body; the Republic of China was a dictatorship under Chiang Kai-shek and all power was in the executive.[19]

Meanwhile, the ROC depended on the United States for its survival. The United States still maintained some ambiguity over the legality of the Guomindang's takeover of Taiwan. Interestingly, in the 1952 Treaty of San Francisco in which the US occupation of Japan ended, Japan renounced any claim to Taiwan, but the treaty did not mention who controlled the island. Since the document was drawn up under the direction of the American government it indicated a lack of commitment in Washington toward the Guomindang's authority over Formosa as it was generally called at that time.

THE FIRST TAIWAN STRAIT CRISIS

In its first years the Republic of China (Taiwan) had a rather precarious existence. The big change came in 1954 when the PRC decided to move aggressively toward China. The Chinese premier Zhou Enlai declared his government's intention of gaining control of the island and putting an end to the Republic of China. The PRC began shelling the offshore islands of Quemoy (or Kinmen) and Matsu held by the ROC. Chinese leaders did not plan to retake the island which they did not have the navy to do so but to put pressure on it.[20] The shelling, nonetheless, alarmed officials in Washington as the American public viewed this as an act of communist aggression. In early 1955, amid the artillery barrages, the US Congress passed the Formosa Resolution establishing an American commitment to protect Taiwan. Shortly after, Taipei and Washington signed a Sino-American Mutual Defense Treaty that formally committed to the United States to the defense of the Republic of China. Some American military commanders called for strikes against the PRC, even the use of atomic weapons if it did not stop their aggression but the Chinese stopped the shelling. Three years later, Taiwan's defense treaty with the United States was tested. In 1958, PRC forces again began shelling Kinmen and Matsu. During this the Second Taiwan Strait Crisis the Americans supplied the Taiwanese with air to air missiles that shot down many PRC planes and Beijing ceased its actions against the two islands. The second crisis left Taiwan more secure.[21]

In what it called its "One China Policy" the PRC insisted that there was only one legitimate Chinese government, its own of course. Beijing regarded the existence of Taiwan as unfinished business from the Chinese Civil War. In its view Taiwan was the last province still held by the defeated, discredited Guomindang regime. It never wavered in its determination to bring that province back under its control but was stalemated by the US support for the ROC. The ROC had its own One China Policy, although it did not call it that. It continued to claim that it was the sole legitimate government of all China. Each year officials would proclaim their desire to "return to the mainland." Over the years this became increasingly unlikely since the Communist regime was well entrenched and there was no obvious desire on the mainland for a return to the rule by Guomindang (Nationalist Party). In fact, over time the ritualistic speeches by ROC leaders that the "situation was becoming ripe for the return to the mainland" became increasingly absurd.

Meanwhile, Taiwan was far from diplomatically isolated. When the Chinese Communist took power in 1949, the United States and its allies refused to recognize it nor allow it to take the Guomindang's seat in the United Nations. Thus, for more than two decades the government in Taipei represented China in the UN. Not only that, but as one of the major Allied Powers at the end of World War II, China was made one of the five permanent members of the Security Council along with the United States, the Soviet Union, Britain, and France. This meant that not only did the regime in Taipei occupy China's seat in the UN, it was one of five UN members to exercise a veto power. It was still recognized by many countries around the world as the legitimate government of China and therefore enjoyed diplomatic influence far beyond its modest size. It also acted to isolate China. The PRC insisted that it would not enter diplomatic relations with any country unless it broke off relations with Taiwan. Taiwan held the same position. Each country had to choose whether it would have formal relations with Beijing or Taipei.

TAIWAN BECOMES MORE ISOLATED

That little Taiwan was regarded by half the world and by the UN as representing all China was an absurdity that was prolonged by the tensions of the Cold

War, especially America's involvement in Vietnam, and China's inward turn during its Cultural Revolution. Inevitably, countries chose to have relations with Beijing, and even close American allies began to switch recognitions. Meanwhile, each year a proposal to allow the PRC to represent China at the UN instead of the ROC was put before the UN. Each year more members voted in favor. In the fall of 1971, there were enough votes in the UN to seat the regime in Beijing. Taiwan was no longer a UN member. This was a turning point. Taiwan was now diplomatically isolated except for its support from the United States. But even that began to waiver somewhat. In 1971, President Nixon, eager to use China as a counterweight to the Soviet Union and perhaps its assistance in getting out of Vietnam, started talks with China which led to his visit to the PRC in early 1972. At that time the two countries issued the Shanghai Communiqué. It stated the commitment of the two countries to work toward better relations. On the sensitive Taiwan issue, the United States acknowledged the One-China policy without actually endorsing Beijing's version of it. It also agreed to cut back on military installations in Taiwan.[22] It was rather ambiguous but still posed a potential threat to Taipei.

It was now a real possibility that the United States would abandon its support for Taiwan. Then in late 1978, what the regime in Taipei feared happened. President Carter decided to begin full diplomatic relations with the PRC which meant that at end of that year it broke off formal relations with the ROC. This was a shock. One newspaper trying to put a positive spin on events came out with the headline "Paraguay Confirms Its Support for the ROC." On the first of January 1980 the Sino-American Mutual Defense Treaty came to an end. This was an enormous blow to Taiwan, since almost every major country by 1979 had chosen to recognize PRC. Many in the United States felt uneasy with suddenly abandoning an ally, although the obvious farce of pretending the regime in Taipei was the sole government of China and not having relations with the world's most populous nation was generally appreciated. As a compromise the US Congress at the end of 1978 passed the Taiwan Relations Act.

The Taiwan Relations Act which is still in effect as of 2020, became Taiwan's lifeline keeping it from the threat of absorption into China. The act's complicated language also illustrates the complexity of the relations between Taiwan, China, and the United States. It states that Taiwan is to be treated under US laws the same as "foreign countries, nations, states, government or similar entities." That is the United States while not formally having relations, not having an embassy or an ambassador would maintain other institutions that acted like them. The de facto US embassy in Taipei became the American Institute in Taiwan. Interestingly, nowhere in the act is the term "Republic of China" mentioned since the United States, like all countries that have relations with Beijing, can no longer admit to such an entity. There is only one China. Instead, the act uses the term "governing authorities on Taiwan." The legislation was intended to provide reassurances to Taiwan that the United States did not abandon them and to serve as a warning to China not to try a military invasion. It states that the "United States will make available to Taiwan such defense articles and defense service in such quantity as may be necessary to enable Taiwan to maintain sufficient self-defense capabilities." The act stipulates that the United States will "consider any effort to determine the future of Taiwan by other than peaceful means, including boycotts or embargoes, a threat to the peace and security of the Western Pacific area and of grave concern to the United States." It does not state explicitly that the United States will come to the island's defense in case of a Chinese invasion. Nor does it clearly commit the United States to its defense. US troops stationed in Taiwan were withdrawn but the United States continued to sell advanced military weapons that would give Taiwan a creditable defense capacity and discourage any attempt by Beijing to reunite the two Chinas by force.[23]

The language of American-Taiwan relations is filled with what has been called "strategic ambiguity." It seeks to reassure Taiwan and its supporters in America that the United States will not allow the PRC to unilaterally take over the country but at the same time recognizes the importance of Beijing's "One China Policy" and of maintaining good working relations with China. At the same time, it seeks to dissuade the government of Taiwan from declaring its independence. If Taiwan were to declare independence, it would undermine the One China Policy and bring about a crisis in Asia that could easily lead to war. In 1982, under the Reagan administration the House of Representatives passed the Six Assurances that stated the United States would continue to abide by the Taiwan Relations Act and would not make deals with China on the status of Taiwan or concerning the defense of Taiwan without consulting the authorities Taipei.[24]

Taiwan's diplomatic isolation can at times borders on the bizarre. For example, Taiwan officials, including the presidents, cannot travel to most countries, in fact, to nowhere but the handful of mostly tiny states that recognize them. When Taiwanese presidents made an occasional overseas trip to the Caribbean or Latin American countries that had diplomatic relations with the ROC, they had to stop in the United States to transit. They could stay in the United States as long as it took to change planes and then only meet local officials. In 2018, the US Congress passed and President Trump signed the Taiwan Travel Act, which allowed senior American officials to visit Taiwan and senior Taiwan officials to visit the United States. Beijing was furious at what it considered a violation of the One China Policy.[25] In July 2018, in an unprecedented move, President Tsai Ing-wen took advantage of the new law to visit Denver and New York on the way to St. Kitts and

Nevis, St. Vincent and the Grenadines, St. Lucia and Haiti, countries that still recognized Taiwan. In New York she met with a delegation from the US Congress. She also met with American businessmen during her two-day stay in New York. This resulted in tensions as Beijing organized demonstrations in New York protesting the visit among pro-Beijing Chinese in the United States while large pro-Taiwan groups came out to support her.[26]

Taiwan desperately tried to maintain as many diplomatic recognitions as possible. But it was a difficult task since most countries were more interested in dealing with China, which became even more that case after the PRC began its period of economic growth in the 1980s and became one of the world's leading trading nations. Almost every major country broke off diplomatic relations. The exceptions were mostly small developing countries who found the benefits of economic trade and especially foreign aid from Taipei worth continuing ties. These included small Pacific Island nations and Central American countries which received generous assistance from Taiwan that made a significant impact on their small economies. Beijing, meanwhile, remained adamant on its position toward Taiwan, its "One China Policy." So important is this issue that it is written into the constitution of the People's Republic of China. The preamble states: "Taiwan is part of the sacred territory of the People's Republic of China. It is the lofty duty of the entire Chinese people, including our compatriots in Taiwan, to accomplish the great task of reunifying the motherland."[27]

THE TAIWAN MIRACLE

One of the ironies of Taiwan was as it gradually became more politically isolated it underwent a remarkable economic transformation. In the 1950s, it was a poor, agricultural land. It relied heavily on generous US foreign aid to finance the government and for general economic support. However, the Guomindang carried out reforms on the island that it had failed to do when it was in power on the mainland. The most important was land reform that converted the peasants into small independent farmers. It then provided assistance to boast agricultural production and living standards. It expanded public education until the country had among the world's highest literacy rates.[28] Thousands of Taiwanese went overseas for advance studies. In 1959, the government began a Nineteen-Point Program for Economic and Financial Reform that laid the blueprint from rapid industrial development. In 1964, it developed an export processing zone in the port of Kaohsiung, encouraging foreign investment into the country. Taiwan under Chiang Kai-shek's Guomindang regime used the state control of banks to lend to export oriented businesses. Under these policies, the economy in the 1960s and especially in the 1970s began booming, becoming at one time the fastest growing in the world. To keep the development momentum, in 1979, the state launched the Ten Major Construction Projects to improve infrastructure.[29]

By the 1980s Taiwan was lumped with South Korea, Hong Kong, and Singapore as one of Asia "Four Little Tigers," third world countries that were quickly transforming themselves into modern industrial states. Most of Taiwan's businesses were family-owned enterprises, small or medium in size rather than the huge conglomerates that characterize Japanese and Korean industry. However, despite their small size, Taiwanese firms were no less internationally competitive. Focusing on exports, starting with industries such those that made shoes for brand name companies and assembled electronic parts for foreign firms it moved on to a wide range of manufacturing.[30] Taiwan became in the 1980s and 1990s one of the world's largest exporters of manufactured goods with a role in the global economy much greater than its modest size would suggest. Graduates of Taiwan's highly competitive schools went on to study at many of the world's leading universities. Between 1954 and 1989, 115,000 Taiwanese earned advanced degrees overseas with United States being the main destination. During much of that time, Taiwan sent more students to American universities than any country, despite its modest size.[31] Some stayed overseas, yet many came back with cutting edge training and advanced knowledge in many fields contributing further to the country's dynamic economy.

While the term "economic miracle" has been used many times to describe spurts of high economic growth, Taiwan's transformation into a modern industrial society was extraordinary. Its economy grew by 9.2 percent annually in the 1960s, 10.2 percent in the 1970s, and 8.2 percent in the 1980s. No country had every grown at that rate. It was double that of Japan at that time, which was famous as an economic powerhouse.[32] Only South Korea came close. By the end of the twentieth century, Taiwan was becoming a first-world nation. By the 2000s, it had a per capita income on par with the richer countries of Europe. So fast did it grow that it is worth asking how it achieved this. It had some capital brought over from the mainland, but this was modest. Most of the growth was due to factors such as careful government planning, investment in infrastructure, technology transfer agreements, and the encouragement of foreign investment. Then there was the work ethic of the Taiwanese people, and perhaps more important their zeal of education that created a highly literate, numerate workforce. And Taiwanese were frugal, saving 26 percent of the income in the 1970s, one of the highest rates in the world.[33]

DEMOCRATIZATION AND "TAIWANIZATION"

Taiwan's economic modernization was accompanied by its political modernization. The corrupt and repressive rule of the Guomindang gave way to governance by competent technocrats. When Chiang Kai-shek died in 1975, he was replaced by his son Chiang Ching-kuo. The younger Chiang had been effectively administering the country in the last years of his father's rule, so the transition was undramatic. Following violent pro-democracy demonstrations in the port city of Kaohsiung in 1979, he undertook steps to liberalize the political system. A major goal of Chiang Ching-kuo was to heal the ethnic bitterness between the Mainland Chinese who politically controlled the country and the Taiwanese majority. This he did by democratizing the political system and by appointing ethnic Taiwanese to positions in the Guomindang Party and the government.[34] In 1984 he appointed a local native-born Taiwanese technocrat, Lee Tung-hui as his successor meaning that the state would no longer be run by the Guomindang gang that came over in 1949. In 1986, the regime permitted the formation of an opposition Democratic Progressive Party. Then martial law was lifted.

When Chiang Ching-kuo died in 1988 Lee Tung-hui became president and carried out further reforms. In 1991, the constitution was amended to make the National Assembly a real assembly and democratic elections were held for the first time on the island. Now all Assemblymen represented districts of Taiwan not phantom provinces on the mainland.[35] In 1998, the state organized the Compensation Foundation for Improper Victims to provide compensation to victims of the White Terror and their survivors. Most censorship was lifted and in 2000 in a freely contested election, the opposition Democratic Progressive Party (DPP) won. Its leader, a strong critic of the Guomindang, Chen Shui-bian, became president. He was re-elected in 2004. Unfortunately for the opposition, Chen and his wife were caught up in scandals that contributed to the victory of the Guomindang candidate Ma Ying-jeou in the 2008 elections, but by this time democratic rule had taken firm root in Taiwan. Under Ma Ying-jeou there was no return to the repressive past. Nor was there a halt to the growing sense of "Taiwaneseness" among the people of the island. Ma proudly called himself Taiwanese, stating he was raised on Taiwan water and Taiwan rice.[36] Nonetheless, in 2016, the DPP came back into power led by the country's first woman president Tsai Ing-wen. Democratic transfers of power were becoming routine.

Until the 1990s, ethnically Taiwanese Chinese, as opposed to the mainlanders, found themselves as second class citizens in their own country, much as they had under Japanese rule. In school Mandarin was the sole language of instruction. Taiwanese students learned all about Chinese history and geography and almost nothing about Taiwan. Mainlanders, that is, the Mandarin-speakers who arrived in the 1940s, received subsidized housing, and were favored for admission into the military and civil service. They often looked down on the Taiwanese speakers as "Taike" which meant country bumpkins or "rednecks."[37] When they became sick they were cared for in veterans' homes called "Homes for Men of Honor."[38] However, these advantages diminished over time as jobs in the private sector began to pay much better, and the subsidized housing became inferior to newer private housing. The former became more shabby overtime.[39] In the late 1980s a Taiwanese language movement began. It aimed at not only encouraging the use of spoken Taiwanese but making Taiwanese a written language.[40] The domination of the Mainlanders was ending, and Taiwan was becoming more Taiwanese.

By the early twenty-first century Taiwan was a democratic, middle-class prosperous society. Most Taiwanese accepted the democratic and free-market economic system. The sharpest political cleavage was over the status of Taiwan and how to deal with China. There were two political groupings: the Pan-Blue Camp (or Coalition) made up of the Guomindang and smaller allied parties, and the Pan-Green Camp (or Coalition) which consisted of the Democratic Progressive Party and the Taiwan Solidarity Party formed in 2001.[41] The Guomindang and of the Pan-Blue group backed what it called the "1992 consensus." This supported the PRC's One China Policy but interpreted it as meaning there was a single sovereign state that included mainland China and Taiwan. It left the question on which government was the legitimate one unstated. The Guomindang policy meant that there would be no permanently separate Taiwan state, and it accepted that both sides of the strait would be eventually be reunited. This position was acceptable to Beijing. What Beijing feared most was an independent Taiwan state that would be forever lost to China.

This ran counter to the Green Coalition position which wanted an independent Taiwan. Not a Republic of China but a republic of Taiwan. This was a sharp break since it meant that Taiwan was a separate nation, not part of China. But such a radical position was too provocative to openly espouse since it could bring about Chinese retaliation or even war. So Instead the Democratic Progressive Party argued that while it agreed with the "one China principle" this meant "One Country on Each Side." It also stated in a contradictory fashion that it believed in "one China, one Taiwan." The confusing, somewhat ambiguous, stand was necessary since an open call for independence was too risky to appeal to any but the most ardent Taiwanese separatists. Yet it was consistent in its main position: that the people of Taiwan have the right to determine their own status.

COPING WITH DIPLOMATIC ISOLATION

How does a country prosper, becoming an international exporter when few countries even acknowledge it as a sovereign state? When it faces a rising superpower determined to terminate its existence? By 2020 only fourteen countries—Belize, Eswatini (Swaziland), Guatemala, Haiti, Honduras, the Marshall Islands, Nauru, Nicaragua, Palau, Paraguay, Saint Kitts and Nevis, Saint Lucia, Saint Vincent and the Grenadines, and Tuvalu plus the Vatican—still had diplomatic relations with Taiwan. That number was dwindling fast as Beijing began an aggressive effort to sign aid agreements or whatever else was necessary to persuade the few holdouts into switching recognitions. The ROC conducted relations other most countries through the Taipei Economic and Cultural Representation Offices and smaller Taipei Economic and Cultural Offices (TECO). These functioned like embassies and consulates issuing visas, work permits, and offering services to Taiwanese living overseas. Countries carried out official business through various indirect channels such as the American Institute in Taiwan, which acts much as a US embassy but officially is a private institution. This author was once issued a visa at a China Airlines office. At international conferences and organizational meetings if the Taiwanese were invited at all they came as representatives of the strange entity: Chinese Taipei.

Meanwhile, the government of the ROC in 1991 modified the constitution so that it applied only to Taiwan. In a subtle way it was effectively abandoning the claim to be the government of all China, at least for now. China and Taiwan developed in the 1990s what both refer to as "cross-straits relations." In Taipei relations with mainland China are not conducted by the Foreign Ministry but by Mainland Affairs Council. The two governments China and Taiwan do not directly engage with each other. Talks are carried out through China's Association for Relations Across the Taiwan Straits (ARATS) and Taiwan's Straits Exchange Foundation.[42] They are theoretically private organizations not official ones, but both are in reality arms of their respective governments.

While China was the cause of Taiwan's diplomatic isolation, it also became its largest trading partner. In the 1990s, trade and contact with China expanded. As Taiwan grew into a mature economy its industries like those of other advanced industrial countries were looking for low wage places to move manufacturing and China was the most enticing choice. Taiwan's businesspeople had many advantages: they were right next door, spoke the same language, and shared much of the same culture. The PRC government saw Taiwanese business operations in China as not only a source of foreign investment and expertise but a way of integrating the economy of Taiwan into its own. Taiwan firms became among the major investors in China, especially in Fujian Province just across the Strait. The PRC did not issue visas to Taiwanese because this would suggest Taiwan was a foreign country, and likewise Taiwan didn't issue visas to businesspeople and travelers from the PRC for the same reason. There was only one China after all. So instead each issued special identity cards so that its nationals could travel back and forth.

President Ma after 2008 encouraged more cross-strait trade. Opinion polls showed the most Taiwanese supported this, but the majority were opposed to too much liberalization of trade with the mainland.[43] Meanwhile, the future of Taiwan was suggested by events in Hong Kong. In 1997, after long negotiations Britain turned Hong Kong over to Beijing, two years later the Portuguese colony of Macau also reverted to Chinese ownership. Now part of the PRC the two territories there were governed by the policy of "one state, two systems." Hong Kong and Macau were treated as special districts with their own laws, governments, and customs while China controlled their foreign affairs and defense. Ultimate authority over the two was in Beijing but the Chinese government pledged to minimize interference in their local affairs. This was seen as a model for administering Taiwan once it was reunited. Beijing after 1997 proudly pointed to Hong Kong's continued prosperity, its free press, and open lifestyle as an inducement for the Taiwanese.

However, Taiwan's future became more clouded by the more aggressive behavior of China under Xi Jinping. In January 2019, the Chinese leader declared "Taiwan must and will" be united with the mainland. He stated that reunification should be peaceful under the "One Country, Two Systems" arrangement for Hong Kong, but that independence would not be tolerated and that China "reserves the option of taking any measures that are necessary," to prevent outside forces that interfere with reunification and against Taiwanese separatists.[44] But the One Country Two Systems policy in Hong Kong began to look much less appealing. Under the hardline Xi who cracked down on any dissent and sought to strengthen the role of the Chinese Communist Party in directing and controlling the people, Hong Kong's freedom was being eroded. Beijing attempted to stifle free speech by kidnapping and arresting publishers who wrote books critical of the Chinese regime and its leaders. Then events in Hong Kong took a dramatic turn. An attempt by the Hong Kong authorities to pass an extradition treaty would allow Hong Kong citizens to be sent for to the mainland for trial resulted in massive protest demonstrations in 2019. Begun as a protest against the treaty, the movement widened to include demands for a democratically elected government in Hong Kong instead of the Beijing-appointed or Beijing-approved officials that governed the autonomous city. Beijing massed forces along the border and threatened to intervene. It was clear that the freedoms Hong Kong enjoyed since 1997 were being eroded. Then in the spring of 2020 Beijing placed Hong Kong under new national security laws and allowed its internal security forces to operate in the territory, effectively ending its political freedom. This could hardly be encouraging to those in Taiwan who thought some sort of similar arrangement might be an acceptable alternative to independence. The repression of the demonstrators by the Beijing-backed, widely hated government of Hong Kong led to a surge of support for the pro-independence DPP. In January 2020, the previously unpopular President Tsai won reelection in a landslide victory.

Taiwan was vulnerable to any aggressive measures by China. It could not compete with it militarily. Taiwan was a rich, technologically advanced country with modern, sophisticated armed forces equipped with advanced US weaponry. But China's military capacity far surpassed it. In 1996 during the major Straits crisis China's defense spending was twice that of Taiwan but by 2019 it was sixteen times. China developed its own advanced weaponry. To defend itself the United States advised Taiwan to follow what was called the "porcupine strategy" of smaller, cheaper and more mobile weapons. The policy was endorsed by the Tsai Ing-wen administration in 2017. It included intelligent sea mines that could evade sweeping, remote-controlled sentry guns for outer islands, armed drones to patrol its coastline, churning out hundreds of missiles placed on speed boats and unmarked trucks.[45] All these would not be able to stop a Chinese invasion but simply make one very costly. However, China would not need a military invasion to take the island but could simply cripple its economy by stopping trade with it and pressuring other countries to do the same. In practical terms, Taiwan was largely defenseless against a concerted effort by Beijing to retake the island.

BEING TAIWANESE VS BEING CHINESE

Are the people of Taiwan Chinese or Taiwanese? One of the oddities of the Republic of China is that it is the Republic of China, not the Republic of Taiwan. But Taiwan is different from the rest of China for several reasons. It has its own history. From 1895 to 1945 it was not part of China but part of the Japanese Empire, during which time the people evolved along their own path. Since 1949 it has had a very different history and trajectory than the rest of China. In fact, in the past 123 years it was only part of China for four years. China developed a communist system, went through the Great Leap Forward and the Cultural Revolution, experiences that profoundly impacted the people. Taiwan's recent history has been radically different. China made war with its own cultural traditions denouncing Confucianism as feudalistic, destroying much of its cultural heritage as backward and promoting atheism. None of this happened in Taiwan that saw itself as the preserver of the country's cultural heritage. While the PRC in more recent times has embraced much of its past culture, even Confucianism or elements of it, there is still a sharp difference in the way one society rejected and another worked within its cultural heritage. Another difference is that much more than China, Taiwan was profoundly influenced by the more open democratic societies of Japan and the West, especially the United States.

The Guomindang discouraged strong identification with Taiwan and emphasized a pan-Chinese identity with the people on the mainland. This began to change when under the Lee Tung-hui administration in 1988 in what was called "localization" promoted Taiwanese history and culture. The administration of Chen Shui-bian further promoted "Taiwanization." These efforts reflected the democratization of the country, but they also reflected a reassertion of Taiwanese identity that is increasingly shared by most of the population including the minority groups.

Then there is the fact that most of the people of Taiwan speak Taiwanese and identify with Taiwan, often more than they do with being Chinese. Since 1992 National Chengchi University has been conducting a survey every six months as to whether people identify as "Chinese," Taiwanese," or both. The data show a clear trend. In 1992, 17.6 percent identified as Taiwanese, and the number has grown over the years—in June 2016 it was 59.3 percent. The number who claim they are Chinese has declined from 25.5 percent in 1992 to 3.0 percent in 2016.[46] Another survey published in 2015 found 61 percent regarded themselves as Taiwanese only and 32 percent as Taiwanese and Chinese.[47] Analysis of surveys of identities finds that the younger people are more likely to identify strongly with being Taiwanese than are older ones.[48] In all surveys only a very small number, between 3 and 8 percent, considered themselves as Chinese only. What these all suggest is that for a majority of Taiwanese their Taiwanese identity is stronger than their Chinese identity. This appears to be truer of younger people. It suggested that after so many years as a separate country, despite the decades-long effort by the ROC government from 1949 to 2000 to promote a common Chinese identity, most people feel they are different. They might share a broader Chinese cultural identity, but their nation is Taiwan.

Taiwan, it should be pointed out, is not an ethnically homogenous society as some of our de facto states such as Nagorno Karabakh or Somaliland are, but is divided into Mainland Chinese, ethnically Taiwanese and smaller groups such as the Hakka and the indigenous peoples. The last are known today as *yuanzhumin* (original inhabitants).[49] The big division was between the politically dominant Mainland Chinese and the Taiwanese majority. Taiwanese went into business, Mainlanders into government. Mainlanders did not bother to learn Taiwanese and often lived in their own neighborhoods. But the divisions began to diminish over the years of rapid economic growth when the gap in wealth disappeared.[50] Even attitudes among the indigenous people of Taiwan have changed. Despite their small numbers, they have been active in asserting their identity. Interestingly, the attitude to Taiwanese of Chinese descent has changed too from seeing indigenous Taiwanese as an alien group to embracing them as part of the mix of cultures and historical traditions that makes Taiwan different from China.[51]

Chapter 9

TAIWAN STUCK IN INTERNATIONAL LIMBO

Taiwan started out as something akin to a government-in-exile, a government that once ruled one-quarter of the humanity found itself clinging to a small island off the coast, waiting for the day it could return to the mainland. Over the decades it evolved into a nation-state. But that evolution coincided with its increasing diplomatic isolation, its descent into de facto state status. What is the future of Taiwan? As of 2020 this was not clear. With a strong and growing sense of national identity, a large and dynamic economy, a democratic political order and an important member of the world economy, Taiwan is a significant, clearly defined state. In the past there were two reasons why Taiwan was not a nation-state. One was that the government was dominated by mainlanders who regarded the island as part of China and dreamed of returning to the "mainland." The other reason was that China regarded it as a province of China. Oddly both the government in Taipei and in Beijing agreed on the second point. Yet, today the mainlanders are no longer the dominate group; there has been a resurgence of Taiwanese cultural identity, and a substantial majority of the population regards their nation as Taiwan and would like to see a sovereign Republic of Taiwan. The problem is the People's Republic of China has become more determined than ever to "reunite" the country. Beijing can live with a Taiwan that still officially regards itself as part of China or at least is ambiguous about its status, that is, a Taiwan which would eventually become administratively absorbed into the PRC. It cannot accept an independent Taiwan that might be a de jure sovereign state and recognized by the international community as such.

The question then is, why not? And the answer is complex, but as we have seen it is difficult for countries to accept a loss of part of their sovereign territory. We can see this in other cases, for example, Serbia, or Georgia or Moldova. China's national agenda has included regaining all the territories "lost" during the age of imperialism when it was weak and backward. Regaining them is a symbol of its recovery, of its reemergence as a great political, economic, military, and cultural power. There is another factor as well. Along its periphery, lies groups that do not strongly identify with Chinese culture and have their own separatist tendencies—notably the Tibetans and the Uighurs. More recently separatist sentiment has emerged in Hong Kong. If Taiwan slips away it could encourage other disaffected parts of the state to try to do so. Furthermore, Taiwan was the product not of a secessionist conflict as is the case of most de facto states, but a civil war. Its absorption by the mainland is, in a sense, the last unfinished business of that war.

China is a great power. This means that Taiwan, whose economic prosperity should give it political influence, is isolated in the international community and unlikely to get much support. It seems highly unlikely that the Taiwanese people will ever seek to trade their de facto independence and personal freedom to be an outpost of an authoritarian China. Nor would China wish to create an international crisis or even military confrontation by retaking Taiwan by force, although this cannot be entirely ruled out. Thus, in 2021 it appeared that its strange ambiguous status is likely to remain in place for the conceivable future.

NOTES

1. John F. Copper, *Taiwan: Nation-State or Province?* (Boulder, CO: Westview Press, 2003), 2.
2. Steven Crook, *Taiwan* (Guilford, CT: Bradt Travel Guides, 2014), 6.
3. Copper, *Taiwan*, 2.
4. Copper, *Taiwan*, 9.
5. Copper, *Taiwan*, 14.
6. Copper, *Taiwan*, 32.
7. Shelly Rigger, *Why Taiwan Matters: Small Island, Global Powerhouse* (Lanham, MD: Rowman & Littlefield, 2011), 15.
8. John E. Wills, Jr., "The Seventeenth-Century Transformation: Taiwan Under the Dutch and the Cheng Regime," in Murray A. Rubinstein, editor, *Taiwan: A New History* (Armonk, NY: M.E. Sharpe, 1999), 84–106, p. 85.
9. Copper, *Taiwan*, 34–35.
10. Wills, "The Seventeenth-Century Transformation," 42–43.
11. James Davidson, *The Island of Formosa: Past and Present* (Oxford, UK: Oxford University Press, 1989), 52.
12. Copper, *Taiwan*, 40–42.
13. Steven Phillips, "Between Assimilation and Independence: Taiwanese Political Aspirations Under Nationalist Chinese Rule, 1945–1948," in Murray A. Rubinstein, editor, *Taiwan: A New History* (Armonk, NY: M.E. Sharpe, 1999), 275–319, 277.
14. Peter Chen-main Wang, "A Bastion Created, A Regime Reformed, An Economy Reengineered, 1949–1970," in Murray A. Rubinstein, editor, *Taiwan: A New History* (Armonk, NY: M.E. Sharpe, 1999), 320–38, 321.
15. Copper, *Taiwan*, 47.
16. Hsiao-ting Lin, *Accidental State: Chiang Kai-shek, the United States, and the Making of Taiwan* (Cambridge, MA: Harvard University Press, 2016), 2.
17. Phillips, "Between Assimilation," 285.
18. Phillips, "Between Assimilation," 292–96.
19. Copper, *Taiwan*, 118–19. Chiang's son Chiang Ching-kuo increased Taiwan's representation to 10 percent in 1980.
20. Pang Yang Huei, *Straits Rituals: China, Taiwan, and the United States in the Taiwan Strait Crises, 1954–1958* (Hong Kong: Hong Kong University Press, 2019), 94–95.
21. Huei, *Straits Rituals*, 280.

22. Rigger, *Why Taiwan Matters*, 178–79.

23. American Institute in Taipei, *Taiwan Relations Act*, https://www.ait.org.tw/our-relationship/policy-history/key-u-s-foreign-policy-documents-region/taiwan-relations-act/, Retrieved July 8, 2018.

24. The Taiwan Documents Project, *The Six Assurances to Taiwan*, http://www.taiwandocuments.org/assurances.htm, Retrieved July 9, 2018.

25. David Brunnstrom, "Trump Signs Taiwan Travel Act Angering China," *Reuters*, March 16, 2018, https://www.reuters.com/article/us-usa-taiwan-china/trump-signs-u-s-taiwan-travel-bill-angering-china-idUSKCN1GS2SN, Accessed July 31, 2018.

26. Rick Gladstone, "Taiwan President Risks Infuriating China with U.S. Visit," *New York Times*, July 11, 2019, imes.com/2019/07/11/world/asia/taiwan-president-united-states-china.html, Accessed July 28, 2018.

27. USC US-China Institute, *The Constitution of the People's Republic of China, 1982*, https://china.usc.edu/constitution-peoples-republic-china-1982, Accessed July 9, 2018.

28. Murray A. Rubinstein, "Taiwan's Socio-Economic Modernization, 1971–1996," in Murray A. Rubinstein, editor, *Taiwan: A New History* (Armonk, NY: M.E. Sharpe, 1999), 366–402.

29. Rubinstein, "Taiwan's Socio-Economic Modernization," 372–73.

30. Rubinstein, "Taiwan's Socio-Economic Modernization," 370–71.

31. Copper, *Taiwan*, 95.

32. Copper, *Taiwan*, 178.

33. Frank S. T. Hsiao and Mei-Chu Wang Hsiao, *Economic Development of Emerging East Asia: Catching Up of Taiwan and South Korea* (London: Anthem Press, 2017), 14.

34. Copper, *Taiwan*, 52–53.

35. Copper, *Taiwan*, 119.

36. J. Bruce Jacobs, "Introduction," in J. Bruce Jacobs and Peter Kang, editors, *Changing Taiwanese Identities* (London: Routledge, 2018), 1–11, 3.

37. Rigger, *Why Taiwan Matters*, 33.

38. Rigger, *Why Taiwan Matters*, 30–31.

39. Rigger, *Why Taiwan Matters*, 31.

40. Wi-run Taiffalo Chiung, "Languages under Colonization: The Taiwanese Language Movement," in J. Bruce Jacobs and Peter Kang, editors, *Changiing Taiwanese Identities* (London: Routledge, 2018), 39–63.

41. Rigger, *Why Taiwan Matters*, 81.

42. Saryu Shirley Li, *Taiwan's China Dilemma: Contested Identities and Multiple Interests in Taiwan's Cross-Strait Economic Policy* (Stanford, CA: Stanford University Press, 2016), 100–1.

43. Lin, *Taiwan's China Dilemma*, 181.

44. "Xi Jinping Says Taiwan Must and Will Be United with China," *BBC News*, January 2, 2019, https://www.bbc.com/news/world-asia-china-46733174.

45. *Economist*, "Dire Strait: Defending Taiwan," January 26, 2019, 31–33.

46. Jacobs, "Introduction," 5–6.

47. Wei-chen Tseng and Wei-han Chen, "'Taiwanese' Identity Hits Record Level," *Taipei Times*, January 25, 2015.

48. Tanguy Lepesant, "Taiwanese Youth and National Identity under Ma Ying-jeou," in J. Bruce Jacobs and Peter Kang, editors, *Changing Taiwanese Identities* (London: Routledge, 2018), 64–86.

49. Rigger, *Why Taiwan Matters*, 33.

50. Copper, *Taiwan*, 76–79.

51. In Chris Berry, "Taiwan's Indigenous Peoples and Cinema: From Colonial Mascot to Fourth Cinema?" in Bi-yu chang and Pei-yin Lin, editors, *Positioning Taiwan in a Global Context: Being and Becoming* (London: Routledge, 2019), 228–41.

Chapter 10

Not Quite De Facto States

INTRODUCTION

We have examined some of the de facto states in the twenty-first century, states that are on borderline between "real" countries and not countries at all. There are other self-proclaimed states that can be called "not quite *de facto* states." Although some have obtained a degree of legal recognition, they possess fewer of the features of a sovereign state. Some are governments in exile that have no territory or population at all. Some are part of active rebellions with fluctuating borders. Sometimes called "ephemeral states," the latter lack the territorial stability and endurance of our de facto states. Most have not developed the institutional capacity to carry out the basic functions of government. This chapter will look at some of these, noting that some come closer than others to being de facto states.

VATICAN CITY: RECOGNITION WITHOUT STATE

One of the world's geopolitical oddities is the Vatican City. Rather than a state with limited recognition the Vatican City is a case of recognition with limited state, that is, it is a de jure state but not a real country. It is recognized by most of the international community as a sovereign state and maintains formal diplomatic recognition with most of the world's countries. With an area of only 110 acres (44 hectares) and less than 1,000 residents, it is the smallest in size and population of any sovereign state. It also has the world's lowest birthrate. A tiny city state, surrounded by the much larger city of Rome, and ruled by the Roman Catholic pope, it is truly a geopolitical oddity. It is the world's lone ecclesiastical state, its last sacerdotal-monarchical state, that is, a state where the absolute ruler holds priestly as well as temporal authority.

This tiny state, so small that eight would fit in New York's Central Park was created by the Lateran Treaty of 1929 between the Italian government of Mussolini and the Roman Catholic Church. From the eighth century to 1870, the Bishop of Rome, better known as the Pope, was not only the head of the Roman Catholic Church but the ruler of territories in central Italy also. The Papal States covered quite a large chunk of Italy including the city of Rome. When Italy was unified in 1861 much of these territories were absorbed into the new Kingdom of Italy. This happened under Pope Pius IX who resented the loss of papal territory. Once regarded as a liberal reformer, he became a staunch supporter of tradition and the power and privileges of the papacy. Pius issued the *Syllabus of Errors* in 1864 denouncing liberalism, modernism, secularization and the separation of state; a few years later he decreed the doctrine of papal infallibility. This, however, did not prevent him from losing the rest of his political domain when in 1870 the last remaining Papal territory, the city of Rome and some area around it was also annexed. Pius IX, the longest reigning pope in Church history, stayed in the Vatican section of Rome where the vast Basilica of St. Peter and the papal residence was located. The Italian state left him and his successors alone. A kind of standoff between the Italian state and the Vatican began. Benito Mussolini resolved this by recognizing the sovereignty of the Holy See and placing the Vatican City outside the authority of the Italian government.

We mentioned the Vatican City as a sovereign state but that is not correct. It is the Holy See that is sovereign. The Holy See and the Vatican City are considered two separate entities under international law. The Holy See, a strange term, refers to the Bishop of Rome, that is the Pope, and it also refers the Roman Curia, the central government of the Roman Catholic Church. The Holy See manages a vast international organization that administers the spiritual needs of the world's one billion Catholics and runs the largest private education and healthcare system in world. It also maintains bilateral diplomatic relations with 172 sovereign states, signs agreements and treaties with them, engages in international diplomacy, and is a member of many international governmental organizations. At the UN it has permanent observer status, the only other entity to have this is Palestine. It may seem odd that the Holy See has a status in international law nearly the same a sovereign state, but this has proved useful for the Catholic Church in managing its international network of charities and holdings. And the Holy See often plays a useful role as a sort of neutral broker in international diplomacy.

But for all its de jure status and wide recognition, the Holy See is a person and an organization not a state. Nor is the Vatican City itself really a state. It has territory, a government, the capacity to enter into relations with other states, but it has no permanent population. Its status as a state, is simply a useful legal fiction.

PALESTINE: LIMITED STATE WITH RECOGNITION

The other permanent observer state in the UN is the State of Palestine. Also like the Vatican City, or more properly the Holy See, it has more recognition as a sovereign state than the reality of one. As of 2021, it was recognized as a sovereign state by 138 countries. It is a member of many international organizations including the International Olympic Committee, the G77, the Arab League, and the Organization of Islamic Cooperation. However, despite this diplomatic support, Palestine is far from a sovereign state. Palestinian Liberation Organization, an umbrella group of various Palestinian nationalist groups, declared the independence of the State of Palestine in 1988 with Palestine Liberation Organization (PLO) chairman Yasser Arafat as president. But this was only a gesture typical of national independence movements. However, in the 1990s, with the creation of a semiautonomous Palestinian Authority that was governing parts of Palestine, the state began to have some semblance of reality.

Palestine by any measure is a curious entity. It is made of two disconnected territories: the West Bank and the Gaza Strip. The West Bank, that is on the west bank of the Jordan River which separates it from the state of Jordan, is surrounded on three sides by Israel with a border with Jordan on its east marked not only by the Jordan River but also by the Dead Sea. The second piece of territory, the Gaza Strip, is a sliver of land wedged between Egypt and Israel. The two are separated by more than 160 kilometers (100 miles) of Israel but, that might be thousands of miles apart since direct travel between the two is not permitted by Israel. The total area is of Palestine is 6,020 square kilometers (2,320 square miles) of which 5,860 square kilometers (2,262 square miles) is in the West Bank and 365 square kilometers (141 square miles) is in the Gaza Strip. It has a population as of 2019 of 5 million. 3.2 million people live in the West Bank and 1.8 million in the Gaza Strip. It claims Jerusalem as its capital, however, Jerusalem is the official capital of Israel which doesn't recognize Palestine's claim to the city. The West Bank city of Ramallah functions as the administrative center.

The entire area of what is now Israel, Palestine, and Jordan was part of the Ottoman Empire for centuries and then became the British Mandate of Palestine at the end of World War I. When the British were planning to withdraw the UN's plan was to partition Palestine west of the Jordan River into Israel and a Palestinian state. This plan was rejected by the Arabs which opposed the creation of an Israeli state in what they considered Arab land. When Israel became independent in May 1948, its Arab neighbors invaded and were defeated by the Israelis. Some of the intended state of Palestine was annexed by Israel some by Jordan. The area of the Gaza Strip was under Egyptian authority. While with the collapse of the European colonial empires after World War II most their imperial subject became independent, the Palestinians remained a people under foreign rule. An All-Palestine Government Authority was established in Gaza but had little real independence and was abolished in 1959 when Egypt assumed direct rule over it. All the Palestinian territories fell under Israeli occupation during the Six Day War in 1967.

The State of Palestine was officially proclaimed by the PLO under its chair Yasser Arafat at a meeting in Algiers on November 15, 1988. It was only a government in-exile, there was no Palestinian state. But the Israeli government and the PLO began secret negotiations in Oslo that led to the Oslo I Accord and the Oslo II Accord. The first signed between Israel and the PLO in Washington in 1993 was held by many as a breakthrough in the Palestinian-Israeli conflict.[1]

The Oslo II Accord signed in Taba, Egypt in 1995 spelled out the process by which the Palestinians and the Israeli would share the administration of Palestine. The West Bank was divided into Areas A, B, and C. Area A is exclusively administered by the Palestinian Authority. In Area B the Palestinian Authority and Israel shared administration, and Area C is exclusively under Israeli control. The later area is majority Israeli—home to nearly 400,000 Israelis living in 135 settlements and well as 100 other outposts not recognized by the Israeli government. About 300,000 Palestinians live in Area C. The Palestinian Authority administers education and medical care for the Palestinians in Area C but does not control public works and has no authority over the settlements. Area C contains the most territory containing 60 percent of the West Bank's territory. Thus, the Palestinian Authority has administrative authority over only about 40 percent of the West Bank's land area.[2]

The Oslo Accords gave limited administrative autonomy to the Palestinians, or most of them, but did not deal with many contentious issues. These included: what the borders of the Palestine State would be, the status of Jerusalem which both sides claim as their capital, and especially contentious was the issue of Israeli settlements. The UN has repeatedly condemned the settlements as illegal, but the Israelis have not recognized this legal argument. Things became even more complicated when in 2007 the Gaza Strip came under the rule of Hamas, an organization that Israel regards as a terrorist group that has links with Iran which does not recognize Israel's right to exist, and that is a rival to the PLO.

Palestine if it were a sovereign state would be among the world's geographically strangest. Not only is it divided into two parts separated by Israel, the West Bank areas A and B that are under or partially under the Palestinian Authority are divided into 165 areas of land that are not contiguous. This is a contrast to the Israeli settlements that form a connected swathe of land that isolate the Palestinians into little pockets. Since the West Bank fell under Israel's control in 1967, Jewish settlements have been established. The Palestinians, the United States and the international community has periodically called for a halt to these, but Israeli religious conservatives who see this as part of the chosen land, and more nationalist elements have pressured the democratic government of Israel to allow these. As these have expanded, they have further fragmented the territory under the Palestinian Authority.[3]

In some ways Palestine as a state resembles the Sahrawi Arab Democratic Republic, an Arab state with considerable political recognition and support, although the SADR does not have as much of either. Yet, in some ways Palestine is less of a state. It does not have a uniform government since the Gaza Strip is under a different administration than the West Bank, it is as much as two states as one. The Palestinian Authority does not completely control any territory; the Polasario government in the SADR at least has sovereign control over a perhaps 40,000 square kilometers (16,000 square miles) of desert. And although mostly controlled by Morocco, the Western Sahara has more clearly defined borders.

Since 2007, the Gaza Strip has had a separate government from the West Bank. In elections in 2006 the Hamas party won control over the rival Fatah group that dominated the Palestinian Liberation Organization and the Palestinian Authority. In following year Hamas ousted Fatah for Gaza. The United States, Israel and the EU all regard Hamas as a terrorist organization with links to Iran. Sanctions were placed on the Gaza Strip that isolated it and resulted in considerable hardship. In some ways the Gaza Strip became a de facto sovereign state on its own. Its internal affairs were not controlled by anyone. If it is regarded as a state it would be the third most densely populated one after Monaco and Singapore. Close to 2 million people are packed into its tiny area 41 kilometers (25 miles) long and 6–12 kilometers (3.7–7.5 miles) wide. And even part of this is an uninhabitable buffer zone. But it neither claims to be sovereign nor is it recognized as such. Instead it is regarded as under "indirect occupation" by Israel. Israel commands the air and maritime space, as well as six of the seven land crossings (the seventh is controlled by Egypt). Gaza is also dependent on Israel for water electricity and telecommunications links, and the Israelis claim the right to move troops into the territory anytime they feel it is necessary. So, it cannot be considered a state in any real sense.

As of 2021 the State of Palestine is not yet a state, not even a de facto one. It has only limited autonomy, most major decisions still need Israeli approval. It has the potential for a nation-state. Palestinians have a strong sense of collective national identity; they feel themselves to be a nation. It is not a nationalism with a long history but one the emerged with the creation of the state of Israel and the shared sense of loss, suffering and struggle to achieve independence that followed. It has a population of 5 million, many well educated and with some experience in self-governance. One could easily see a dynamic, independent nation-state of Palestine becoming part of the international community. But not within its present unworkable borders. And there is the problem of the Palestinian diaspora; in 2020, 400,000 Palestinians were living in southern Lebanon and 1.9 million in Jordan. A few returned to Palestine after the Palestinian Authority was set up but these needed the permission of Israel to do so, and in any case the limited economic opportunity does not make it a very attractive place to return.[4] Would an independent Palestine include parts of Jordan and Lebanon which are mostly Palestinian?

The Israeli-Palestinian conflict has been a seemingly intractable one, with hardliners on both sides making a solution very difficult. In this way, it is not very different from those that revolve around the other de facto states which also are complicated by decades or even generations-long conflicts such as among Armenians and Turks, between Greeks and Turks, Georgians and Abkhaz, or between Chinese on Taiwan and the mainland. Yet although people involved in these ethnic/tribal conflicts often trace them back to ancient enmities they are mostly modern conflicts, created by modern events and encased in modern identities. And they can change.

KURDISTAN

Another candidate for a de facto country is the Kurdistan Regional Government (KRG) in northern Iraq. It has many of the characteristics of a real country but does not claim to be independent. It has a territory, a government that effectively controls that territory with minimum outside interference, and a population that recognizes the government and identifies with the territory. It has an army, as well as a flag and a strong sense of nationhood. But the KRG does not claim to be or is recognized as anything but an autonomous region. Many of its people see themselves not as Iraqi or even as members of the KRG but as part of a larger non-existent country: Kurdistan.

Kurds are, it is often said, the largest nation without a state. Kurds live in the mountains and highlands of the Middle East extending across eastern Turkey, northern Iraq, western Iran, and northeastern Syria and spilling over a bit into the Caucasus. Like the peoples of the Caucasus, the mountains have protected them from assimilation by the larger groups around them: the Turks, Arabs, and Iranians. As a popular saying goes, "the Kurds have no friends but the mountains"[5] Historically a rural folk of nomadic or semi-nomadic livestock herders and of farmers, today most Kurds live in cities. No one quite knows how many Kurds there are since afraid of discrimination, many do not make their cultural identity clear, 30 million is a good guess. Around 15 million live in Turkey where they make up nearly 20 percent of the population. Eight million are in Iran accounting for 11 percent of the nation's total, 2 million reside in Syria constituting about 10 percent of that country's population. There are also 200,000 Kurds in the former Soviet Union and about 1 million in Europe.[6] All speak Kurdish which is really not one, but several closely related languages that are more distantly related to Persian. Mostly Sunni Muslims, for all their differences they share a common culture, traditions, and sense of themselves as distinct from their Arab, Turkish, and Iranian neighbors.

In the early part of the twentieth century the wave of nationalism that swept across the non-Western world reached many of them who developed a concept of being a nation-Kurdistan. The British promised them creation of a homeland for then during World War I but this did not happen. Instead the Kurds found themselves eventually divided into: Turkey, with the largest share, Iraq, Iran, and Syria. For three generations various Kurdish groups have arisen in each of these countries with the aim of national self-determination. Because of these nationalist secessionist movements, Kurds have found themselves a persecuted, discriminated against minority in all the states they live. In more recent decades, nationalist sentiment has only increased in response to the centralizing tendencies of the Turkish, Iraqi, and Syrian governments and their attempts to create a "state nationalism."[7]

Kurdish aspirations for national independence can be compared to that of the Poles before World War I. Like the Kurds, the Poles had a strong sense of being a distinct people with a shared cultural identity and a desire for national liberation but found themselves divided by three empires: the German, the Austro-Hungarian, and the Russian. Independence at the start of the twentieth century seemed improbable. Yet opportunity occurred when at the end of World War I all three empires simultaneously collapsed and a Polish state emerged. It might take a similar and unlikely upheaval in all the four states they find themselves for a unified Kurdish nation to emerge. In Turkey, the Kurds have faced a strong, stable, highly nationalistic Turkish state that denied even the existence of Kurds, labeling them "Mountain Turks." A Kurdish resistance movement the PKK has carried on a decades-long struggle for autonomy but has not been very successful. In Iran, at the aftermath of World War II, the Kurds succeeded with the help of the Soviet Union in creating a short lived Kurdish Republic of Mahabad in 1946, but when the Soviets withdrew from Iran it collapsed.[8] The Iranian state has been too strong and repressive for Kurdish separatist movements to flourish. Kurds in Iraq and Syria, however, were able to create two semi-states: the KRG and Rojava as the result of wars and civil conflicts that engulfed their host countries.

THE KURDISTAN REGIONAL GOVERNMENT

The Kurdistan Regional Government (KRG) was established in 1992 in the aftermath of the Gulf War. Iraq itself was a creation of British colonialism when three Ottoman vilayets or provinces—those of the Arab-speaking Basra and Baghdad and the predominantly Kurdish vilayet of Mosul—were united in the 1920s. Initially the Kurdish region had some autonomy, but this disappeared over time. Iraqi Kurds revolted against the government of Baghdad in 1961 led by Mulla Mustafa Barzani. A peace was arranged in 1970 but when Iraq went to war with Iran a decade later, many Kurdish leaders supported Iran with hopes of achieving independence. Kurdish nationalist sentiment in Iraq only grew. A factor in creating a sense of nationalism in Iraqi Kurdistan has been the urbanization of the country. In a process roughly similar to Western Sahara, rapid urbanization brought people of different tribes and clans together. In the 1960s, 1970s, and 1980s the mechanization of agriculture, the growth of the oil industry, as well some other industries such as the tobacco industry changed the country from a rural land of shepherds and farmers to a predominantly urban society.[9]

Kurdish independence fighters in the mountainous north of Iraq were brutally attacked by the Saddam Hussein regime but not decisively defeated. The most notorious incident was the Iraqi government's use of poison gas to kill thousands of villages during its Anfal campaign. An appalling 100,000 civilians were killed, 3,000 villages were destroyed, and 500,000 people, about a sixth of the population, became homeless.[10] When the Kurds rose up again in the Gulf War, the US-led coalition forces carried out Operation Provide Comfort which cleared the Kurdistan of Iraqi troops and provided a no-fly zone. This was done mainly as a humanitarian effort to prevent another mass slaughter of Iraqi Kurds but with effective Iraqi rule in the region at an end the Kurds set up the Kurdistan Regional Government 1992, a state within a state. In 2003 following the Iraq War, a new Iraqi constitution guaranteed its autonomy. For an entire generation, the Kurds from their capital in Erbil have managed their own affairs. It is a substantial state of 48,861 square kilometers (18,093 square miles) and a population of about 6 million. It has its own armed forces, the Peshmerga.

The Kurds wanted full independence, but this was denied to them by the United States that held to the principle of maintaining stable international borders. The United States may have promoted regime change in Iraq but was committed to the territorial integrity of the country. This is the same pattern we have seen in other cases. The international community of states after the breakup of the colonial empires which so many members enthusiastically encouraged has been reluctant to see any changes in the borders of the UN members. So, like the Somalilanders or the Abkhaz there has been little support for their independence cause. Meanwhile, while the rest of Iraq was in turmoil, the KRG was an island of relative stability, semi-democratic government, and prosperity. The prosperity came from oil which under a revenue sharing agreement with the government in Baghdad it earned enough money to carry out a construction boom. For all its autonomy and obvious desire for independence the KRG is still part of Iraq, and Kurdish officials had a junior role in the central government. Erbil and Baghdad quarreled out the division of oil revenues. A particularly contentious issue was the dispute with Baghdad over the city control of Kirkuk. Kirkuk was once a Kurdish city, but Saddam moved Arabs into the city and it became ethnically mixed.

Besides enjoying some stability and prosperity, the KRG has also been one of the more politically open societies in the region. The is a free press and elections. However, internal politics, has been marred by a struggle between two ruling groups: the Kurdistan Democratic Party KDP and dominated by the Masoud Barzani and his family and the Patriotic Union of Kurdistan PUK dominated by Jalal Talabani. The two parties KDP and PUK in the 1990s had at one time rival governments in Irbil and the second city of Sulaymaniyah. The two factions fought a civil war that cost 3,000 lives until the United States brokered a peace in 1998. In 2006 the two rival governments were unified.[11] The KRG has moved a long way from toward creating a national identity that has overridden tribal and clan ones but its politics has been still dominated by two families and their patronage networks. Not all Kurds have been happy with this and demonstrations took place in 2011 protesting corruption and the family dominated political system.[12] There is an emerging civil society and a relatively free press, at least by Middle Eastern standards. The Kurds have gone further than most Middle Eastern people in promoting gender equality and in many ways the KRG is a model progressive state in the region.

The rise of ISIS gave the Kurdistan a good scare. In 2014 ISIS captured the neighboring city of Mosul then advanced within 20 miles of Erbil before being stopped with the help of US air strikes.[13] ISIS was driven out of the region and Mosul was recaptured by the Iraqi government with American assistance, however, the defeat of the Islamic Caliphate did not bring peace to the region. Instead a resurgent Iraqi government threated to chip away at the KRG's autonomy. Then the 2017 the KRG carried out a referendum on independence; 92 percent voted in favor. It was declared illegal by the Iraqi government and received no international support. Iraqi forces then retook control over Kirkuk. As a punishment Baghdad cut Erbil's share of oil revenue, this along with the fall in oil prices was a severe economic below to what had been a booming economy.

KRG proved to be still dependent on the government in Baghdad as well as US support, and it remained surrounded by potential hostile states: Turkey,

Iran, and an Arab-dominated Iraq and its foremost military protector, the United States, was eager to disengage from the region, while Turkey, its most important trading partner and main avenue to the outside world, remained hostile to the idea of an independent Kurdish state on its border. The Turks feared that would encourage its own Kurdish minority to seek the same for themselves. As of 2020, independence for the KRG in the foreseeable future appeared unlikely.

ROJAVA: THE OTHER KURDISTAN "NEAR STATE"

For a few years another Kurdish state was emerging. Officially named the Autonomous Administration of North and East Syria, it was a de facto autonomous region if not a de facto state in northeastern Syria. The Kurds called it Rojava "where the sun sets." Covering 48,000 square kilometer (19,000 square miles) and 2 million people it was large enough to function as state. Rojava contained some of the most fertile land in Syria as well as most of Syria's modest oil reserves.[14] Its capital was the city of Qamishli. The region is considered by many Kurdish nationalists as one of the four parts of their homeland.

As elsewhere, Syrian Kurds suffered from ethnic discrimination and persecution. In the 1970s, the government in Damascus seized land from tens of thousands of Kurds, evicted families from their villages, and gave the land to Arab families in an effort to absorb the region. Many Kurds were stripped of their citizenship becoming stateless. As in the case of Iraq, persecution by the central government only increased nationalist sentiment. Then in 2012, early in the Syrian Civil War, Syrian forces withdrew from the area. In the vacuum the underground Kurdish group took over. The main group the Democratic Union Party (PYD) joined with another, the Kurdish National Council, to form the Kurdish Supreme Committee. This government created the People's Protection Units the (YPG). Both have links with the PKK, the Kurdish resistance movement in Turkey. The YPG aided by the United States proved to be effective fighters capturing important strategic towns and becoming a part of the resistance to both the Syrian regime of Bashir Assad and ISIS.

By 2019, Rojava began to function more and more like an independent state. With the help of international aid agencies, infrastructure was being repaired, schools were functioning, and its towns were enjoying a mini-boom in construction. Like the KRG, Rojava pursued a fairly progressive agenda, being more open, democratic and tolerant than its neighboring states (except perhaps Turkey). It is secular, and women enjoy greater rights and freedom than in most of the Middle East. Polygamy is outlawed and every government office is co-led by both a man and a woman.[15] But there were some major differences with the KRG. Unlike the northern Iraq state which is ethnically overwhelmingly Kurdish, Rojava had a more mixed population. Although the government was dominated by the Kurdish PYD and protected by the Kurdish YPG, the population was divided roughly equally by Arabs and Kurds. In fact, Arabs may have made up a majority, although with the population in flux in the region hard statistics were difficult to obtain.

In response the government in late 2018 renamed the country the "Autonomous Administration of northern and eastern Syria," and moved the capital from the Kurdish city of Qamishli to the Arab town of Ain Issa. Still the Kurds were very much in charge and reports were that the Arabs felt alienated.[16] Rojava, to use the less awkward name, was especially precarious. Unlike the KRG it did not have UN recognition (as an autonomous entity) and it faced threats from ISIS, from the Syrian government as it regained control over the country, and from Turkey which regarded it as a potential base for PKK terrorism. In fact, there were ties with between the PYD and the PKK although the government of Rojava aware of the danger of a hostile Turkey was careful to disassociate itself from the Kurdish rebels in Turkey.

Rojava in 2019 appeared to be even less likely to achieve independence than the KRG. Even its status as an autonomous region seemed to be problematic as the government of Bashir Assad with Russian and Iranian support succeeded in regaining control over the country, and Turkey remained suspicious of an autonomous Syrian Kurdish government that had historic ties to the PKK. Even the KRG was unable to lend much support for fear of alienating Turkey. Furthermore, complicating the efforts by the Kurds of Rojava to achieve autonomy, was the fact that unlike mostly ethnically homogeneous KRG, Rojava had a large Arab minority as well as smaller Assyrian and Turkmen ethnic groups. Isolated, and largely friendless, the Kurdish Syrian region did not have very good prospects for becoming even a de facto state. Then in late 2019 President Trump in a surprise move decided to permit Turkey to move into the border regions and to withdraw US troops that had been protecting the Kurds. Turkish forces entered and the retreating Kurdish forces looked to its former foe, the Assad regime, for help. Any dream of an independent Syrian Kurdish state seemed to have come to an end. Rojava then turned out to another "ephemeral state," too impermanent to be considered a sovereign state even if it had claimed to be one.

LUHANSK PEOPLE'S REPUBLIC AND THE DONETSK PEOPLE'S REPUBLIC

Ukraine has been a country torn between a desire to be associated with the West and with Russia. Roughly speaking, the central and western parts of the country are overwhelmingly Ukrainian speaking and tend to be pro-Western. The eastern region is majority Russian speaking and pro-Russian. Pro-Russian sentiment was especially strong in the eastern Donbass region that was added to the Ukrainian Soviet Socialistic Republic when it was created in 1922. In February 2014, a popular uprising in Kiev overthrew the pro-Russian Ukrainian government of Viktor Yanukovych after he withdrew from talks with the EU. A pro-Western government emerged. In the Donbass region pro-Russian separatists seized control of the Donbass cities of Luhansk and Donetsk and in April proclaimed the People's Republics of Luhansk and Donetsk.

The People's Republic of Donetsk established on April 7, 2014, is the larger of the two self-proclaimed states. Its claims authority over the entire province of Donetsk, however, the separatist government controlled the two principle cities of Donetsk and Horlivka, most of the territory of the province was held by the Ukrainian government. The other state, the Luhansk People's Republic occupies several thousand square miles of territory and has perhaps, 1.5 million people. On May 11, 2014, both breakaway republics held referendums in which they reported overwhelming majorities favoring independence from Ukraine. With Russian support they have been fighting the government of Ukraine since.[17] The war between the central government in Kiev and the rebel regions remained stalemated as of early 2020. It has been a costly drain on Ukraine and also on Russia which has supported the two militarily and economically. Hundreds of Russian troops supposedly acting as volunteers have died in the conflict.

While Russia supports the two republics surreptitiously sending military equipment and Russian volunteers to help, it does not officially recognize either. It does recognize identity papers, driver's licenses and other documents issued by the two republics. Donetsk and Luhansk are recognized only by each other and by South Ossetia. Abkhazia was going to recognize them but decided against it after the breakaway regions entered talks with Ukraine about autonomy. And this reflects the fact that the people of the two regions do not wish to be sovereign states but to be free of direct control from Kiev. The first choice for many would be joining Russia, but since Moscow has already assumed costly international sanctions for annexing Crimea it was reluctant to annex these two areas.

In the fall of 2014 members of the OSCE and representatives from the rebel regions met in Minsk to work out a settlement. This failed and a second attempt was made in 2015 when Russia, Ukraine, Germany, and France worked out a series of protocols called Minsk II that it hoped would end the fighting. The agreement, a very complex one that aimed at providing greater autonomy for the regions in return for their acceptance as part of the state of Ukraine, was never fully implemented and the fighting continued. By 2020, more than ten thousand had been killed in the conflict, a third of them civilians. According to US State Department estimates from 2014 to 2018 about 400–500 Russian troops have been killed. Moscow officially denies that its armed forces are directly involved in the conflict. The future of the two states seemed uncertain. A possible outcome would be for the two republics with perhaps Russia's blessing to gain partial or full autonomy within the Ukraine state.

The case for considering the two breakaway separatist states as de facto sovereign states is shaky. Other than their core cities they control an indeterminate amount of territory. That is, they do not have clearly defined borders but shifting battle lines. Furthermore, it has not been the desire of the rebels to create permanents states but to be annexed to Russia. However, Russia has not shown any intention of doing so.

KACHIN STATE

One rebel territory that comes close to being a de facto state is Kachin State in northern Myanmar. This breakaway political entity controls most of the Kachin province of Myanmar, a rugged mountain region of bordering Yunan province of China. It's a territory of about 89,000 square kilometers (34,000 square miles), with about million and a half people; 300,000 live in the capital, its main city of Myitkina. The majority are Kachins, a mostly Christian minority group, numbering about 1 million living in a predominantly Buddhist country. Kachin is under the administration of the Kachin Independence Organization (KIO). Formed in 1961 with the goal of creating a separate state. The KIO has through its armed wing the Kachin Independence Army been fighting the government of Myanmar (formerly Burma) ever since. There was a ceasefire from 1994 and 2011, but as of 2021 fighting has continued with the Myanmar military carrying out air attacks on both fighters and civilians. That such a small group has been able to resist the Myanmar forces for over half a century in this little reported conflict is remarkable. Partly it is a tribute to the discipline of the Kachin fighters. The rugged mountainous and forested terrain of their homeland and the border with China with which they carry out trade has also enabled the Kachins to survive despite many military campaigns by the Myanmar army.

The Kachins are a group of six related peoples, the largest and dominant one is the Jingpaw (also known as Jingpo). They live in the highest mountains of Myanmar, wedged up against the border of Yunnan Province in China. Although their language (or languages since opinion differs if there is one language with many dialects or if they are different languages) is related to Burmese, their culture is not. By religion, ethnicity and tradition they are quite different from the dominant Burmese or Bamar ethnic group that makes up 70 percent of the people of Myanmar and dominates the political life of the country. The remoteness of their homeland, and traditions of independence, typical of many mountain folk, meant they were never fully under effective control of either the British colonial rulers or the Burmese government after Burma's independence in 1948. In the late nineteenth and early twentieth century, Western missionaries, mostly American Baptist converted them to Christianity and created a written language.[18] Based on the Jingpo dialect it is written in the Latin rather than in the Burmese alphabet. The religion and writing system only reinforced their differences with the Burmese, and it has assisted in fostering a sense of their own nationhood.

The origins of the Kachin State can be traced to World War II. During this time northern Burma briefly had great strategic value. The territory of the Kachins was a key link between Republic of China fighting the Japanese and its British and American allies. The famous Stillwell Road (also called the Ledo Road) ran through it. Myitkyina airport may have been the busiest in the world between 1942 and 1944. The allies recruited many Kachin who were pitted against the Burma Independence Army under Aung San the father of Aung San Suu Kyi.[19] Kachins have been fighting the Bamar/Burmese off and on ever since then. After independence, relations between the Kachins and many other non-Bamar peoples along the Myanmar's frontiers remained tense. These hill people resisted control and assimilation into Burma and wanted if not independence, a high degree of ethnic autonomy as well as a sense of equality with the Bamar majority.

Outright civil war began in 1961. That year the Kachin Independence Army was created. The situation between the central government and the people of the mountainous frontier further worsened when General Ne Win came to power and ended the democratic government. New Win's Burmese Programme Party attempted to create a socialist state what he called the "Burmese Way to Socialism." It was inward looking, isolationist but also authoritarian. To resist Ne Win's government various minority groups formed the National Democratic Front in 1976 with the aim of creating a federal state in which each minority would have a high degree of autonomy. The Kachin Independence Organization and its armed wing the Kachin Independence Army played a leading role in it.[20] Then Ne Win's government was replaced by a military junta the State Peace and Development Council which went by the wonderfully disagreeable sounding acronym SLORC in 1988. In 1994, SLORC worked out a ceasefire.[21]

Kachin has many of the attributes of a real country. The central government in Myanmar has never effectively controlled much of the Kachin State; the Kachins have been largely self-governing with their own schools, government administration, radio and television stations. Since 1994 a key center has been Laiza on the Chinese border. Yet, despite Kachin state's remarkable resilience for over half a century, its continued existence remains precarious. Its borders fluctuate with the outcomes of armed conflict, and it hangs on in part because it is along the Chinese border and the Chinese have permitted trade and smuggling. In fact, its economy depends on trade with China, including gemstones and timber exports.[22] It has survived also because the Myanmar government has struggled to control almost all its peripheral territories and has had to deal with more threatening secessionist groups such as the Karens.

Kachin State does not seek or expect to become a sovereign state. Rather the goal of the Kachins is autonomy within Myanmar.[23] The Kachin Independence Organization and its Independence Army has fought to achieve autonomy and preserve their culture within the larger state of Myanmar. The fact that the Kachin State does not really want to be an independent state does not disqualify it from our list. Neither Nagorno Karabakh nor Northern Cyprus wished to come separate states. But it has never claimed to be sovereign, rather it has been as much an insurgent movement as a real country.

OTHER WOULD-BE STATES

Insurgent States

Kachin, along with Donetsk and Luhansk, is an example of an insurgent state, that is, an entity created by rebel groups that control some territory and people. While some of these groups such as the Kachins are not trying to create new states but overthrow an old one or simply achieving autonomy, others proclaim themselves to be new states. They set up much of the apparatus of government administration, but they generally do not have stable borders. Instead their boundaries fluctuate; the territory they control is actively contested, and often ill-defined. Communities under their authority sometimes pay allegiance to both the rebel groups and to the internationally recognized state that the rebels are fighting, depending on the frequently changing situation. While most de facto states are products of frozen conflicts, these rebel entities are usually located in active conflict zones.

One of the best-known insurgent states was the Islamic State of Iraq and the Levant (ISIL) also known as the Islamic State if Iraq and Syria (ISIS). It was more of an organization though than a state. It had its origins in 1999 as a militant Islamic group which pledged allegiance to al-Qaeda. After the US invasion of Iraq in 2003 it became part of the Iraqi insurgency. In 2006 it declared itself a state in the territory it controlled in Iraq and in 2013 it claimed itself the government of both Iraq and Syria. In 2014 it ended its association with al-Qaeda and in rebranded itself the Islamic State claiming to be a caliphate—that is the legitimate government of all Muslims. By the end of 2015 it controlled large parts of northern Iraq and northeast Syria. By this time, it had a functioning government administration over perhaps eight million people. It established the Syrian city of Raqqa as its capital.

A US supported counter-offensive in 2017 greatly reduced its territory. In July 2017 Iraqi forces recaptured Mosul the largest city under Islamic State control. Three months later, in October, Syrian rebel forces with American support took Raqqa. By 2018, the Islamic State had reverted to largely a guerilla organization tenuously controlling only scattered areas. No government ever recognized the state. The Islamic State never fitted the definition of a de facto state. It did not exercise sustained administration of a clearly defined territory. Its borders were also shifting and even its control over its administration of its core at around the capital Raqqa functioned for only three years.

The Islamic State also deviated from the norms of statehood by proclaiming itself a caliphate in the traditional sense, that is, as a political and spiritual authority of all Muslims. In fact, it belonged to a radical tradition in modern Islam that rejects the very concept of the state and the state system as it has evolved in modern times. Rather it harkened back to the premodern concept of universal rulership. Interestingly it claimed to be the governing authority in parts of Libya, West Africa, the Caucasus and elsewhere, wherever local Muslim insurgents pledged allegiance. The most notable example was in northeastern Nigeria where the radical Islamic group Boko Haram gave its allegiance. Thus, besides falling more in the category of insurgent groups that exert control over an unstable swathe of territory, the Islamic State was a would be state that rejected the concept of state in its modern sense.

AZAWAD

Another ephemeral political entity was Azawad. This was created by the Tuareg minority of northern Mali. The bulk of the population of Mali are farmers living in the dry but still arable Sahel that spreads across the southern part of their country. The north is mostly desert or desert steppe and is ethnically and culturally different from the rest of the country. This is the home of the Tuaregs, a Berber speaking people, scattered throughout the Sahara that are linguistically, ethnically, and culturally linked with the peoples of North Africa more than with West Africa. Primarily a pastoral people, they have little in common with the people of in the south. The region they live in takes up 60 percent of Mali's territory but had only one tenth of the country's 16 million inhabitants.

The Tuaregs, impoverished, politically marginalized and culturally different have been restless for years. In January 2012, the Tuareg rebels defeated a Malian army force. Soon they had effective control of the region. The rebels organized themselves as the National Movement for the Liberation of Azawad (NNLA), Azawad being the name they call their region.[24] On April 6, 2012, they declared the Republic of Azawad with the legendary city of Timbuktu its capital. Leaders of Azawad declared that their new state would abide by UN charter and called on Tuaregs abroad to come home and build its institutions. If they had any chance of success it was undermined it when the government of Azawad allied itself with the Islamicist group Ansar Dine. This proved to be their undoing. In the summer of 2012, the Ansar Dine turned on the MNLA and captured the three largest cities in northern Mali, Kindal, Gao as well as the Azawad capital of Timbuktu. Ansar Dine did not stop there but sought to gain control of all Mali. This led to the intervention of France which sent forces to assist the Mali Army. By the end of 2013 they succeeded in regaining control of most of the north. The MNLA cooperated with the French troops, announcing that it sought only greater autonomy within Mali. In 2016 members of the MNLA formed the Movement for the Salvation of Azawad (MSA). While still seeking some form of autonomy the MSA cooperated with the French in fighting Islamic militants.[25] While the first attempt at an independent state was a disastrous failure, it is not impossible that the call for an independent Azawad will reemerge.

AMBAZONIA AND DAR EL KUTI

Ambazonia is another potential state but in 2020 it was a rebel cause not a country. Located in western Cameroun, Ambazonia has clearly defined borders, based like Western Sahara and Somaliland on earlier colonial ones. It covers 42,710 square kilometers (16,490 square miles) and an ethnically diverse population of five million. Ambazonia too it the product of colonialism and collapse of empire. After World War I the German colony of Kameroun was divided into a smaller British and a much larger French territory. As the preparations began for independence the people of the British Cameroun indicated they wanted an independent state. But a report in 1959 argued that the territory was not economically viable and recommended that it be attached to Nigeria or have a federation with the rest of Cameroun. So, it became part of French speaking Cameroun, yet it never gained the autonomy promised at independence in 1960. Rather there has been a pressure to assimilate into the main culture. This has created a backlash and a strong movement for independence emerged.

A group of local leaders declared the independent state of Ambazonia in 2017 which has led to a violent and largely ignored conflict. It could in fact become an independent country someday, certainly the secessionist movement in the years 2017 to 2020 was gathering strength.[26] But it faced the same problem all African separatist movements have deal with, the commitment of

African governments to maintain the colonial boundaries. Like Somaliland it could be argued that it is based on colonial boundaries since it was part of the British zone of Cameroun. However, there is no support for the breakup of African states. And unlike Somalia, Cameroun, did not descend into anarchy but is a stable, if somewhat fragile, political unit with a government that is modestly effective by African standards in governing the land within its boundaries.

Then there is the Republic of Logone or known as Dar El Kuti proclaimed in December 2015 by Muslim rebels in the Central African Republic. It was the product of the chaos that took place when in 2013 Muslim rebels known as the Seleka overthrew the Christian government in the CAR capital of Bangui. A civil war followed and one of the factions of Seleka led by Noureddin Adam who controlled a vast swath of territory in the northeast broke with the other Muslim insurgents and formed his own autonomous region. Dar El Kuti was too unstable and is too lacking in the real functions of government to be taken seriously as a state. Nor was the intention of this group to create a truly independent state but to have its own autonomous region which could possibly be used someday to take over the entire country.

NAGALIM

Most insurgencies are unable to carry out the functions of government or hold steady control over territory. Some like in Kachin have held some territory for long periods. Another example has been Nagalim. Since the 1950s there has been an insurgency in the small northeastern Indian state of Nagaland, also called Nagalim. Bordering Burma, Nagaland has only 16,579 square kilometers (6,401 square miles) and a population of 2 million, 90 percent who are Nagas. The Nagas are a group of fourteen tribes who have different languages, yet all share the Naga language, a lingua franca among them that is a pidgin based on Assamese, Hindi, and Bengali. They differ from their non-Naga neighbors in being mostly Christian rather than Hindu or Muslim, and culturally more Southeast Asian than South Asian. Many Nagas have hoped for an independent state but their small size, geographic isolation, and India's determination not to allow any separatist movements begin a process of unraveling the union, all have made that unlikely.[27]

DE FACTO STATES ARE RARE

There are many other movements, transient political entities that seek nationhood or at least autonomy but none of these qualify or are likely to become members of the global community of states. Even a brief survey of all them would make for a lengthy book. Between 1992 and 2002, two did become states: Timor Leste and South Sudan. But before independence they never quite fit the definition of de facto state. In other words, de facto states such as Somaliland, Transnistria, or Taiwan are rare anomalies.

NOTES

1. Charles D. Smith, *Palestine and the Arab-Israeli Conflict* (Boston, MA: Bedford/St Martin's, 2004), 437–41.
2. Smith, *Palestine and the Arab-Israeli Conflict*, 444–45.
3. Samih F. Farsoun and Naseer H. Aruri, *Palestine and the Palestinians*, 2nd Edition (Boulder, CO: Westview Press, 2006), 293–94.
4. Farsoun and Aruri, *Palestine and the Palestinians*, 135.
5. Michael M. Gunter, *The Kurds: A Divided Nation in Search of a State* (Princeton, NJ: Markus Wiener Publishers, 2019), xvii.
6. Gunter, *The Kurds*, xvii.
7. Gunter, *The Kurds*, 15–16, 21.
8. Gunter, *The Kurds*, 70.
9. Gunter, *The Kurds*, 72–73.
10. Gunter, *The Kurds*, 70.
11. Gunter, *The Kurds*, 76.
12. Gunter, *The Kurds*, 80.
13. Gunter, *The Kurds*, 84.
14. Gunter, *The Kurds*, 88.
15. "The Kurds are Creating a State of Their Own in Northern Syria," *The Economist*, May 23, 2019.
16. "The Kurds are Creating a State of Their Own in Northern Syria."
17. Tymur Korotkyi and Natalia Hendel, "The Legal Status of the Donestsk and Luhansk 'Peoples' Republics'," in Sergey Sayapin and Evhen Tsybulenko, editors, *The Use of Force at Ukraine in International Law* (Spring, 2019): 145–70, https://link.springer.com/chapter/10.1007/978-94-6265-222-4_7, Accessed December 31, 2019.
18. Donald M. Seekins, *Historical Dictionary of Burma (Myanmar)* (Lanham, MD: Scarecrow Press, 2006), 236–37.
19. Robert Anderson and Many Sadan, "Historical Perspectives on War and Peace in Kachin Space: The First Kachin Ceasefire 1944–1961," in Mandy Sadan, editor, *War and Peace in the Borderlands of Myanmar: The Kachin Ceasefire, 1994–2011* (Copenhagen, Denmark: NIAS Press, 2016), 29–54.
20. Martin Smith, "Reflection on the Kachin Ceasefire: A Cycle of Hope and Disappointment," in Mandy Sadan, editor, *War and Peace in the Borderlands of Myanmar: The Kachin Ceasefire, 1994–2011* (Copenhagen, Denmark: NIAS Press, 2016), 57–91, 59.
21. Smith, "Reflection on the Kachin Ceasefire," 60–61.

22. Lee Jones, "Understanding Myanmar's Ceasefires: Geopolitics, Political Economy and State-building," in Mandy Sadan, editor, *War and Peace in the Borderlands of Myanmar: The Kachin Ceasefire, 1994–2011* (Copenhagen, Denmark: NIAS Press, 2016), 95–113.

23. Nehginpao Kipgen, *Myanmar: A Political History* (New Delhi: Oxford University Press, 2016), 130–31.

24. Gregory Mann, "The Mess in Mali," *foreign policy.com*, April 5, 2012, https://foreignpolicy.com/2012/04/05/the-mess-in-mali/, Accessed September 18, 2019.

25. *Crisis Watch*, "Mali," 2019, https://www.crisisgroup.org/crisiswatch/print?page=1&location%5B0%5D=26&date_range=cust&t=CrisisWatch+Database+Filter, Accessed January 18, 2020.

26. *Deutche Welle*, "Who are Cameroon's Self-Named Ambonia Successionists?" September 30, 2019, https://www.dw.com/en/who-are-cameroons-self-named-ambazonia-secessionists/a-50639426, Accessed January 19, 2020.

27. *Unrepresented Nations and Peoples Organization*, "Nagalim," April 26, 2019, https://unpo.org/members/7899, Accessed January 21, 2019.

Conclusion

What Can We Learn from De Facto States?

Our de facto states are the products of unresolved international conflicts and the current rather rigid (and stable) state system that makes it hard for new states to gain recognition. Each has sought to gain international acceptance, although some have tried more than others. In all, their governments and their citizens have had to overcome the many obstacles to establishing normal life created by being excluded from the international community. They are all directly or indirectly products of disintegrating empires. They are all secessionist states (Taiwan might be considered an exception) and face an unwelcoming international community that supports the claims of their parent state. With the exception of Somaliland, they have a patron to survive. For Nagorno Karabakh, it is Armenia; for Abkhazia, South Ossetia, for Transnistria, it is Russia; for Northern Cyprus, it is Turkey; for the Sahrawi Arab Democratic Republic (SADR), it is Algeria; for Taiwan, it has been the United States; Kosovo has been protected by North Atlantic Treaty Organization and assisted by the European Union. Yet, they are also quite different from each other, emerging from different historical contexts, posing different questions about the international state system.

NAGORNO KARABAKH: CAN A COUNTRY NOT WANT TO BE A COUNTRY AND STILL BE ONE?

Nagorno Karabakh is a country not because its people or their leaders sought independence but because of a historical accident. What all the Armenian-Karabakhis wanted was to be a part of the Armenian state, not Azerbaijani state. The chaos that accompanied the fall of the Soviet Union was an opportunity to achieve their long-held aim of joining their fellow Armenians and they declared their independence in December of 1991 as a tactical move to achieve this. The Karabakh War, 1992–1994 made what they intended to be a temporary independence a long-term situation. Nearly three decades later Karabakhis still saw their country as an orphaned province of Armenia. Yet at what point does a country become one because it is accustomed to governing itself?

As far as being a de facto state, Nagorno Karabakh has a strong case for being one. Nonetheless, although it enjoys self-government it remains dependent on Armenia for its defense, and its communication and transportation links with the outside world. Economically, it is not especially viable but gets by with the support of donations from the Armenian diaspora (which to some extent is true of Armenia itself). In any case, it would be geopolitically difficult for Armenia to annex Nagorno Karabakh since that would anger all the countries that it has good relations with including the United States and Russia. After the 2020 Armenian-Azerbaijani war its position became even more precarious.

Countries have become independent states against their will. An example is Singapore which was part of the federal system of Malaysia when the country became independent from Britain in 1963. Certainly, Singapore, an island separated by a narrow passage from the peninsular Malaya, makes more sense as a part of Malaysia than the Sarawak and Sabah (formerly British North Borneo) separated by hundreds of miles of ocean. However, the new government of Malaysia dominated by ethnic Malays did not want to share power with predominately Chinese Singapore and its ambitious leader Lee Kwan Yew. So, it forced Singapore out in 1965. Lee announced the decision in tears. But the little city state of Singapore has prospered becoming one of the wealthiest societies on earth, and a cohesive, Singaporean nationalism emerged. Nagorno Karabakh, small, isolated, poor, and ethnically akin to Armenia, seemed less likely to develop its own national identity.

ABKHAZIA: CAN A MINORITY BECOME A NATION BY EXPELLING A MAJORITY?

If Nagorno Karabakh became a country by accident, Abkhazia did so by design. In many ways it was a typical secessionist movement in which a minority group within a nation sought to withdraw and create their own nation-state. Abkhazia is the homeland for a distinct ethnic group the Abkhaz, an ancient people with their own language and traditions. It therefore makes sense as a nation-state. While small it has the basis to be a viable state. It is not as isolated as Nagorno Karabakh and has the potential for a prosperous economy based on agriculture and even more so on tourism. However, like Nagorno Karabakh, its independence is based on the presence of a protector, in its case Russia. Russian troops are stationed there, and Russia subsidizes the state, providing the government with much of its funding. It is easy, therefore, to dismiss it as a puppet state of Moscow. Yet, unlike Nagorno Karabakh, public sentiment is for separate status; Abkhazians appear to want their own country and their support for Russia is tactical. Government leaders have shown interest in broadening their support by developing ties with the EU and other countries but have not been successful in doing this.

Abkhazia as an internationally recognized state, however, poses a problem. In the process of becoming a national state the ethnic Abkhaz expelled over half its population, either deliberately chasing them out or creating a situation where they felt like they had to flee. It was a case where a minority, albeit one that had previous been a majority, ethnically cleansed a majority. When does a country deserve to be a country? And if the state is based on popular sovereignty—whose sovereignty is that? Certainly, the ethnic Georgians who made over two-fifths of the population in 1989, did not want secede from Georgia. Nor is there any indication that the Russian and Armenian minorities sought independence. The status of the refugees it created is a major obstacle in achieving recognition, a problem it shares with Nagorno Karabakh. And it is not just a practical problem of offending Georgia or of supporting international law, but a moral dilemma for any nation recognizing it.

South Ossetia's situation resembles Nagorno Karabakh more than Abkhazia. It became an independent state as a step toward joining its fellow Ossetians in the north. Like Nagorno Karabakh it was historically part of another land, although (also like Karabakh) an outer part of it separated by mountains. It was then placed into another state by an imperial power—a move that might make sense geographically but not make ethnic-historical sense (again like Karabakh). Its independence is less viable than Abkhazia, isolated and almost totally dependent on Russia it is difficult to imagine the country as ever becoming a truly sovereign state nor is there any indication its population seeks sovereignty. Rather like the people of Karabakh South Ossetians hope to unite with the republic of their kin. In this case, the republic they seek to join, North Ossetia, is an autonomous region of Russia. Thus, they would be part of Russia.

TRANSNISTRIA: CAN A SECESSIONIST STATE WITH FLUID IDENTITIES BE VIABLE?

Transnistria is still another secessionist state created from the collapse of the Soviet Union or perhaps better labeled the Soviet Empire. Its leadership and population appear to be ambivalent or perhaps uncertain whether they wish to be a real country like Abkhazia or part of another like Nagorno Karabakh and South Ossetia. As with most de facto states it relies on a protector to maintain its autonomy. Russian troops protect it although it might be able to survive without Russia. Its viability as a state would depend on the willingness of Moldova to accept it as one. This is not impossible. Like our other states it was born of violent conflict. But it was a shorter less violent conflict and did not involve ethnic cleansing or a large embittered refugee population. Relations between Transnistria and Moldova are uneasy but lack the tension and hostility seen in the Caucasus states.

Transnistria also differs in that it is a land of fluid identities. Predominantly Russian, it has substantial Romanian and Ukrainian populations many of whom identify with the state—so it is less a case of an ethnically based nationalism than being attached to a different economy, a different dominant language and a rejection of a Moldovan identity. If there is a Transnistrian identity, it is based as much as on a nostalgia for the past—a clinging to the Soviet identity long after the Soviet Union has gone. This makes it a strange place, an anachronism. Yet, fluid identities are not so strange. It is in fact, possible, that Transnistria will simply become an autonomous region of Moldova. But it could be a separate state or less likely a part of Russia. After three decades of independence there was no obvious future course for Transnistria.

KOSOVO: WHAT RIGHT DOES A COUNTRY HAVE TO DENY RECOGNITION OF ANOTHER?

Kosovo differs from our other de facto states in that it enjoys diplomatic recognition from much of the international community and its full membership into the world state system appears to be inevitable. It is not because of Serbia. In this way it resembles the de facto states of the Caucasus, a breakaway region whose recognition is blocked by the state it seceded from.

However, unlike them, the parent state is not overwhelmingly supported by the international community. While most of the international community supports Azerbaijan, Georgia, and Moldova, only a few support Serbia's claim to Kosovo. It is only because Serbia's supporters include Russia and China both of which have a veto power in the UN that prevents Kosovo from joining. In another respect, Kosovo is much like the other states we have examined; it also relies on a foreign protector—NATO—to maintain its autonomy.

Kosovo is also dissimilar from most of our other de facto states in that people have heard of it. It is located closer to Western Europe, NATO was involved in its creation, and it has the economic and political support of the

EU. It was part of the wars that accompanied the breakup of Yugoslavia, wars, that because they occurred close to the center of Europe, drew more Western attention. Serbia already cast as the villain in Bosnia carried out a horrific campaign of ethnic cleansing that caused international outrage. Kosovo's victimization gained it international sympathy. Yet, Kosovo's legitimacy and international support have been compromised by the thuggish behavior and criminality of some of its independence fighters and their leaders, and by its persecution of the small Serbian minority. So like Abkhazia, South Ossetia, Nagorno Karabakh, and to a lesser extent Transnistria, its actions have displayed the same intolerant nationalism that it rebelled against.

Kosovo also resembles Nagorno Karabakh and South Ossetia in that it became a country because it couldn't join another. Kosovars are Albanians, but Albania failed in the early twentieth century to create a state that united all Albanians. Kosovo was a large northern chunk of the Albanian speaking lands that became part of Serbia. Many Kosovars sought union with Albania as much as independence, but after a long separation, several generations of a different historical experience, the struggle for independence and the indifference or even opposition of Albania to unification, Kosovo is likely to be a separate nation-state. It is a reality that most Kosovars have begun to accept.

Kosovo raises a question—how is it possible for the claims of one country to block the right of statehood of another? There are many examples of this: China's opposition to an independent Taiwan is one. Greece for a while blocked the entry of Macedonia into the UN and undermined its bid to join the EU because it objected to the name, Macedonia. Since Macedonia was the name of a region of northern Greece, this implied to the Greeks an irredentist claim on its sovereign territory, although Macedonia never made such a claim. Perhaps more seriously by naming itself after the kingdom of Alexander the Great it undermined the Greek claim to be heir to that ancient state. It had to change names twice. It was admitted to the UN as the Former Yugoslav Republic of Macedonia, and then became North Macedonia to apply for EU membership. For Serbia, the acceptance of Kosovo which was the heartland of the Serbian state in its medieval glory days runs against its very national identity and the two-century project of restoring Serbia to its ancient boundaries and greatness. Unlike Macedonia, a simple name change is unlikely to work. But Kosovo's lack of recognition is also a product of the general fear of secessionist movements. It is not just Serbia and Russia's support of Serbia that stands in the way to UN membership, but other states such as Nigeria and India, uncomfortable in legitimizing insurgency, had not established diplomatic relations either.

TRNC: HOW CAN A COUNTRY BE DEPENDENT ON ANOTHER AND SURVIVE WITHOUT BEING ABSORBED?

The Turkish Republic of Northern Cyprus is another accidental as well as de facto state. Turkish Cypriots did not seek secession from the Republic of Cyprus and remained hopeful of entering some form of federation with it after they did set up their own government. There have been questions about how independent it really is but, in most respects, it has functioned as a de facto state. Like Transnistria it benefits from the country that it is not a part of. Because the Republic of Cyprus is a member of the EU and the Northern Cyprus is regarded by the EU as part of the Republic of Cyprus, its citizens can get a Cypriot passport which is an EU passport even though the state itself is unable to enjoy the privileges of being part of the European Union. Like our other de facto states, it has a protector—Turkey. In fact, it can be argued that the TRNC was a creation of the 1974 Turkish invasions. Yet if it were not for its diplomatic isolation Northern Cyprus could be a viable state. As a popular tourist destination it could stand alone economically or even prosper if it were a recognized independent state. But in its current state of geopolitical limbo it needs Turkey.

The TRNC depends on Turkey for its defense, for its communications, for financial support, even for some of its fresh water. But the problem for the TRNC is how can it enjoy Turkey's support without being absorbed into its protector? Unlike the ambivalent attitude of Transnistrians and the open desire of most Karabakhis and South Ossetians to join their ethnic brethren, few Turkish Cypriots want to be part of Turkey. Despite the shared language and religion, their the cultural differences are too great. Most feel more Cypriot than Turkish. Yet an increasingly authoritarian, Islamic Turkey has been interfering more rather than less in the affairs of the TRNC while Ankara's general drift toward anti-Western, conservative Islam only further alienates Turkey from people it protects in Cyprus.

SAHRAWI ARAB DEMOCRATIC REPUBLIC: MORE RECOGNITION THAN COUNTRY?

Western Sahara, or the SADR, belongs in a class by itself. In many ways it is more of an insurgency than a state, resembling the Kurds, Kachins, Nagas, and Tuaregs. The Polisario is an independence movement that governs from a refugee camp. Ruling over only small sparsely populated patches of desert, it does not have control over most of its homeland or its people. For this reason, its inclusion in our list of de facto states is problematic. Yet in some ways Western Sahara, to give it the more popularly used name, is a real country that in a very short time developed a strong sense of nationhood within clearly defined geographical boundaries. Like our other states it has a patron/protector—Algeria—without which there would not be even the semblance of a state. Western Sahara occupies a position closer to Palestine, which has a government that is recognized by a number of countries, leads a national movement that has the support of the population, but exercises no control over the vast majority of its territory. Unlike the Palestinian Authority, however, it has real control of the small bits of land it occupies.

However, international sympathy, the support of some nations, and the recognition by some others are not enough to make the SADR real. And it faces a problem that raises an issue. Is it possible to create a state when "your people" have become a minority in their own land? We have seen this issue in Abkhazia. It would probably have happened to Albanian Kosovars if it had not been for foreign interference. And it has happened to many would-be nation-states in the past. By the late 2010s, Moroccans outnumbered Sahrawis in the Western Sahara. Would an independent SADR mean the expulsion of these settlers? At what point is the Western Sahara the home for not only those Moroccans who have recently settled there but for their children who have grown up in the territory?

SOMALILAND: JUST WHAT DOES A COUNTRY HAVE TO DO TO BE RECOGNIZED?

No country better exemplifies the contradictions in the international state system than Somaliland. More than any other of our de facto states, except perhaps Taiwan, it has all the features of a "real" country. Somaliland meets every criterion for a sovereign state except recognition. It is true that the borders, especially with Puntland, are unclear and the central government does not exercise effective control over some of these areas. But most of the country—certainly its core—has one of the more effective governments in the region. Somaliland differs from some of the rest of our de facto states in two regards. First, it does not have a protector. Ethiopia is sympathetic, and helps link the country to the outside world, but Somaliland does not depend on Ethiopia or any other country. It is largely on its own. Second, although it is a secessionist state, it seceded from an ineffective failed state that exerts little control over most of the country. Somalia which barely functions as a country at all, has little ability to regain its hold over the northern breakaway region. This is why Somaliland does not need an external protector.

It can be argued that Somaliland is an artificial country, based on an arbitrarily drawn set of borders in colonial times, that the Somalis in Somaliland are of the same language and ethnicity as those in Somalia and are not a separate people. But then nations are based on shared historical experiences and the people of the former British Somaliland have theirs, which have proven strong enough to develop a distinct collective identity. The country is no more artificial or unnatural than Austria, Canada, or Colombia.

Somaliland has done almost everything imaginable to gain international recognition but has failed. Yet, there seems to only the weakest arguments for not accepting it into the international community. Not only has it failed to gained support from the outside world, it has failed to have been noticed by it. Somaliland's very existence is remarkably unknown, as if it were a secret country. In fact, its very stability has resulted in little attention being drawn to it. It is hard to make the case for recognition as an independent state when the world is so little aware of its existence. So, what does it have to do? If the international community is committed to the fiction of a united Somalia, if the African Union is opposed to secessionist movements, if a country has no international constituency, if no great power is willing to support it—how can it secure membership into the club of sovereign states?

TAIWAN—CAN A COUNTRY BE A COUNTRY IF IT INSISTS IT IS NOT?

Taiwan is the most egregious and best-known case of a modern country with effective and efficient governing institutions that labor under the burden of being diplomatically isolated. It differs from our other de facto states by being a major industrial nation, an important player in the international economy, a dynamic, wealthy, democratic society.

Taiwan, like all our de facto states except Somaliland, has a protector—the United States, albeit one whose relations with its client are rather ambiguous and uncertain. It can be seen as a secessionist state although that needs qualifying. Since 1895 it has been part of mainland China for only four years. As with most of our de facto states it is recognized by the majority of the international community as a part of the country it seceded from (the SADR and Kosovo being exceptions). Yet Taiwan is also a peculiar case. It officially does not claim to be a separate state. For the first decades of its existence it declared itself to be the legitimate government of all China; as we have seen it went to absurd lengths to keep up this pretext. In more recent times Taiwan has dropped this claim replacing it with a very ambiguous status: one China, two states. More than any other country it has walked a thin, sometimes barely coherent line between declaring itself a nation and arguing that is something less than one. Public opinion surveys, however, make it clear that most citizens feel that their country is Taiwan. Their link with China has become a bit like Canada or Australia's connection with Britain, acknowledging a shared cultural heritage but also a different modern history and identity.

IS DE FACTO STATE A MEANINGFUL CATEGORY?

Our nine states are all so different that it calls into question whether de facto statehood is a meaningful category, whether they might be better described as miscellaneous geopolitical oddities. If we narrow the definition of de facto statehood down to two fundamental features—(1) having all the characteristics of recognized sovereign states but general international recognition, (2) being enduring rather than ephemeral entities—then most would fit that label but still require a lot of qualifications. Rather it might be easier to refer to degrees of "stateness" based on the following: (1) the degree which the de facto state has compromised its sovereignty, (2) the degree it maintains effective internal control, (3) the degree the government and the people it rules see themselves as a sovereign state, (4) and the degree it has achieved the capacity to enter into diplomatic relations with other states.

Taiwan and Somaliland have probably compromised their sovereignty the least. All the others have ceded some freedom of action to a patron or in the case of Kosovo to the UN, the EU, and NATO. Although all have demonstrated a willingness to act independently of their patrons, none are puppets of the patron states, even if like the TRNC that are heavily dependent on them. As for the second measure of "stateness," the SADR controls little of the territory it claims, and its population is mainly confined to refugee camps. Somaliland's control over its periphery is somewhat compromised. Taiwan scores well on this point, Abkhazia, Transnistria, TRNC also do well. The degree to which the government and the people it governs see themselves as a sovereign state varies. Yet, surely the people of the SADR do even if in all other respects they are less like a "real state" than the others. So do Somalilanders and Kosovars. Increasingly this is true of the people of Taiwan too. The case of Nagorno Karabakh is muddier since annexation by Armenia remains their main goal. Abkhazia, South Ossetia, Transnistria also show an ambivalence about being a sovereign nation. The citizens of TRNC have demonstrated their will to forfeit sovereignty for autonomy. Yet, they also have shown a strong sense of their own identity as a people and accept their government as the legitimate representative of that people. All have the capacity, if not the success, to enter in diplomatic relations with other states.

If we see the unrecognized states as being on a continuum of "stateness" then the SADR is at the low end and could be dropped from the list. Based on all these four categories, Somaliland, Taiwan, and Kosovo have the highest degree of "stateness." With Kosovo, widely recognized, its full membership seems only a matter of time. But for Taiwan and Somaliland the future in 2021 is less clear. These two states, it can be argued, are the most egregious cases of nations being victimized by the international state system.

All our de facto states, however, are victims of the international state system. In an era of unprecedented geopolitical stability, it has been increasingly difficult for new states to emerge and for recognized boundaries to alter. The struggles of our de facto states illustrate this, it has been extremely hard for them to gain international recognition, and the failure to do so creates enormous obstacles for their people to carry on with their lives in a modern world. And there are only a few of them. Unrecognized entities at the high end of "sovereign stateness" are true outliers in the global political landscape. Because they are rare anomalies, they are fascinating places, worthy of examination, even if they are not always on the map.

Bibliography

Abi-Mershed, Osama, and Adam Farrar. "A History of the Conflict in Western Sahara," in Anouar Boukhars and Jacques Rousellier, editors. *Perspective on Western Sahara: Myths, Nationalism, and Geopolitics.* Lanham, MD: Rowman & Littlefield, 2014, pp. 3–27.

Aida Ammour, Laurence. "The Algerian Foreign Policy on Western Sahara," in Anouar Boukhars and Jacques Rousellier, editors. *Perspective on Western Sahara: Myths, Nationalism, and Geopolitics.* Lanham, MD: Rowman & Littlefield, 2014, pp. 91–117.

Anderson, Benedict. *Imagined Communities: Reflections on the Origin ad Spread of Nationalism.* London: Verso, 1991.

Anderson, Robert, and Many Sadan. "Historical Perspectives on War and Peace in Kachin Space: The First Kachin Ceasefire 1944–1961," in Mandy Sadan, editor. *War and Peace in the Borderlands of Myanmar: The Kachin Ceasefire, 1994–2011.* Copenhagen, Denmark: NIAS Press, 2016, pp. 29–54.

Armstrong, John. *Nations before Nationalism.* Chapel Hill, NC: University of North Carolina Press, 1982.

Berry, Chris. "Taiwan's indigenous Peoples and Cinema: From Colonial Mascot to Fourth Cinema?" in Bi-yu chang and Pei-yin Lin, editors. *Positioning Taiwan in a Global Context: Being and Becoming.* London: Routledge, 2019, pp. 228–241.

Boum, Aomar. "Refugees, Humanitarian Aid, and the Displace Impasse in Sahrawi Camps," in Anouar Boukhars and Jacques Rousellier, editors. *Perspective on Western Sahara: Myths, Nationalism, and Geopolitics.* Lanham, MD: Rowman & Littlefield, 2014, pp. 261–275.

Brezianu, Andrei. *Historical Dictionary of Moldova.* Lantham, MD: Scarecrow Press, 2007.

Briggs, Philip. *Somaliland,* Second Edition. Guilford, CT: Bradt Travel Guides, 2019.

Cakaj, Gent, and Gezim Krasniqi. "The Role of Minorities in the Serbo-Albanian Political Quagmire," in Leandrit I Mehmeti and Branislav Radeljic, editors.

Kosovo and Serbia: Contested Options and Shared Consequences. Pittsburgh, PA: University of Pittsburgh Press, 2016, pp. 149–166.

Caspersen, Nina. *Unrecognized States: The Struggle for Sovereignty in the Modern International System*. Cambridge, UK: Polity, 2012.

Chirigov, Fuad. "The Nagorno Karabakh Conflict is Destroying Armenia." *National Interest*, June 9, 2019. https://nationalinterest.org/blog/buzz/nagorno-karabakh-conflict-destroying-armenia-61407. Accessed August 17, 2019.

Chiung, Wi-run Taiffalo. "Languages under Colonization: The Taiwanese Language Movement," in J. Bruce Jacobs and Peter Kang, editors. *Changing Taiwanese Identities*. London: Routledge, 2018, pp. 39–63.

Christou, George. *The European Union and Enlargement: The Case of Cyprus*. New York, NY: Palgrave Macmillan, 2004.

Clark, Howard. *Civil Resistance in Kosovo*. London: Pluto Press, 2000.

Cojocaru, Natalia. "Nationalism and Identity in Transnistria." *Innovation: The European Journal of Social Science Research* 19, no. 3–4 (2006): 261–272.

Copper, John F. *Taiwan: Nation-State or Province?* Boulder, CO: Westview Press, 2003.

Cornell, Svante E. *The Nagorno Karabakh Conflict*. Uppsala: Uppsala University Press, 1999.

Coufoudakis, Van. *Cyprus: Contemporary Problem in Historical Perspective*. Minneapolis, MN: University of Minnesota Press, 2006.

Coulie, Bernard. "The Quintessential Conflict-A Cultural and Historical Analysis of Nagorno Karabakh," in Michael Kambeck and Sargis Ghazaryan, editors. *Europe's Next Avoidable War: Nagorno Karabakh*. New York, NY: Palgrave Macmillan, 2013, pp. 35–42, 35.

Council of Foreign Relations. "The Horn of Africa's Breakaway State." February 1, 2018. https://www.cfr.org/backgrounder/somaliland-horn-africas-breakaway-state.

Crawford, James. *The Creation of States in International Law*, Second Edition. Oxford, UK: Oxford University Press, 2006.

Crisis Watch, "Mali." 2019. https://www.crisisgroup.org/crisiswatch/print?page=1&location%5B0%5D=26&date_range=cust&t=CrisisWatch+Database+Filter.

Crook, Steven. *Taiwan*. Guilford, CT: Bradt Travel Guides, 2014.

Davidson, James. *The Island of Formosa: Past and Present*. Oxford, UK: Oxford University Press, 1989.

Deutche Welle. "Who are Cameroon's Self-Named Ambonia Successionists?" September 30, 2019. https://www.dw.com/en/who-are-cameroons-self-named-ambazonia-secessionists/a-50639426.

De Waal, Alex. *The Real Politics of the Horn of Africa: Money, War and the Business of Power*. Cambridge, UK: Polity Press, 2015.

De Waal, Thomas. *Black Garden: Armenia and Azerbaijan through Peace and War*. New York, NY: New York University Press, 2003.

De Waal, Thomas. "Uncertain Ground: Engaging with Europe's De Facto States and Breakaway Territories." *Carnegie Europe*, December 3, 2018. https://carnegieeurope.eu/2018/12/03/introduction-strange-endurance-of-de-facto-states-pub-77841.

Dbar, Roman. "Geography & Environment," in George Hewitt, editor. *The Abkhazians: A Handbook*. Richmond, UK: Curzon Press, 1999, pp. 23–36.
Dima, Nicholas. *Moldova and the Transdnestr Republic*. Boulder, CO: East European Monographs, Distributed by Columbia University, 2001.
Economist. "The Black Hole that is Transnistria." *Economist*, May 3, 2007. https://www.economist.com/node/9116439. Retrieved June 11, 2018.
Ekici, Tufan. *The Political and Economic History of North Cyprus, A Discordant Polity*. New York, NY: Palgrave Macmillan, 2019.
Farsoun, Samih F., and Naseer H. Aruri. *Palestine and the Palestinians*, Second Edition. Boulder, CO: Westview Press, 2006.
Felgenhauer, Pavel. "After August 7: The Escalation of the Russia-Georgia War," in Svante E. Cornell and Frederick Starr, editors. *The Guns of August 2008: Russia's War in Georgia*. Armonk, NY: M.E. Sharpe, 2009, pp. 162–180.
Fiddian-Qasmiyeh, Elena. "The Pragmatics of Performance: Putting 'Faith in Aid' in the Sahrawi Refugee Camps." *Journal of Refugee Studies* 24, no. 3 (2011): 533–547.
Forsyth, James. *The Caucasus*. New York, NY: Cambridge University Press, 2013.
Fowkes, Ben. *Ethnicity and Ethnic Conflict in the Post-Communist World*. New York, NY: Palgrave, 2002.
Ghazarayan, Sargis. "Background: Setting the Geopolitical Stage," in Michael Kambeck and Sargis Ghazaryan, editors. *Europe's Next Avoidable War: Nagorno Karabakh*. New York, NY: Palgrave Macmillan, 2013, pp. 10–23.
Gellner, Ernest. *Nations and Nationalism*. Ithaca, NY: Cornell University Press, 1983.
Geukjian, Ohannes. *Ethnicity, Nationalism and Conflict in the South Caucasus: Nagorno Karabakh and the Legacy of Soviet Nationalities Policy*. Burlington VT: Ashgate, 2012.
Goltz, Thomas. "The Paradox of Living in Paradise: Georgia's Descent into Chaos," in Svante E. Cornell and Frederick Starr, editors. *The Guns of August 2008: Russia's War in Georgia*. Armonk, NY: M.E. Sharpe, 2009.
Grant, Thomas D. *The Recognition of States: Law and Practice in Debate and Evolution*. Westport, CT: Praeger, 1999.
Gunter, Michael M. *The Kurds: A Divided Nation in Search of a State*. Princeton, NJ: Markus Wiener Publishers, 2019.
Halback, Uwe. "A Case Sui Generis: Nagorno Karabakh in Comparison with Other Ethnic Conflicts in Eastern Europe," in Michael Kambeck and Sargis Ghazaryan, editors. *Europe's Next Avoidable War: Nagorno Karabakh*. New York, NY: Palgrave Macmillan, 2013, pp. 43–60.
Heidenrich, John G. *How to Prevent Genocide: A Guide for Policymakers, Scholars and the Concerned Citizen*. Westport, CT: Greenwood, 2001.
Herz, Manuel, editor. *From Camp to City: Refugee Camps of the Western Sahara*. Zurich, Switzerland: Lars Uller Publishers, 2013.
Hewitt, George, editor. *The Abkhazians: A Handbook*. Richmond, UK: Curzon Press, 1999.
Hewitt, George. *Discordant Neighbors: A Reassessment of the Georgian-Abkhazian and Georgian-South Ossetian Conflicts*. Leiden: Brill, 2013.

Hill, William H. *Russia, the Near Abroad, and the West: Lessons from the Moldova-Transdniestra Conflict.* Washington, DC: Woodrow Wilson Center Press, 2012.

Hodges, Tony. "The Origins of Sahrawi Nationalism," in Richard Lawless and Laila Monahan, editors. *War and Refugees: The Western Sahara Conflict.* London: Pinter Publishers, 1987, pp. 31–62.

Hoehne, Markus Virgil. *Between Somaliland and Puntland: Marginalization, Militarization and Conflicting Political Visions.* London: Rift Valley Institute, 2015.

Hsiao, Frank S. T., and Mei-Chu Wang Hsiao. *Economic Development of Emerging East Asia: Catching Up of Taiwan and South Korea.* London: Anthem Press, 2017.

Huei, Yang. *Straits Rituals: China, Taiwan, and the United States in the Taiwan Strait Crises, 1954–1958.* Hong Kong: Hong Kong University Press, 2019.

Isachenko, Daria. *The Making of Informal States: Statebuilding in Northern Cyprus and Transdniestria.* New York, NY: Palgrave Macmillan, 2012.

Isidoros, Konsantina. *Nomads and Nation-Building I the Western Sahara: Gender, Politics and the Sahrawi.* London: I.B. Taurus, 2018.

Jacobs, J. Bruce. "Introduction," in J. Bruce Jacobs and Peter Kang, editors. *Changing Taiwanese Identities.* London: Routledge, 2018, pp. 1–11.

Jenson, Erik. *Western Sahara: Anatomy of a Stalemate?* Boulder, CO: Lynne Rienner, 2012.

Jones, Lee. "Understanding Myanmar's Ceasefires: Geopolitics, Political Economy and State-building," in Mandy Sadan, editor. *War and Peace in the Borderlands of Myanmar: The Kachin Ceasefire, 1994–2011.* Copenhagen, Denmark: NIAS Press, 2016, pp. 95–113.

Judah, Tim. *Kosovo: War and Revenge.* New Haven, CT: Yale University Press, 2000.

Kaplan, Seth. "The Remarkable Story of Somaliland." *Journal of Democracy* 19, no. 3 (July 2008): 143–157.

Kapteijns, Lidwien. *Clan Cleansing in Somalia: The Ruinous Legacy of 1991.* Philadelphia, PA: University of Pennsylvania Press, 2013.

Keating, Joshua. *Invisible Countries: Journeys to the Edge of Nationhood.* New Haven, CT: Yale University Press, 2018.

Ker-Lindsay, James. *The Cyprus Problem: What Everybody Needs to Know.* Oxford, UK: Oxford University Press, 2011.

Ker-Lindsay, James, and Eiki Berg. "Introduction: A Conceptual Framework for Engagement with de Facto States." *Journal of Ethnopolitics* 17, no. 4 (July, 2018): 335–342.

King, Charles. *The Moldovans: Romania, Russia, and the Politics of Culture.* Stanford, CA: Hoover Institution Press, 2000.

Kipgen, Nehginpao. *Myanmar: A Political History.* New Delhi: Oxford University Press, 2016.

Kosto, Pal. "Biting the Hands that Feed Them." *Journal of Post-Soviet Affairs* 36, no. 2 (December 2019): 140–158. https://www.tandfonline.com/doi/full/10.1080/1060586X.2020.1712987.

Kolsto, Pal, and Helge Blakkisrud. "From Secessionist Conflict Toward a Functioning State: Processes of State- and Nation-Building in Transnistria." *Post-Soviet Affairs* 27, no. 2 (May 2013): 178–220.

Kolstø, Pal, and A. Malgin. "The Transnistrian Republic: A Case of Politicized Regionalism." *Nationalities Papers* 26 (March 1, 1998): 103–128. https://www.tandfonline.com/doi/full/10.1080/1060586X.2020.1712987.

Kraus, Verena, and Gail Warrander. "Updated by Bridget Nurre Jennions and Larissa Olenicoff," in *Kosovo the Bradt Travel Guide*. Guilford, CT: Bradt Travel Guides, 2017.

Kucera, Joshua. "Russian Troops in Transniestria Squeezed by Ukraine and Moldova." *Eursianet*, May 25, 2015. https://eurasianet.org/node/73586. Accessed June 12.

Kyris, George. *The Europeanisation of Contested Statehood: The EU in northern Cyprus*. London: Routledge, 2015.

Laitin, David, and Said Samatra. *Somalia: Nation in Search of a State*. Boulder, CO: Westview Press, 1987.

Land Mine and Munition Cluster Monitor, August 2, 2017. http://www.the-monitor.org/en-gb/reports/2017/nagorno-karabakh/view-all.aspx.

Lepesant, Tanguy. "Taiwanese Youth and National Identity under Ma Ying-jeou," in J. Bruce Jacobs and Peter Kang, editors. *Changing Taiwanese Identities*. London: Routledge, 2018, pp. 64–86.

Lewis, Ioan M. Lewis. *A Modern History of the Somali: Nation and State in the Horn of Africa*, Fourth Edition. Oxford, UK: James Currey, 2002.

Lewis, Ioan M. *Understanding Somalia and Somaliland: Culture, History, Society*. Columbia, SC: New Columbia University Press, 2008.

Li, Saryu Shirley. *Taiwan's China Dilemma: Contested Identities and Multiple Interests in Taiwan's Cross-Strait Economic Policy*. Stanford, CA: Stanford University Press, 2016.

Lin, Hsiao-ting Lin. *Accidental State: Chiang Kai-shek, the United States, and the Making of Taiwan*. Cambridge, MA: Harvard University Press, 2016.

Mackinlay, John, and Peter Cross. *Regional Peacekeepers: The Paradox of Russian Peacekeeping*. New York, NY and Paris: United Nations University Press, 2003.

Malcolm, Noel. *Kosovo*. New York, NY: New York University Press, 1998.

Mann, Gregory. "The Mess in Mali." *foreign policy.com*, April 5, 2012. https://foreignpolicy.com/2012/04/05/the-mess-in-mali/.

McLean, Ruth. "Build a Wall Across the Sahara-That's Crazy but Someone Did It." *The Guardian*, September 22, 2018. https://www.theguardian.com/world/2018/sep/22/western-sahara-wall-morocco-trump.

Menabde, Giorgi. "Georgians in Abkhazia: A Choice Between Assimilation and Emigration." *Eurasian Daily Monitor*, August 6, 2019. https://jamestown.org/program/georgians-in-abkhazia-a-choice-between-assimilation-and-emigration/.

Michaelis Stavrou, Michael. *Resolving the Cyprus Conflict: Negotiating History*. New York, NY: Palgrave Macmillan, 2009.

Middleton, Nick. *An Atlas of Countries that Don't Exist: A Compendium of fifty Unrecognized and Largely Unnoticed States*. San Francisco, CA: Chronicle Books, 2015.

Miller, Donald E., and Lorna Touryan Miller. *Armenia: Portraits of Survival and Hope.* Berkeley, CA: University of California Press, 2003.

Noutcheva, Gergana. "Contested Statehood and EU Actorness in Kosovo, Abkhazia and Western Sahara." *Journal of Geopolitics* 25, no. 2 (December 2018): 449–471.

Niarchos, Nicholas. "Is One of African's Oldest Conflicts Finally at an End?" *The New Yorker*, December 29, 2018. https://www.newyorker.com/news/news-desk/is-one-of-africas-oldest-conflicts-finally-nearing-its-end.

Njoke, Raphael Chijioke. *The History of Somalia.* Santa Barbara, CA: Greenwood, 2013.

Oberling, Pierre. *The Road to Bellapais.* Ann Arbor, MI: Social Science Monographs, 1982.

Ohanian, Karine. "Karabakh Defends New Constitution." *Global Focus: Caucasus*, January 11, 2007. https://iwpr.net/global-voices/karabakh-defends-new-constitution. Retrieved June 13.

Papousti, Aimilia. *Frozen Conflict Zones: The Case of Transnistria.* Saarbrucken, Germany: Lambert Press, 2016.

Payaslian, Simon. *The History of Armenia: From the Origins to the Present.* New York, NY: Palgrave Macmillan, 2007.

Pazzanita. Anthony G. *Historical Dictionary of Western Sahara*, Third Edition. Lanham, MD: Scarecrow Press, 2006.

Pegg, Scott. *International Society and the De Facto State.* London: Routledge, 1998.

Pham, Peter. "Somalia: When a State is not a State." *The Fletcher Forum for World Affairs.* http://www.fletcherforum.org/home/2016/9/6/somalia-where-a-state-isnt-a-state?rq=somalia.

Phillips, Steven. "Between Assimilation and Independence: Taiwanese Political Aspirations Under Nationalist Chinese rule, 1945–1948," in Murray A. Rubinstein, editor. *Taiwan: A New History.* Armonk, NY: M.E. Sharpe, 1999, pp. 275–319.

Polyakov, Anton, Anya Galatonova, and Chloe Coleman. "In this Unrecognized Republic, It's not a matter of if the Children Leave, it's When." *Washington Post*, March 7, 2018.

Popjanevski, Johanna. "From Sukumi to Tskinvali: The Path to War in Georgia," in Svante E. Cornell and Frederick Starr, editors. *The Guns of August 2008: Russia's War in Georgia.* Armonk, NY: M.E. Sharpe, 2009, pp. 143–161.

Qirezi, Arben. "Settling the Self-Determination Dispute in Kosovo," in Leandrit I. Mehmeti and Branislav Radeljic, editors. *Kosovo and Serbia: Contested Options and Shared Consequences.* Pittsburgh, PA: University of Pittsburgh Press, 2016, pp. 37–62.

Richards, Rebecca. *Understanding Statebuilding: Traditional Governance and the Modern State in Somaliland.* Burlington, VT: Ashgate Publishing Company, 2014.

Rigger, Shelly. *Why Taiwan Matters: Small Island, Global Powerhouse.* Lanham, MD: Rowman & Littlefield, 2011.

Rubinstein, Murray A. "Taiwan's Socio-economic Modernization, 1971–1996," in Murray A. Rubinstein, editor. *Taiwan: A New History.* Armonk, New York, NY: M.E. Sharpe, 1999, pp. 366–402.

Samatar, Abdi Ismail. *The State and Rural Transformation in Northern Somalia, 1884–1986*. Madison, WI: University of Wisconsin Press, 1989.
Saparov, Arsene. *From Conflict to Autonomy in the Caucasus: The Soviet Union and the making of Abkhazia, South Ossetia and Nagorno Karabakh*. London: Routledge, 2015.
Seekins, Donald M. *Historical Dictionary of Burma (Myanmar)*. Lanham, MD: Scarecrow Press, 2006.
Shaw, Malcolm Nathan. *International Law*. Cambridge, UK: Cambridge University Press, 2003.
Shelly, Toby. *Endgame in the Western Sahara: What Future for Africa's Last Colony?* London: Zed Books, 2004.
Smith, Anthony D. *The Ethnic Origins of Nations*. Oxford, UK: Blackwell, 1986.
Smith, Charles D. *Palestine and the Arab-Israeli Conflict*. Boston, MA: Bedford/St Martin's, 2004.
Smith, Martin. "Reflection on the Kachin Ceasefire: A Cycle of Hope and Disappointment," in Mandy Sadan, editor. *War and Peace in the Borderlands of Myanmar: The Kachin Ceasefire, 1994–2011*. Copenhagen, Denmark: NIAS Press, 2016, pp. 57–91.
Smolink, Franziska, Andrea Weiss, and Yana Zabanova. "Political Race and Borderland practices in Abkhazia and Adjara: Exploring the Role of Ottoman Legacies and Contemporary Turkish Influences," in Franziska Smolnik and Andrea Weiss, editors. *Reconfiguration of Political Space in the Caucasus: Power Practices, Governance and Transboundary Flows*. London: Routledge, 2019, pp. 89–99.
Toal, Gerard, and John O'Loughin. "How People in South Ossetia, Abkhazia and Transnistria Feel about Annexation by Russia." *Washington Post*, March 20, 2014.
Trier, Tom, Hedvig Lohm, and David Szakonyi. *Under Siege: Inter-Ethnic Relations in Abkhazia*. New York, NY: Columbia University Press, 2010.
UN Refugee Agency. "Abkhazia's Attempts to Bring Expatriates Home Meets Major Obstacles." *UNRFA*, March 16, 2016. https://www.refworld.org/docid/56ec0bae4.html.
UN Office for the High Representative for the Least Developed States. "The Role of Remittances in the Development of the Economy of Somaliland." *UN-OHRLLS*, 2019. http://unohrlls.org/news/the-role-of-remittance-in-the-economic-development-of-somaliland/.
United States Department of State. "Background Briefing on the Nagorno Karabakh Conflict." *U.S. State Department*, May 16, 2016. https://2009-2017.state.gov/r/pa/prs/ps/2016/05/257263.htm.
Unrepresented Nations and Peoples Organization. "Nagalim." April 26, 2019. https://unpo.org/members/7899.
Unrepresentative Nations and Peoples Organization. "Somaliland: Surviving the Agonizing Process of International Recognition." *UNPO*, November 11, 2009. https://unpo.org/article/10322.
Vujacic, Veljko. "Kosovo: A Case Study in the Unintended Consequences of Communist Nationality Policy, 1968–1986," in Leandrit I. Mehmeti and Branislav

Radeljic, editors. *Kosovo and Serbia: Contested Options and Shared Consequences.* Pittsburgh, PA: University of Pittsburgh Press, 2016, pp. 14–36.

Wang, Peter Chen-main. "A Bastion Created, A Regime Reformed, An Economy Reengineered, 1949–1970," in Murray A. Rubinstein, editor. *Taiwan: A New History.* Armonk, NY: M.E. Sharpe, 1999, pp. 320–338.

Wills, John E., Jr. "The Seventeenth-Century Transformation: Taiwan Under the Dutch and the Cheng Regime," in Murray A. Rubinstein, editor. *Taiwan: A New History.* Armonk, NY: M.E. Sharpe, 1999, pp. 84–106.

World Bank Group. *Somaliland's Private Sector at a Crossroads: Political Economy and Policy Choices for Prosperity and Job Creation.* Washington, DC: World Bank, 2015.

Zartman, Willian. "Morocco's Saharan Policy," in Anouar Boukhars and Jacques Rousellier, editors. *Perspective on Western Sahara: Myths, Nationalism, and Geopolitics.* Lanham, MD: Rowman & Littlefield, 2014, pp. 55–70.

Zunes, Stephen, and Jacob Mundy. *Western Sahara: War, Nationalism, and Conflict Irresolution.* New York, NY: Syracuse University Press, 2010.

Index

"1992 consensus," 185

Abkhaz: historical origins, 40; language, 39
Abkhazia, 2, 3, 13, 37–53, 216–17; autonomous republic of Georgia, 42–43; economy, 51–52; ethnic composition, 53, 53; geography, 38–39; historical background, 40–43, 46; independence wars, 43–46, 46–48; independent state, 48–52; prospects for recognition, 52–53; relations with Georgia, 48–49, 52–53; relations with Russia, 50–51, 52, 53; viability as a state, 51–52
Adan, Edna, 162
"Aden's Butcher Shop," 151
African Union. *See* Organization of African Unity (OAU)
Akinci, Mustafa, 118
Albania, 86–89, 91–92, 100, 101; ethnic ties with Kosovo, 86–87; relations with Kosovo, 100–101; under Italian occupation, 91
Albanian language, 86, 101
Algeria, 131, 137, 138, 139, 142; reasons for supporting the SADR, 138
Aliyev, Heydar, 29
Aliyev, Ilham, 29

Ambazonia, 211–12
Anna, Kofi, 115
Ardzinba, Vladimir, 48–49
Armenia, 17; history and culture, 17–19; relations with Nagorno Karabakh, 30–34
Armenian genocide, 18–19
Armenian-Tatar War, 21
Artsakh, 16
Azawad, 210–11
Azerbaijan, 21–24, 25–27, 33; refugees, 27
Azeris defined, 23–23. *See also* Azerbaijan

Bagapsh, Sergei, 48, 49
Baker Plan, 135
Bassiri, Mohammad, 132
Battle of Kosovo Field, 88
Bender, 67
Berbera, 158
Berbers, 127–28
Bessarabia, 68, 69
Biafra, 11
Border Wall (Western Sahara), 132
Brezhenev, Leonid, 70
British Somaliland, 151–52

Catalans, 165

Caucasus region: geography, 16–17; linguistic diversity, 16–17
Chen Shui-bian, 184, 189
Chiang Ching-kuo, 184
Chiang Kai-shek, 175–77, 183
China, 6, 7. *See also* Taiwan
Chinese Civil War, 176
Clerides, Glaicos, 114
Community Assembly of Kosovo and Metohija, 102
constitutive principle of state sovereignty, 6
Crimea, 12
Cyprus: geography, 107–8; history, 109–13; independence, 112–13; under British rule, 109–11. *See also* Turkish Republic of Northern Cyprus (TRNC)

Dar El Kuti, 212
Darood clan, 156
Dayton Agreement, 94
declarative principle of state sovereignty, 5
de facto states, 2, 214; defined, 2–3, 12–13, 223; as a meaningful concept, 223–24
Democratic League of Kosovo, 99
Democratic People's Party (DDP), 184
Democratic Union Party (PYD), 204
Denktash, Rauf, 111–12, 115
divided states, 119–20
Djibouti, 147
Donetsk People's Republic, 205–7
Dushan, Stefan, 93

East Timor, 13
Egal, Muhammad Jaji Ibrahim, 156
enosis, 110
EOKA, 111
Erbil, 203
Eroglu, Dervis, 116
Ethiopia, 148, 149, 160, 219, 220

European Union (EU), 28, 165, 199, 223; role in Cyprus, 116, 121; role in Kosovo, 96–98

February 28th (2-28) Incident, 177
First Taiwan Strait Crisis, 178–79
Formosa. *See* Taiwan
Formosa Resolution, 178
Four Little Tigers, 183
Fourteenth Soviet Army, 71, 73
"frozen conflict" zone states, 3

Gadaym Izik, 136
Gagauz, 72–73
Gaza Strip, 197–99
Georgia, 37–68. *See also* Abkhazia; South Ossetia
Germany as divided country, 120
Gorbachev, Mikhail, 22, 71
Guomindang, 176–78, 183–85
"Greater Morocco" agenda, 137
Greece, 107–22. *See also* Turkish Republic of Northern Cyprus (TRNC)
Greek Cypriots, 107, 114, 116. *See also* Cyprus; Turkish Republic of Northern Cyprus (TRNC)
Green Line, 115
Green March, 132
Guurti, 159

Haidar, Aminatou, 141
Hargeisa, 148, 154
Hassan II, 132, 137
Holy See, 196
Hong Kong, 187, 190

insurgent states, 209–10
International Court of Justice, 96
Iraq, 202, 203
Isaaq clan, 150
Islamic State (ISIS), 203, 205, 209–10
Israel, 197–200
Italy. *See* Somaliland

Jashari, Adem, 95
Japan, rule of Taiwan, 174–75
Jingpaw, 207

Kachaks, 91
Kachin Independence Army, 207
Kachin Independence Organization (KIO), 207
Kachin State, 207–9
Kahin, Dahir Riyale, 159, 162, 164
Karabakh Committee, 23
Khadjimba, Raul, 49
Khatumo, 157
Kocharian, Robert, 31
Kodori Gorge, 47
Kokoity, Eduard, 58
Korea as divided country, 120
Korean War, 176
Kosovo, 2, 3, 13, 85–103, 218–19; future prospects, 102–3; geography, 85–86; historical background, 87–90; independence movement, 94–98; as part of Yugoslavia, 91–93; since independence, 100–103; treatment of Serbian minority, 97, 101–2; under Serbian rule, 88–91, 93–94
Kosovo, Battle of, 88
Kosovo Force (KFOR), 97, 102
Kosovo Liberation Army, 95, 99
Kosovo War, 94–96
Kurdistan, 200–205; historical background, 200–201
Kurdistan Regional Government, 200, 202–4; economy and politics, 203; future prospects, 205
Kurds, 200–201
Kyrenia (Girne), 118

Laas Geel, 158
Laayoune, 129, 140, 142
Laiza, 209
League of Prizren, 89
Lebed, Alexander, 74
Lee Tung-hui, 184
Luhansk People's Republic, 205–7

Lykhny Letter, 44
Lykhny uprising, 41

Ma al Aynayn, 128–29
Macedonia, 219
Madrid Agreement, 133
Mahabad, Republic of, 201
Makarios, Archbishop, 111, 112
Mao Zedong, 176
Mauretania, 130–33, 138
Ma Ying-jeou, 184, 187
Medieval Monuments of Kosovo, 88
Megali idea, 110
Metohija, 92
Milosevic, Slobodan, 93, 96
Minsk Group, 28
MINURSO (United Nations Mission for the Referendum in Western Sahara), 135
Mogadishu, 147
Mohammad VI, 135, 136
Moldavian Soviet Socialist Republic, 69
Moldova, 65–81
Morocco, 125–43; claims to Western Sahara, 136–38; occupation of Western Sahara, 132–38, 142
Movement for the Liberation of the Sahara, 130
muhajirs, 53
Myanmar, 207–9
Myitkyina, 207

Naga, 212
Nagalim, 212
Nagorno Karabakh, 1, 2, 3, 12–34, 215–16; economy, 32; geography, 16; history of, 19–23, 25–27; independent state, 27–34; meaning of name, 16; politics of, 27–29; status as a state, 30–32; under Soviet Rule, 21–23
Nagorno Karabakh War, 25–27
Nakhchivan, 21
nationalism: definition, 8; origins of, 8–9

nation-state, 10–12
NATO: role in Kosovo, 95, 96–97, 101; war with Serbia, 95
Nicosia, 107
Nineteen-Point Program for Economic and Financial Reform, 182
Northern Cyprus. *See* Turkish Republic of Northern Cyprus (TRNC)
North Ossetia-Alania, Republic of, 59. *See also* Ossetianization

Ogaden, conflict over, 153
One China Policy, 179, 180, 181, 182, `85
"One Country, Two Systems," 187
Operation Provide Comfort, 202
Organization of African Unity (OAU), 163, 166
Organization of Security and Cooperation in Europe (OSCE), 46, 47, 59
Oslo Accords, 198
Ossetianization, 50
Ottoman Empire, 17, 40, 67, 88, 109

Palestine, 197–200
Palestinian Liberation Organization (PLO), 198, 199
Pan-Blue Camp, 185
Pan-Green Camp, 185
Peoples Protection Units (YPG), 204
People's Republic of China (PRC). *See* China
Peshmerga, 202
Polisario, 131, 132, 133, 134, 135, 136; founding of, 130; governing refugee camps, 138–42
Pope Pius IX, 196
Popular Front of Moldova, 72
Pristina, 86, 100, 101
Prizren, 86, 88, 100
Puntland, 156–57, 221

Quebec, 2, 165

refugee camps in Algeria. *See* Tindouf
Republic of China (ROC). *See* Taiwan
Republic of Somaliland: 1960 declaration, 152; 1991 declaration, 155. *See also* Somaliland
Rio de Oro, 129
Rojava, 204–5
Romania, 68–70, 72
Romanian language, 68, 70, 72
Rugova, Ibrahim, 95, 98–99
Russia, 4, 16, 40, 41, 42, 50, 67, 68; conquest of Caucasus, 17, 20, 21, 41; patron of Abkhazia, 50–51; patron of South Ossetia, 59, 61; support of Luhansk and Donetsk, 205–7; support of Serbia, 98, 102; support of Transnistria, 78; war with Georgia, 46–48. *See also* Soviet Union

Saakashvili, Mikhail, 48
Saguia el-Hamra, 129
Sahrawi: ethnic origins, 127–28; national consciousness, 131–32
Sahrawi Arab Democratic Republic (SADR), 2, 3, 13, 125–43, 220–21; administration in Tindouf, 138–42; declaration of, 133; future prospects, 143; population of. *See* Western Sahara
Sampson, Nikos, 113
"Sand War," 137
sangar (fortresses), 138
Sayed, El-Ouali Mutapha, 132
"Scramble for Africa," 128, 151
Serbia, 85, 87–90, 93, 94, 95; ethnic cleansing, 94, 95–96; opposition to Kosovo, 9, 97, 98, 102–3
Serbs minority in Kosovo, 101–2
Sheriff company, 79–80
Shushi, 27, 30
Siad Barre, 153, 154, 165
Silanyo, 159
Singapore, 216
Sino-American Mutual Defense Treaty, 178, 180

Six Assurances, 181
Smara, 129
Smirnov, Igor, 76–77
Somalia, 147–49; historical background, 150–52. *See also* Somaliland
Somaliland, 2, 3, 13, 147–66, 221–22; creation of independent state, 161–66; declaration of independence, 147; as a de facto state, 13, 166; diaspora, 158; droughts and hunger, 160–61; economy, 158–59; efforts to gain recognition, 161–62; first republic, 152–53; geography, 147–49; historical background of region, 149–56; human rights, 160; political system, 159–61; reasons it has not gained recognition, 162–65; since independence, 156–66
Somali National Movement, 154–56
Somalis, 149–50; clan structure, 150; language, 149
South Ossetia, 2, 3, 13, 53–61, 217; as a de facto state, 13, 60–61; geography, 54; historical background, 55–56; independence wars, 56–58; independence state, 58–61; relations with Georgia, 59–60; relations with Russia, 59–61; under Soviet Union, 55–57
South Sudan, 12
Soviet Union, 10, 11. *See also* Abkhazia; Nagorno Karabakh; Russia; South Ossetia; Transnistria
Spain, 125, 132–33, 141; colonization of Western Sahara, 128–30
Spanish Morocco, 129
Spanish Society of Commercial Geography, 128
state definitions of, 3–6; modern state, 7–9
state sovereignty, 5, 6, 9
state system, 9–10
Stepanakert, 15, 31–32
Sukhumi, 37, 50

Taipei, 172
Taiwan, 2, 3, 13, 171–91, 222–23; as de facto state, 13, 171, 190–91; democratization, 183–85; economy, 182–83; ethnic composition, 173, 189; foreign affairs, 185–88; future prospects, 190–91; geography, 172–72; historical background, 173–82; politics, 185; relations with China, 180, 181, 186–88, 190–91; relations with the United States, 178–82, 186, 188; Taiwanese ethnic identity, 188–89; trade with China, 186; under Japanese colonial rule, 174–75
Taiwanization, 189
Taiwan Miracle, 182–83
Taiwan Relations Act, 180, 181
Taiwan Travel Act, 181
"tented state," 138
Thaci, Hashim, 97, 99
taksim (partition), 111
Ter-Petrosian, Lev, 32
Thaci, Kahim, 99
Tindouf, 133, 139–42
Tiraspol, 67, 69, 76, 78
Tirotex, 79
Transnistria, 2, 3, 13, 65–81, 217–18; economy, 78–80; geography, 65–66; historical background, 66–71; human rights record, 77; independence conflict, 73–75; independence state, 75–81; politics, 76–77; Russia as patron, 78; shady reputation, 78–80; Soviet period, 69–73; viability as a state, 80–81
Tsai Ing-wen, 184, 188
Trust Territory of Somaliland, 152
Tskhinvali, 54, 57, 58
Turkey, 107, 112; intervention in Cyprus, 113–14; role in Northern Cyprus, 117, 118, 119
Turkish Republic of Northern Cyprus (TRNC), 2, 3, 13, 107–22, 220; creation of, 114–16; declaration of

independence, 114; economy, 118; future prospects, 120–22; geography, 108; as independent state, 116–22; politics and human rights, 116–17
Turkish Resistance Organization, 111
Tuur, Abdirahman Ahmed Ai, 154, 156

Ukraine, 206–7
United Nations, 6, 7, 180, 223
United Nations Interim Mission in Kosovo (UNMIK), 96
United States, 165, 199, 202–5
Unrepresented Peoples Organization, 161

Vatican City, 195–97

West Bank, 197–99
Western Sahara, 125; early history, 126–26; geography, 125–26, 142; independence movement, 131–32; Moroccan takeover of, 132–33; Spanish colonial period, 128–32; under Moroccan rule, 142. *See also* Sahrawi Arab Democratic Republic (SADR)
Western Sahara Authority, 135
White Terror, 184

Xi Jinping, 187

Yedinstvo Movement, 72
Yemen as divide country, 120
yuanzhumin, 189
Yugoslavia, 91–94

Zemla Intifada, 130
Zheng Chenggong, 174

About the Author

Michael J. Seth is a professor of history at James Madison University. There he teaches East Asian and World history. His research has focused on South Korea's economic, social, and educational development. Seth is the author of *Education Fever: Society, Politics and the Pursuit of Schooling in South Korea* (2002), *A Concise History of Korea* (third edition, 2020), *North Korea: A History* (2018), *Korea: A Very Short Introduction* (2020), and the editor of *The Routledge Handbook of Modern Korean History* (2016).

In addition to his scholarship on Korea, Seth has been involved in workshops on world history. Combining his study of world history with his love of travel, he and his wife have been to many parts of the globe. In recent years, he has been visiting some de facto countries becoming fascinated by their ambiguous roles in the international state system, an interest that led to this book.

www.ingramcontent.com/pod-product-compliance
Lightning Source LLC
Chambersburg PA
CBHW020742020526
44115CB00030B/844